AGAINST SUSTAINABILITY

Against Sustainability

Reading Nineteenth-Century America
in the Age of Climate Crisis

Michelle C. Neely

FORDHAM UNIVERSITY PRESS

New York 2020

Fordham University Press has no responsibility for the persistence or accuracy of URLs for external or third-party Internet websites referred to in this publication and does not guarantee that any content on such websites is, or will remain, accurate or appropriate.

Fordham University Press also publishes its books in a variety of electronic formats. Some content that appears in print may not be available in electronic books.

Visit us online at www.fordhampress.com.

Library of Congress Cataloging-in-Publication Data

Names: Neely, Michelle C., author.
Title: Against sustainability : reading nineteenth-century America in the age of climate crisis / Michelle C. Neely.
Other titles: Reading nineteenth-century America in the age of climate crisis
Description: First edition. | New York : Fordham University Press, [2020] | Includes bibliographical references and index.
Identifiers: LCCN 2020000622 | ISBN 9780823288229 (hardback) | ISBN 9780823288205 (paperback) | ISBN 9780823288212 (epub)
Subjects: LCSH: American literature—19th century—History and criticism. | Environmentalism in literature. | Human ecology in literature. | Nature—Effect of human beings on—United States. | American literature—20th century—History and criticism. | American literature—21st century—History and criticism.
Classification: LCC PS217.E55 N44 2020 | DDC 810.9/36—dc23
LC record available at https://lccn.loc.gov/2020000622

Printed in the United States of America
22 21 20   5 4 3 2 1
First edition

CONTENTS

Oh Matchless Earth—We underrate the chance to dwell in Thee
    —Emily Dickinson to Susan Gilbert Dickenson, about 1870

what has been made
can be unmade
                —Lucille Clifton, "the message from The Ones"

The Unlikely Environmentalisms of Nineteenth-Century American Literature

Nineteenth-Century Environmentalisms in the "Anthropocene"

According to a sobering October 2018 report from the United Nations' Intergovernmental Panel on Climate Change, humans have just ten years left to radically reduce greenhouse gas emissions if we are to avoid the +1.5 degree Celsius threshold widely predicted to bring on the most apocalyptic environmental consequences: devastating droughts, food shortages, hurricanes, sea rise, the death of coral reefs, millions of climate refugees. Despite the increasingly dire timeline, this is old news to the American public, which has been hearing and mostly not heeding such warnings since the late 1980s. Why have US environmental ethics so spectacularly failed to curb our well-publicized descent into "the sixth extinction" and a catastrophically warmer world?

Against Sustainability responds to our environmental crisis not by seeking the origins of our environmental problems but by returning to the nineteenth-century literary, cultural, and scientific contexts that gave rise to many of our most familiar environmental solutions. In readings that juxtapose nineteenth- and late-twentieth- or twenty-first-century writers such as Walt Whitman and Lucille Clifton, George Catlin and Louise Erdrich, and Herman Melville and A. S. Byatt, the book demonstrates that cherished environmental ethics such as recycling and preservation are compromised beyond instrumentality because they are hopelessly imbricated with the very systems they need to address if they are to be efficacious. Yet it is not enough simply to levy critiques of our environmental paradigms—we must embrace alternatives. Thus, the other half of *Against Sustainability* explores alternative paradigms for mitigating wasteful consumerism and living in just community with human and nonhuman life. Through the work of writers such as Emily Dickinson, Henry David Thoreau, Hannah Crafts, and Harriet Wilson, the book explicates the value of embracing unusual and perhaps even provisional environmentalisms from unlikely sources as the first step to a more fundamental reworking of Anglo-American environmental ethics. The alternative environmentalisms seem initially counterintuitive, perhaps even strange, making it easy to dismiss them as "unlikely" at best. However, each is more reliably positioned to guide us toward more genuine forms of solidarity and community—with one another and with other forms of life. Neither of these ethics is necessarily ideal or even helpful at all times and for all people. Instead, they are provocative environmentalisms that might goad early-twenty-first-century, mainstream US culture in particular to embrace more ethical responses to our increasingly compromised world. Ultimately, this book demonstrates that building more just, environmentally sound futures means deepening our understanding of the histories of Anglo-American environmental ethics and paradigms and then consciously embracing environmental paradigms that interrupt rather than sustain systems of oppression.

I use the term "Anglo-American" here and throughout the book to signal the transatlantic origins of critical aspects of US environmental thought and to distinguish mainstream, majoritarian environmental culture, which has historically been led by relatively wealthy, white Americans, from the vibrant veins of US environmental activism and culture led by Black, Indigenous, and other people of color, organized labor, and so on. I certainly do not mean to suggest that Anglo-American environmental culture is the only environmental culture in the United States but rather to signal that it is the environmental culture *Against Sustainability* will examine and assess.

Against Sustainability's commitment to transformative solutions is what drives the book's sustained focus on the nineteenth century, the period in which many of our touchstone environmental paradigms took their definitive shape. While this book takes the antebellum period in particular as

its focal point, the story of the rise of US environmentalism has more typically focused on the late-nineteenth-century iterations of conservationist
and preservationist principles by figures such as George Perkins Marsh and
John Muir.[1] This now-familiar environmental history narrates the rise of
conservation and preservation ethics as part of a triumphalist account of a
late-nineteenth-century, Anglo-American shift away from utilitarian and
exploitative attitudes and policies and toward nonhuman nature. The story
begins with "a definitive shift in the balance of wilderness and civilization"
in the nineteenth century, which produced new forms of nostalgia for the
"howling wilderness" that settlers had sought to eradicate since seventeenth-
century colonization.[2] The postbellum perception of a threatened wilderness generated many of the movements, organizations, and institutions
upon which modern environmental activism still rests. The Yosemite Valley gained federal and state protection beginning in 1864, and Yellowstone would become the first national park in 1871. Theodore Roosevelt's
conservation group, the Boone and Crocket Club, began organizing on behalf of US nature in the 1870s and had won National Wildlife Refuges by
1903 and the National Forest Service by 1905. John Muir, instrumental in
preserving Yosemite and Sequoia as national parks during the 1870s,
founded the Sierra Club in 1892, now one of the most influential environmental organizations in the world. By the early twentieth century, preservation and conservation were powerful paradigms capable of driving public
policy. In this scholarly and popular telling, preservation and conservation
are the celebrated ethics that helped usher in more liberal environmental
protections and more complex ideas about ecological community; as such,
they necessarily remain the relatively uninterrogated heroes of US environmental culture.

More recently, interest in the nineteenth-century emergence of modern environmental ethics has been overshadowed by an explosion of environmentally minded scholarship done under the sign of the Anthropocene,
the proposed geological epoch defined by the beginning of significant
human impact on the planet. The Anthropocene proposal has encouraged
scholars across disciplines to focus on the difficult problem of which historical period or set of events catalyzed the twenty-first-century ecological crisis. In literary studies, significant scholarship has highlighted the
consequences of ecological imperialism and colonial violence in the seventeenth century, the Industrial Revolution in the nineteenth century, and
the advent and use of nuclear weapons in the twentieth century.[3] Important as this work has been, the focused attention on the cultural-historical
origins (or, at least, prehistory) of our environmental *problems* has tended

to preclude in-depth exploration of our agreed-upon *solutions* to those same problems.

By contrast, *Against Sustainability* takes as its starting point a conviction that the origin of our responses to environmental crisis deserves a second look. Timothy Clark has argued that the Anthropocene "may name a kind of threshold at which modes of thinking and practices that were once self-evidently adequate, progressive, or merely innocuous become, in this emerging and counter-intuitive context, even latently destructive."[4] Rather than accepting as a given the progressiveness of familiar environmental paradigms such as preservation, I focalize the nineteenth-century cultural formation and logic of these paradigms through the "counter-intuitive context" of twenty-first-century environmental crisis. What results are topsy-turvy portraits. Antebellum celebrations of material recycling that appear prescient at first glance turn out to enable unfettered appetite rather than suggest limits to consumption. Profound respect for the ocean's unmasterable power helps explain our current difficulty to respond appropriately to plastic pollution and other threats to oceanic life. On the other hand, antebellum Americans emerge as surprisingly complex theorists of consumer desire under capitalism and of radical forms of multispecies solidarity. The counterintuitive findings in *Against Sustainability* are the result of centering the logic of environmental paradigms as they appear and are theorized in poems and prose—literary, scientific, and popular.

In other words, this book's primary aim is not to measure the environmental soundness, by contemporary standards, of particular antebellum literary representations of nonhuman animals, landscapes, or ecosystems.[5] Nor am I sifting nineteenth-century literature for the origin point of the "Anthropocene" or even for early hints of contemporary environmental woes such as smog or petroculture.[6] These ways of reading nineteenth-century literature and culture are essential to a robust nineteenth-century literary studies and a vibrant ecocriticism and Environmental Humanities. Yet an exclusive focus on these ways of reading the period has tended to obscure recognition and reckoning with nineteenth-century Americans as the masterminds of many of our most familiar and influential environmental paradigms. In *Against Sustainability*, I treat the poets and writers that I consider as theorists of consequential environmentalisms—principles that either open up or foreclose modes of living and of living with. Thus, my emphasis is on the logic of the environmental paradigms and on the forms of pleasure, justice, and community (human and multispecies) that each calls into being. This emphasis on forms of solidarity and "living with" that a given environmental ethic makes possible or disallows is at base an exercise in defamiliarization and thus an exercise in imagination, one that allows us to evaluate even our most beloved environmental ethics from uncomfortably fresh vantage points.

Against Sustainability's methodology takes seriously its core nineteenth-century texts' ability to theorize environmental ethics, which allows for the novel or counterintuitive readings of the twentieth- and twenty-first-century literary texts that also appear in each chapter. All too often, scholarship has taught readers to expect that it is primarily twentieth- and twenty-first-century texts that theorize and thus help us interpret literature of past centuries; this relationship is reversed in *Against Sustainability*, and this reversal helps demonstrate the debt that contemporary US environmental thought owes to the nineteenth century and to nineteenth-century literature in particular.

Making visible the cultural, literary, and scientific forges in which US environmental topoi took shape during the nineteenth century defamiliarizes these topoi in order to make space for us to imagine and enact more just and capacious futures in the present. While this kind of "strategic presentism" has recently been the subject of debate in a range of fields, including Victorian, Renaissance, early modern, and postcolonial literary study, the methodology is common in pre-twentieth-century scholarship in the fields of ecocriticism and Environmental Humanities.[7] As Jesse Oak Taylor has observed, ecocritics have long been willing to "atten[d] to the particularities of the past as a means to intervene in contemporary debates over the state of the world and our responsibility to the future."[8] Moreover, strategic presentism has a particular purchase on transatlantic and hemispheric nineteenth-century literary study; as Anna Kornbluh and Benjamin Morgan have argued, "To study the nineteenth century is to be struck almost daily by the sense that it never really went away: ours is also a gilded age of income inequality, of financial speculation, of de facto debtor's prisons, of capitalist exploitation, of global inequity, of misplaced faith in evolutionary psychology, of widespread reliance on coal-based energy."[9] As I have been arguing, it is not just these and other nineteenth-century problems that "never really went away" but many of our common responses to them, as well.

This book's approach is also deeply informed by critical theoretical work—by Donna Haraway, Anna Lowenhaupt Tsing, Kyle Powys Whyte, Zoe Todd, Maria Puig de la Bellacasa, Thom Van Dooren, Kim TallBear, Ursula Heise, Andreas Malm, and others—that challenges models of solidarity and community limited by anthropocentrism, white supremacy, capitalism, patriarchy, and our own imaginations.[10] Stacy Alaimo's *Exposed* and Nicole Seymore's *Bad Environmentalism* are also fellow travelers, insofar as each questions the ideals, sensibilities, and assumptions of contemporary mainstream US environmentalism.[11] While these works often limit their scope to the contemporary, *Against Sustainability* contributes an archival, historical foreground that enriches this deeply necessary conversation. The spirit and approach of essays in the imaginative ecotheory collection *Veer Ecology* (2017) are perhaps most consonant with my project in this book, in the sense that they aim to provoke new lines of environmental thought in order to "propel change."[12] Yet very few of the essays in *Veer Ecology* explore the theoretical possibilities of literature, culture, and thought from the nineteenth century.[13] Among its other contributions, *Against Sustainability* aims to demonstrate that the nineteenth century is fertile ground to research and rethink many of our current environmental ethics at the moment of their emergence, as we reimagine and build a more ecologically and socially just culture for the United States.

At the outset, perhaps it seems odd to focus this book specifically on US environmentalisms when so many environmental problems are clearly global in their scope and when the study of "American literature" has been so productively expanded into a transnational, hemispheric, oceanic, and even planetary field of study. My focus on the United States is not parochial myopia but is grounded instead in an awareness of the global impact of dominant, Anglo-American environmental ideas and practices. It is not simply that Americans consume an untenable percentage of the planet's resources at an untenable rate. Americans also export their environmental attitudes and ideals globally: Elites all over the world increasingly imitate or aspire to imitate American patterns of consumption, and US companies and NGOs seek to export and impose American environmental paradigms such as wilderness preservation worldwide.[14]

A focus on the particular failures and possibilities of US environmental culture leads *Against Sustainability* to join the growing body of scholarship uneasy with the Anthropocene proposal. Even as the Anthropocene has been the impetus for a great deal of significant scholarly work, the proposal has also been criticized and at times rejected for its Eurocentrism; its reliance on an undifferentiated, abstract humanity; and its mystification of systems of power, among other charges. Jason Moore, in particular, has argued that any search for a singular historical source for anthropogenic (or, as Moore terms it, "capitalogenic") climate change courts "historical myopia" and an intellectually deadening focus on effects rather than the systems that produce those effects (for Moore, capitalism).[15]

I agree with Moore and with Donna Haraway,[16] Joni Adamson,[17] and the many other critics of the Anthropocene proposal who claim that the concept occludes as much as it makes visible. For that reason I favor Moore's "Capitalocene," and I use that term throughout the book, except when I am referring to the Anthropocene proposal specifically (as I do here and in Chapter 4).

For all that the Anthropocene has opened up, its origin-of-crisis focalization and its difficulty singling out the systems and cultures most directly responsible for our twenty-first-century crisis mean that it is unlikely to reorient an Anglo-American environmental culture that is failing not just US citizens but the whole planet. Most Americans now recognize that our planetary situation is dire, and most of us recognize that many US environmental beliefs and practices are retrograde. Yet even for those in the United States who have confronted the reality of where we are and want to act, change can feel impossible. Frequently, we have some idea about how to address contemporary environmental crises; Americans' inability to enact these solutions—individually or politically—reflects not merely a failure of will but, more profoundly, a failure of imagination. As Andrew Dessler, a climate scientist at Texas A&M has remarked, responding effectively to climate change by 2030 is "going to take a reimagining of how the world is constructed around us and we are lacking imagination."[18] Our lack of imagination is grounded in the stories Americans tell and are told about our history, which make change seem impossible. If the quintessence of the American dream is capitalist acquisition, if Anglo-Americans' relationship to land remains one of settler-colonial resource extraction, what hope can we have for change—for a meaningful environmental culture? Yet other dreams have been dreamed, and other modes of living have been tested, all along.

Against Sustainability: Building Antipastoral Paradigms

The manifest difficulties of centering transformative environmental ethics in mainstream US environmental culture are only compounded by the hegemonic force of the sustainability paradigm. Definitions of sustainability are famously vague, making its outcomes difficult to measure.[19] At the same time, there are two common ways of defining sustainability, each of which makes visible crucial failures of the paradigm, and each of which helps explain its inability to orient mainstream environmental culture toward radical justice. By briefly treating each definition in turn, I will articulate not only grounds on which one might be "against sustainability" but also some of the core methodological commitments of *Against Sustainability*.

The first common way that sustainability is defined is with a Venn diagram or a triangle in which sustainability constitutes the space of overlap between economic, environmental, and social goods.[20] This triangle is often understood to mean that the interests of global capitalism may be balanced with economic and social justice, which means that sustainability discourse is frequently in the peculiar position of trying to weigh questions of human justice and saving the planet against the financial interests of the global elite, despite the fact that these aims can be in conflict with one another. As the planet edges toward disaster, sustainability's tendency to look for a middle ground that protects the portfolio interests of the few over the present and future well-being of the many comes to seem more and more absurd. For this reason, *Against Sustainability* privileges ethics over economics in its analysis of environmental paradigms, an approach that allows the book to take a critical look at the growth imperative of capitalism and the kinds of communities that capitalism-compatible paradigms such as sustainability, recycling, and preservation produce.

Moreover, the triangle or Venn-diagram model of sustainability visually and theoretically perpetuates the separation of "environmental" issues from "environmental justice," a separation that has long marred mainstream environmental discourse. Such a separation only makes sense from the perspective of a US environmental movement dedicated to "preserving" natural resources for their cultural value to white elites. As Chapter 3 demonstrates, this book is critical of the values and assumptions of that form of environmentalism; *Against Sustainability* rejects the idea that the interests of some or all Black, Indigenous, immigrant, poor, or nonhuman beings (just to name a few) may be separated from the province of environmentalism proper. Truly just, ecological communities must reckon with the needs of all their members, and when those needs conflict (as they often do), flexible and sophisticated ethics and practices must guide any adjudication of the conflicts. Such ethics and practices would need to represent the interests of more than white elites, of course, and they would also need to come from a range of perspectives in order to produce flourishing communities for all. For this reason, questions of racial justice are centered throughout *Against Sustainability*. Chapter 4 in particular explores theorizations of multispecies community in novels by antebellum Black women writers and argues for the significance of Black feminism more generally to a livable "Anthropocene."

Even more common than the triangle definition of sustainability is an extremely general (some might say hazy) definition that also privileges balance and stability. In fact, the most familiar and oft-quoted articulation of sustainability, from "Our Common Future," the United Nations' 1987 Brundtland report, reads as follows: "Sustainable development is development that meets the needs of the present without compromising the ability of future generations to meet their own needs."[21] As this definition makes clear, sustainability comes from a well-meaning impulse to ensure the stable persistence of human societies over time, despite the environmental threats that currently endanger not only the stability but the persistence of human societies in the future. Sustainability offers an appealingly "stable, enduring counterpoint to the disruptive energy and change of human societies."[22]

Yet sustainability's reassuring emphasis on stability comes at a high cost: The paradigm fundamentally prizes not transformation but continuity. This means that at its core, sustainability discourse enshrines continuity with environmentally and ethically problematic pasts as the ongoing ideal of present and future environmental cultures. As Steve Mentz has argued, "behind our shared cultural narratives of sustainability sits a fantasy about stasis, an imaginary world in which we can trust that whatever happened yesterday will keep happening tomorrow. . . . In literary studies, we name this kind of fantasy *pastoral*."[23] Mentz is describing a fantasy of unchanging stability that depends upon a misreading of the past so fantastical it produces "an imaginary world" divorced from history. This way of understanding the pastoral is indebted to Raymond Williams, whose *The Country and the City* demonstrates that the pastoral is not simply a preference for the middle landscape between the city and the wilderness; it is also an idealized representation of the life that takes place in the middle landscape, one that frequently obscures the hard reality of country life and labor. Moreover, Williams argues that the cultural politics of the pastoral manifest in an antihistorical nostalgia: Each generation identifies the golden age or ideal form of simple, rural life as having existed sometime in a generation before itself, whether the pastoral ideal is being spun by an ancient Roman or a nineteenth- or twenty-first-century American.[24]

The pastoral is not one of the core paradigms this book explores but is rather a key aspect of its critique and the impetus for studying the nineteenth century through an environmental lens. This same impetus has animated other studies that are in fact dedicated to illuminating lineages of the pastoral. Williams, in observing that nostalgia characterizes the pastoral imagination, notes that it abets "a well-known habit of using the past, the 'good old days,' as a stick to beat the present."[25] In a related vein, Leo Marx's *The Machine in the Garden* describes the pastoral ideal as a "turn[ing] away from the hard social and technological realities," one that "has been used to define the meaning of America ever since the age of discovery."[26] Marx's study definitively establishes the strong hold pastoralism had on nineteenth-century US literature and culture; it follows that many of the ideals and environmentalisms inherited from the period might be tinged with pastoral thinking as well. *Against Sustainability* builds on Marx, Williams, and other theorists of the pastoral insofar as it values historical knowledge as critical to meaningful environmental paradigms. In the chapters that follow, the book seeks to interrupt specific pastoral fantasies about "the good old days" of material consumption and multispecies community in the nineteenth-century United States because such fantasies are obstacles to meaningful environmental theory and action.

Pastoral fantasies turn out to be a useful litmus test by which to judge environmental paradigms: To the extent that a paradigm is constricted by pastoralism, it cannot be future oriented or truly transformative. Herein lies the problem with sustainability's emphasis on stability: Sustainability's ideal future often takes the form of the recovery of an idyll—a recently lost bountiful present. Critics have observed that this emphasis on continuity in sustainability rhetoric and planning functions as an apologia for continued unfettered growth, at least for wealthy elites. Stacy Alaimo has argued that "sustainability has become a plastic but potent signifier, meaning, roughly, the ability to somehow keep things going despite the economic and environmental crises, that, we fear, may render this impossible."[27] In *Braiding Sweetgrass*, Robin Wall Kimmerer tells the story of an Algonquin ecologist defining "sustainable development" to her tribal council. "This sustainable development sounds to me like they just want to be able to keep on taking like they always have," one elder replies.[28] Each of these critiques highlights the confused temporality of sustainability's pastoral fantasy, its insistence that the future can look like a real or imagined past. As Bill McKibben has suggested, the emphasis on continuity expressed in such a vision is a failure of imagination: "We're so used to *growth* that we can't imagine alternatives; at best we embrace the squishy *sustainable*, with its implied claim that we can keep on as before."[29]

We cannot, in fact, "keep on as before,"[30] yet so many of our environmental paradigms presume, explicitly or implicitly, that we can. If we don't always see this, it's partly because sustainability makes powerful use of another pastoral mode: elegiac lament for a vanished, supposedly more ecologically sound past. Recently, a small number of self-styled "ecomodernists" have argued that the key to sustainability amid our twenty-first-century environmental crisis is to double down on the systems that got us here. According to this position, human thriving depends upon our leaning in to capitalism and a technocratic, profit-oriented management of our planet.[31] As one scholar has put it, "rather than opposing the reckless growth imperative that animates contemporary capitalism . . . ecomodernists believe that unfettered capitalism will save the planet."[32] Far more pervasive, however, are environmental arguments that fabricate pastoral pasts to which they argue we should now return. Such accounts envision future sustainability by narrating cherry-picked histories of past practices born of an unexamined conviction that pre-twentieth-century life was not inextricably mired in growth-driven capitalism. The end result is that sustainability as a principle values continuity, even as the pastoral pasts in which sustainability is awash make it difficult to recognize the *actual* continuities between our real environmental pasts and our present state of crisis and to evaluate our guiding environmental paradigms honestly and holistically going forward.

The example of sustainable food can help demonstrate how sustainability discourse often wields pastoral pasts that exist primarily in imagination rather than history. Robert Kenner's 2008 blockbuster documentary *Food, Inc.*, which costars Michael Pollan (the author of *The Omnivore's Dilemma*) and Eric Schlosser (the author of *Fast Food Nation*), is a typical instance of popular "industrial food critique." In the opening four minutes of the documentary, we hear the rhetoric and claims characteristic of so many food sustainability reformers: Over images of pastoral farmland, Pollan's voice assures us that

> the way we eat has changed more in the last fifty years than in the
> previous ten thousand. But the image that's used to sell the food, it is
> still the imagery of agrarian America. You go into the supermarket
> and you see pictures of farmers, the picket fence, the silo, the '30s farm
> house, and the green grass. It's the spinning of this pastoral fantasy.

The film simultaneously critiques the "pastoral fantasy" spun by US marketing that deceives consumers into thinking that their food "still" comes from small, ethical family farms, even as it leaves intact the notion that there is a real referent for that pastoral fantasy: pre–World War II agricultural practices.[33] As one scholar has argued, *Food, Inc.* and other films and books like it produce "food apocalypse narratives" that oppose the horrors of corporate, industrial agriculture to "pastoral landscapes, farmer's markets, and organic alternatives," and these alternatives are given extra redemptive significance through their association with pre-twentieth-century pastoralism and agrarian virtue.[34] With slight variations, well-known figures such as Pollan, Schlosser, Mark Bittman, Jonathan Safran Foer, and many others have offered this same critical narrative in their work over the last few decades. In bestsellers such as *Fast Food Nation* (2001) and *The Omnivore's Dilemma* (2007), the American public has been taught to believe that every aspect of modern, mainstream eating and farming is indeed a post-1930s phenomenon.[35]

But how true is it that food production was fundamentally more eco-logically sound and less profit driven before the 1930s? How true is it that the ideals and practices that defined US food production before the twen-tieth century might guide us toward more ethical and environmental food production now, in the twenty-first century? A look back at nineteenth-century US food culture, and especially the work of the popular vegetar-ian advocate Sylvester Graham, should destabilize any easy certainty that a return to pre-1900 agricultural, commercial, and domestic food practices will be our salvation. Graham's work will be treated more thoroughly in Chapter Two, but here it is sufficient to say that in addition to being an antebellum antimasturbation kook, Graham was a serious anti-industrial food reformer who advocated for a diet of homegrown, unprocessed, ex-clusively vegetarian foods. Reading Graham's 1,200-page magnum opus *The Science of Human Life*, it is hard not to be struck by how many of his critiques of the US food system, in 1839, rehearse or anticipate familiar twenty-first-century critiques.

For example, one of the reasons Graham flour, which is just whole wheat flour, came to be called Graham flour was because Graham was the first public person to advocate for its consumption. Such flour had not needed a special nomenclature before, let alone a public advocate, because super-fine, refined "white" flour was an antebellum innovation—one that, if you believe Graham, caused a virtual pandemic of constipation.[36] Graham is writing as Americans are discovering and steadily consuming simple, re-fined carbohydrates. Not only that, they're increasingly eating industrial food. Graham complains that "in cities and large towns, most people de-pend on public bakers for their bread," and these bakers "for the sake of securing their own emolument" conduct "various experiments with chemi-cal agents." He quotes "treatises on bread-making" that allege that bakers

> have not only succeeded by such means in making light and white
> bread out of extremely poor flour, but they have also been able to
> disguise their adulterations, as to work in with their flour, without

being detected by the consumers, a portion of the flour of beans, peas, and potatoes; and even chalk, pipe clay, and plaster of Paris have been employed to increase the weight and whiteness of their bread.

"Alum" and "sulphate of copper" are also used, much to the detriment of the health of customers.[37] Graham's complaints make clear that during the antebellum period, bread is a market commodity, and food is being adulterated to make it look and taste more appealing in a manner that increases the profit of the people producing the food commodity, a profit that comes at the expense of consumers' health.

It is not just bread, however. "In making . . . cheese for the market, it is quite fashionable for the manufacturer to put annatto and even arsenic and other poisonous substances, to give it a rich and creamy appearance and taste. It is no uncommon thing for whole families to be made seriously sick by eating cheese which is thus adulterated," Graham claims.[38] Graham is describing commodity food, produced for an increasingly urbanized population, in 1839, a moment when, according to pretty much every twenty-first-century food reformer, journalist, etc., American food was supposed to be preindustrial and wholesome. This is supposed to be the pre-1900 idyllic food culture we are meant to recover, yet already Americans are eating unhealthy, processed food.

The fiction that nineteenth-century food culture was markedly more sustainable than what we eat today is particularly disrupted by a focus on meat and dairy production. Graham, writing in 1839, compares ancient animal husbandry practices with those of his time in order to critique the very elements of animal agriculture that supposedly have only come to characterize meat production in the last fifty or perhaps one hundred years:

> In those days, when tillage was less artificial, and when flocks and herds grazed more at large, and subsisted more upon the spontaneous produce of the uncultivated soil, than in modern times, the flesh of the ox and sheep and other domesticated animals was far less unwholesome than the flesh of the same species of animals fed and fattened on the produce of an exceedingly depraved, and, if I may so speak, morbidly excited soil, which has long been subject to the forcing and depraving practice of modern agriculture. Moreover, the confinement and stall-feeding, and all the other artificial circumstances and educated habits of domesticated animals, render their flesh less wholesome for human aliment. Indeed, as I have already remarked, most of the animals which in modern times are fitted for the slaughter-house and for internment in living sepulchers, are actually in a state of disease

when they are killed; and therefore, shocking as the thought may be, the human stomach in these days of elegant refinement and of science and religion, is actually made a kind of "potter's field" to receive the unknown dead of every disease![39]

I quote at length because the passage disrupts so many pastoral fantasies about pre-twentieth-century meat production in one fell swoop. What Graham is saying here is that meat is unhealthy, in 1839, because the fields the flocks graze are unwholesomely, artificially fertilized—if indeed the animals graze at all. Already, in 1839, meat animals are being produced using practices characteristic of contemporary agriculture: They're being confined and fattened with grain rather than being pastured and grass fed, the animals are diseased from these "unnatural" agricultural practices, and the fatty meat that comes from these sick animals is being eaten by humans who assume their modern diet is natural, ethical, and healthful.

It's not just that farmers are already confining animals in the early nineteenth century, and it's not just that they're already grain rather than grass feeding; they're also trying to industrialize the process. By 1824, newspapers describe "large dairies" that farmers are trying to mechanize through the "use of tubes in milking," an innovation described as having "cruel" consequences for the dairy cattle.[40] Reports of this "new method" of machine-milking cows appear in US newspapers throughout the antebellum period.[41] In addition to industrializing technologically, American animal agriculture was industrializing at the level of scale, as well. Antebellum newspapers describe spectacles in which cows produce milk at a scale totally unrelated to what one family, or one family plus their neighbors, might consume (as in a breathless 1824 report of six cows giving milk sufficient to make "935 pounds of good butter, and upwards of 1100 pounds of cheese")[42] and marvel that slaughterhouses are slaughtering hundreds of thousands of animals per "season": "Hog Slaughter in Cincinnati— During the present season, one hundred and twenty-three thousand one hundred and twenty-eight hogs were slaughtered and 15,823 purchased in pork."[43] In contemporary critiques of the US food system, the desire to maximize animal capital by breeding animals who will fatten in unnaturally short periods of time and who can then be slaughtered at tremendous speed in mind-numbingly great numbers is presented as one of those ways that our food has changed in the last fifty years, to return to the language of *Food, Inc.*'s cold open.

Clearly much has changed in U.S. agriculture over the years, yet we would benefit from observing that capitalism didn't suddenly intrude into animal agriculture in 1950, or 1930, or 1900. It was always there in North American animal agriculture—like the cattle and hogs, it came over with European colonists. From the seventeenth century onward, farmers in New England, for instance, were producing meat for a transatlantic meat market. Live animals were driven to market in Boston, where they were slaughtered, salted, packed, inspected, and shipped to the West Indies.[44] Boston was the chief cattle market of New England during the first century of its existence, and as early as 1638, one hundred head of cattle were being driven from a plantation on the Piscataqua River, in New Hampshire, to Boston; from the 1650s onward, cattle were driven there regularly from the Connecticut Valley.[45] In response to such long-distance cattle transport, the first known colonial anticruelty law designed to protect transported food animals appeared in the 1641 Massachusetts Bay Colony "Body of Liberties": "If any man shall have occasion to leade or drive Cattel from place to place that is far of, so that they be weary, or hungry, or fall sick, or lambe, It shall be lawful to rest or refresh them, for a competent time, in any open place that is not Corne, meadow, or inclosed for some particular use."[46] The meat-export trade was carried on successfully throughout the colonial period, so that just before the American Revolution, meat was second only to fish among New England exports, accounting for 20 percent of the total (versus 35 percent for fish). The industrial and marketing structures that developed to supply this export trade eventually found domestic customers, so that in Boston in the early eighteenth century, the domestic market in meat was large enough to generate complaints about city butchers colluding to keep the price of beef high.[47]

A great deal of the current conversation about problems with the US industrial food system is unconsciously and uncritically presentist, based on a fantasy pastoral past that either never existed or that looked different from what we would suppose. Exposés of the contemporary factory-farm system of animal agriculture in particular tend to suggest, implicitly or explicitly, that before 1900 animal agriculture maintained a pastoral, perhaps even Edenic balance between financial interests, human health, animal welfare, and the environment and to argue that it's to some version of this "preindustrial" domestic-animal economy that the United States should now return. Yet we can challenge that there is any more ethically or ecologically sound past to return to by observing that early national capital was utterly contingent on animal life, an economic reality that encouraged early animal agriculturalists to apply all available technologies to expand and exploit their animal capital. This lens discomfits any pastoral narrative that frames the last fifty years of food industrialization as a dramatic break from what came before and suggests that we understand the current state of factory-farmed animals rather as a fulfillment of the logic of three hundred plus years of North American animal agriculture—a *culmination*, not a divergence.

Observing the continuity of contemporary US agriculture with Anglo-American practices from the colonial period onward matters because narrative matters. Narratives help form our reality; they establish the terms in which we understand the past and the terms in which we imagine the future. When we tell the story of industrial agriculture as the story of a break from a pastoral past, as the story of yet another lost Eden, we're telling a retrograde, antiscience, antiprogress narrative, one too easily punctured by historical inquiry and that anyway ignores the real issue: the long-standing interest animal agriculturalists have in maximizing profit. Technology has allowed us to maximize animal capital in new ways and to new degrees, but with the same old goal.

So long as we conceptualize food sustainability as a recovery of agricultural practices and relationships from a fantasy pastoral past, we limit our ability to imagine and develop the just and environmentally sound food culture that we really need. Significant issues vex human food production going forward. How will we farm enough food to feed 9 billion people amid a changing, unstable climate? And how will we do this in a just and environmentally sound manner? Certainly, we won't do it by returning to premodern agricultural practices; as I have been arguing, there is no simple, more sustainable food past to which we can safely retreat. Whether it is in relation to food production or another aspect of contemporary mainstream US society, recognizing the continuity of our past practices and ideologies with our increasingly disastrous present necessarily undermines sustainability as a useful environmental paradigm.

Unlike critiques of sustainability that frame the principle as having "held out great potential" before it was "appropriated by neo-liberal capitalism,"[48] this book argues that any environmental principle with continuity at its core is bound to fail ethically and environmentally in a US context. When we reckon honestly with the history of US environmental ideas and practices, we are forced to recognize the imbrication of many of our most cherished environmental ideals with the systems that produced the environmental problems to which they apparently respond: capitalism, settler colonialism, and white supremacy. If we want something different—for ourselves and for the planet—we will have to imagine it, and then we will have to build it. Only environmental ethics that foster transformation and that disrupt rather than sustain unjust systems and practices will be radical enough to respond effectively to the social and environmental violence of anthropogenic climate change and looming mass extinctions.

Nineteenth-Century Environmentalisms for a Time of Ecological Crisis

Against Sustainability is divided into two parts, and each part has a dialogic structure: Chapter 1 and Chapter 2 are paired reflections on environmental ethics related to human material consumption; Chapter 3 and Chapter 4 explore paradigms theorizing human coexistence with human and nonhuman others. The first chapter in each pair explores a familiar, cherished environmental paradigm that I argue (like sustainability) fosters continuity and stasis, making it of limited use in the twenty-first century. The second chapter in each pair then nominates an alternative, counterintuitive paradigm that I argue might spark transformative environmental practices that support more just forms of community than the familiar paradigm it would replace. Structuring the book in this dialogic manner is an effort to unsettle our environmental imagination by disrupting narratives that naturalize—and thus render inevitable—destructive values and modes of living.

Chapter 1 takes up the environmental paradigm of recycling in Walt Whitman's first two editions of *Leaves of Grass* (1855 and 1856). While scarcity of materials meant scavenging and reuse were common practices in the nineteenth century (as in previous periods), organic-material recycling first emerged as a scientific principle during the antebellum period. Whitman's journalistic and poetic interests in chemistry and compost have by now been documented, leading scholars to elevate the once-overlooked Whitman into the ecopoetic pantheon. However, this increasingly standard ecocritical reading of Whitman's celebration of material recycling and compost makes sense only so long as Whitman's poetics of appetite are ignored. Chapter 1 places Whitman's interest in compost and organic recycling back alongside his even more famous poetic investment in an indiscriminate, "omnivorous" consumption, in order to evaluate the significance of both to his democratic, environmental, and poetic projects. Compost emerges as the twin of appetite in Whitman's poetic environment, which reveals how recycling authorizes consumption without limits and yields a fundamentally static and therefore nonegalitarian and antiecological vision of community. In the last part of the chapter, I demonstrate what resistance to this paradigm looks like in the poetry of Lucille Clifton, a twentieth-century African American poet self-consciously rewriting

Whitman's vision of democratic and environmental community. Ultimately, I argue that while Clifton resists the dream of cyclical, effortless material recycling and consequence-free consumption, it is nineteenth-century Whitman's fantasy of the earth endlessly recycling and renewing human waste that remains more characteristic of contemporary US life.

Chapter 2 counters the ethic of recycling with an anticonsumerist, joyful frugality theorized in Henry David Thoreau's *Walden* (1854) and the poetry of Emily Dickinson. I begin the chapter by evoking a popular culture of frugality-advice literature that circulated in the antebellum period; I then demonstrate that such advice literature linked refusing to consume with personal happiness and vibrant democratic citizenship. In this nineteenth-century context, Thoreau's experiments in frugal living at Walden Pond emerge as much more central to the book's political and artistic projects than has been recognized. Thoreau's radical minimalism in *Walden* is designed to promote both individual contentment and collective social justice as it challenges a consumerist status quo. In the last part of the chapter, I explore Emily Dickinson's 1860s and 1870s poetry of desire, possession, and consumption. Against readings that have consistently pathologized Dickinson's approach to these topics, I suggest that Dickinson is a complex theorist of consumer desire whose emphasis on the pleasures of anticipation and the disappointments of consumption have much to teach us in the Capitalocene. Ultimately, this chapter suggests that Thoreau and Dickinson together theorize a joyful frugality that shifts the site of pleasure away from consumption, making anticonsumerist lifeways seem not only possible but—more importantly—richly appealing.

My next chapter examines another cherished environmental paradigm emergent in the nineteenth century, preservation, in order to trace its originary logic and effects. The first two parts of this chapter delineate the flawed aesthetic foundation of preservation. I begin with the famed first proposal for a "Nation's Park" in the painter, writer, and showman George Catlin's 1844 *Letters and Notes on the Manners, Customs, and Conditions of North American Indians*, demonstrating that preservation takes shape as an environmental ethic not because value is suddenly understood to inhere in nonhuman nature; rather, as the United States expands and develops, indigenous, "wild" natural spectacles are theorized as beneficial to an increasingly "civilized" white US population. The ecological and ethical stakes for these aesthetic judgments were high, as Francis Parkman Jr.'s 1849 *The Oregon Trail* demonstrates. Where Catlin calls for the preservation of the remarkable beauty he sees in the Plains peoples, bison, and their threatened landscape, Parkman writes of an ugliness in need of violent eradication. In the final portion of the chapter, I turn from preservation's flawed aesthetic logic to its flawed spatial logic. Herman Melville's *Moby-Dick* (1851) considers and rejects the possibility of whale extinction by insisting that whales have ocean sanctuaries to which they can retreat. Melville's portrait of the sea and its creatures as unconquerable rests on a false confidence in discrete, separable spaces and in oceanic and planetary resilience. I explicate the failures of these beliefs through a reading of A. S. Byatt's tale of plastic pollution, "Sea Story" (2013), which plays out the destructive twenty-first-century consequences of *Moby-Dick*'s romantic ideas about nature. Altogether, the chapter suggests that preservation is an environmental ethic imbricated in settler colonialism, incapable of fostering meaningful human or interspecies community and whose meager benefits only continue to diminish as our anthropogenic climate crisis intensifies. If, like recycling, preservation generated some positive practices, the paradigm remained and remains violently complicit in the very problems it is designed to address.

The last chapter counters preservation with radical pet keeping, an unlikely environmentalism keyed to the strengths and the weaknesses of the Anthropocene. The Anthropocene proposal has been so widely embraced during the last decade that despite its drawbacks, it's likely to be with us for some time. One portion of its influence and appeal comes from its sometimes oversimplified claim of human domination of the planet, a claim that makes space for the optimistic possibility that humans might yet embrace our responsibility and capability to fix the environmental messes that (at least some) humans (and some systems) have made. Thus far, attempts to imagine less-oppressive versions of our human-dominated but multispecies communities have either focused on wild animals or theorized nonhuman nature's "domestication" through the figure of the garden. By contrast, I argue for the utility of the figure of the pet by recovering its significance to particular antebellum antislavery theories of community.

The first part of Chapter 4 examines how figures of the animal, beast, pet, and pet keeper typically feature in antislavery literature by authors ranging from David Walker to contributors to the *Liberator*. The next section explores Hannah Crafts's *The Bondwoman's Narrative* (c. 1853–1861), which develops a disturbing vignette of pet and enslaved pet keeper murder that undermines the naturalness of oppression based upon racial and species difference. In this and other scenes, Crafts's novel undermines the supposed naturalness of racial and at times even species difference, even as it represents the violent uses to which such differences are put. The result is a sophisticated attack on chattel slavery and racist ideologies undergirding

Black oppression in the nineteenth century. Ultimately, Crafts offers a model of community-with-difference that hinges on interdependence rather than independence. The last part of the chapter treats Harriet Wilson's *Our Nig* (1859), which depicts an interspecies friendship between an indentured servant, Frado, and Frado's pet dog, Fido. Frado's transgressive sympathy allows her to imagine familial relationships between not only Blacks and whites and servants and masters but between humans and animals, as well. The chapter argues that the radical pet keeping imagined in these two novels rests upon an ethic of care that fosters interracial and interspecies solidarity not dependent on sameness. Radical pet keeping, like Black feminisms, foregrounds interdependence across differences, making it a useful environmental paradigm in the Anthropocene, as climate change increasingly forces all life on Earth to live in the world *Anthropos* has built.

Against Sustainability concludes with a coda that contrasts Anglo-American and certain Indigenous North American approaches to "zero waste." Mainstream contemporary representations of the zero-waste environmental paradigm focus on redesigning and carefully managing the manufacturing and disposal processes for commodities. I explore the limitations of this vision through a brief account of the "zero-waste" meatpacking practices detailed in Upton Sinclair's *The Jungle* (1906). By contrast, Robin Wall Kimmerer's *Braiding Sweetgrass* (2013) links a zero-waste ethic to a decolonized relationship to the earth. Achieving this version of zero waste would require transforming not simply US manufacturing and disposal processes but its culture. Using these examples, the coda suggests that there are contexts in which sustainability works as a paradigm. It makes sense to "sustain" Indigenous environmental cultures that resist rather than perpetuate the systems responsible for our environmental degradation. By contrast, Anglo-American sustainability maintains continuity with capitalism's profit and growth imperatives, with settler-colonial resource extraction, and other values and practices inimical to just biotic community. Radical action will only come from transformative paradigms that help Americans confront our past truthfully and then imagine and act for a more environmentally sound present. The coda ultimately suggests we might dethrone sustainability for an orientation toward a utopianism that centers critique and transformation. Such a utopian orientation, combined with a robust commitment to strategic, provisional ethics—including joyful frugality and radical pet keeping—might help bridge the gap between our deadly present and a more livable future.

CHAPTER I

Recycling Fantasies: Whitman, Clifton, and the Dream of Compost

Recycling and reuse were common features of many Americans' lives during the nineteenth century. While these processes sometimes shade into one another, reuse, the process of fixing or finding uses for damaged or broken items, was particularly standard in all but the wealthiest households (as it had been in earlier periods) given the relative scarcity of materials and the labor richness of rural and urban communities alike. A culture of frugality that found its chief expression in domestic guidebooks promoted reuse practices and provided instruction in some of the more common forms of reuse.[1] Reuse could often be achieved with labor already found in a given home, though items such as clocks might require the care of a specialist to be put back into use. Recycling, on the other hand, had its own economy, one that depended on the poor (and often, poor children) to scavenge and junk dealers to buy and vend. According to *Waste and Want: A Social History of Trash*, scavenging recyclables was "a chore and a common pastime for poor children, who foraged for shreds of canvas or bits of metal on the docks, for coal on the railroad tracks, and for bottles and food on the streets and in the alleys."[2]

Occasionally in the nineteenth century, recycling was a more formal part of industry, as in Melville's "The Paradise of Bachelors and the Tartarus of Maids," whose diptych depicts first the splendor and comfort of wealthy London bachelors and then the squalid lives of the young American women who recycle those wealthy bachelors' castoff clothing into cheap paper. This recycling activity means the young women must breathe "fine, poisonous particles, which from all sides darted, subtilely, as motes in sunbeams, into the lungs."[3] In the twenty-first century, as in the nineteenth, recycling frequently takes place on the backs of the poor, and recyclers are typically distant from the sites of consumption (if not always production) of the objects they recycle. Wealthy countries often outsource some or most of their e-waste, used car batteries, unwanted clothing, and more to be recycled in countries from Mexico to China to Pakistan to India, often at great economic, health, and environmental cost to the recyclers and those who live adjacent to their recycling activity.[4] Increasingly, countries are rejecting imports of recyclables, refusing to become a "dumping ground" for the contaminated waste of wealthy countries.[5] In the United States, the loss of these overseas dumping grounds means that higher percentages of recyclables are being incinerated or heaped in landfills, setting up environmental-justice disasters for the communities who live near disposal sites and putting increasing pressure on the American public to confront the consequences of their consumption habits.[6]

Recycling became increasingly state organized in the twentieth century as the value of scrap increased during the first two world wars, and by 1970 recycling's familiar logo and rhetoric was in place.[7] Scavenging activities of the nineteenth-century poor certainly had economic and environmental benefits, but they were not yet touted by the wealthy as part of an environmental vision. Organic-material recycling did emerge as a scientific paradigm during the antebellum period, however, as chemists such as Humphry Davy and Justus Liebig explained the process and significance of decomposition.[8] Despite lacking the sophisticated "microbiological, biochemical, and pedological techniques and concepts" that would emerge in the 1880s, scientists such as Liebig were increasingly able to describe the nitrogen cycle, the significance of minerals to agriculture, and so on.[9] As organic recycling emerged as scientific fact in the nineteenth century, it caught the attention of many nonscientists, not least Walt Whitman. Whitman's poetry is committed to the proposition that all life—all matter, even—is intimately interconnected. This commitment is expressed in his boundless sympathy, in his claims to inhabit imaginatively not just other human subjects but animals of all kinds, trees, plants, rocks, and so on. The

proposition is emblematized in Whitman's obsession with compost, particularly evident in the first few editions of *Leaves of Grass*. The central mystery of grass, summed up in the child's famous query of "what is the grass?"
turns out to be, more than anything else, compost or, to put it another way,
decomposing corpses. After four brief stanzas that offer suggestive but
abstract possibilities as answers to the mystery of the grass ("the flag of my
disposition," "the handkerchief of the Lord," etc.), the poem suddenly provides a concrete answer in the form of an extended, eight-stanza medita-
tion on the grass as "the beautiful uncut hair of graves" full of "hints about
the dead young men and women," "hints about old men and mothers, and the
offspring taken soon out of their laps."[10] Such "hints" famously culminate
in the claim that the dead "are alive and well somewhere; / The smallest
sprout shows there is really no death."[11] This rejection of death is not just
an optimistic metaphor; Whitman means it—matter doesn't disappear, it
simply gets recycled.

As scholars from David Reynolds onward have amply demonstrated,
Whitman's interest in the recycling of matter was stoked by the work of
Justus Liebig in particular.[12] Whitman glowingly reviewed one of Liebig's
major publications, *Organic Chemistry in Its Application to Agriculture and
Physiology*, in the *Brooklyn Daily Eagle* in 1847, touting "Chemistry—that
involves the essences of creation, and the changes, and the growths, and
formations and decays, of so large a constituent part of the earth, and the
things thereof!"[13] Critics who have treated Whitman's writing about compost have almost uniformly tied it to progressive democratic and environmental attitudes. Mark Noble has argued that "for Whitman, Liebig
discloses the organism as a fact of the recombination of smaller bodies, the
immortality of materials perpetually recycled and rearranged, and the pure
democracy and thus broad possibility that are both inherent in and constitutive of nature."[14] Paul Outka has taken Whitman's use of compost in
Leaves of Grass to "undo the distinction between the living and the dead, a
radical decentering of the anthropomorphic that aligns Whitman here
with the deep ecological view of the human as very much a subset of the
larger biotic community."[15] M. Jimmie Killingsworth, reading Whitman's
"This Compost," finds that "faith in the earth's bounty . . . is based in this
poem not upon the pioneer's sense of the world as an inexhaustible store-
house for human exploitation but upon respect for the power of the
earth's processes to restore health and complete its mighty cycles."[16] Maria McFarland has connected Whitman's writings about compost to his
interest in urban sanitary reform and what we would now call environmental health.[17] Serpil Opperman has argued that Whitman's poetic use

of compost emblematizes what it means "to be mutually environed in nature's cyclical rhythms."[18] Through the lens of compost, Whitman has increasingly emerged as a model of ecopoetics, contradicting earlier dismissals of his work by environmentally minded critics.[19]

To foreground compost is thus to beg the question of Whitman as an environmental poet. How can a poet who pays such respect to natural cycles, who repeatedly celebrates the interconnection of living and nonliving objects, fail to be one of the United States' most important environmental writers? In fact, Whitman has been increasingly read in just this way. To be sure, he has not yet received the same degree of attention as contemporaries such as Thoreau or Emerson, but ecocritical interest in Whitman has not been lacking.[20] Whitman's corpus is fertile ground for environmentally minded critics who observe Whitman's attention to the particular sights, sounds, and rhythms of the nonhuman landscapes and creatures he describes, his interest in waste and decay, and—given ecocriticism's own expanding and overdue attention to representations of urban space—his portraits of city life.[21] Such ecocritical work has added richness to our sense of Whitman as a poet and to our understanding of the nineteenth-century US environmental imagination. Yet for all his celebration of "feuillage," his ecstatic sexual congress with the sea, and his mystical take on material recycling, if we keep Whitman's famously undiscriminating appetite front and center, he remains an unlikely environmental poet.

In its own time, the heavy emphasis on appetite in the early editions of *Leaves of Grass* would have been underscored by how its public encountered it: marketed and distributed (and, by the second edition, published) exclusively by the phrenological firm Fowler and Wells. Potential readers might have first met with the book through an advertisement in the columns of Fowler and Wells' popular health-reformist magazine *Life Illustrated*, listed among their catalogue of "New and Miscellaneous Books" available by mail or for sale in their New York City "Cabinet," as the reformers called their storefront and offices on Nassau Street in Manhattan. Imagine the experience of entering Fowler and Wells' phrenological cabinet to buy one of the first editions: Surrounded by busts and casts of heads, death masks, paintings and drawings of animals and humans, the "savage" and the civilized, the criminal and the virtuous; nestled between the writings of the vegetarian reformer Sylvester Graham and sacks of his coarse, whole wheat "Graham flour"; between books on mesmerism, the water cure, temperance, and the dangers of ladies' lacing; amid these and other self-help, health-oriented publications and products you would find Whitman's thin volume of ninety-five pages, "shaped like a small atlas," as the anonymous 1855 reviewer described it in *Life Illustrated*.[22] In other words, the early editions of *Leaves of Grass* were sold in what were essentially protomodern health stores, to people shopping for a brand of do-it-yourself self-knowledge and physical perfectionism. Such a consumer history should remind us that for the "poet of the body," as Whitman denominates his speaker in "Song of Myself," an interest in intake, consumption, and digestion were literal.

In this chapter, I juxtapose Whitman's interest in compost with his poetry's obsession with appetite, exploring the connections between consumption and material recycling and the relationship of both of these to Whitman's democratic and poetic projects. First I explore the relationship between omnivorous appetite and egalitarianism in order to argue that Whitman's commitment to indiscriminate consumption and sympathy is fundamentally antireformist: His purposeful determination to incorporate everything and everyone is precisely what prevents *Leaves of Grass* from modeling a more transformative, egalitarian version of poetic and political community.

Next I connect Whitman's appetitive poetic stance to his interest in compost, arguing that although compost affords an organic foundation for Whitman's poetic project of unification, it also authorizes the unlimited appetite—for goods, bodies, sights, sounds, pleasure, and for nonhuman nature itself—so characteristic of *Leaves of Grass*. In Whitman's hands, the cyclical quality of compost yields a fantasy of perfect material recycling, of an earth that can convert everything discarded, dead, or used up back into something alive, clean, and usable again. Appetite is thus the twin of compost in Whitman's poetic environment.[23] At the end of the chapter, I read Whitman's approach to biotic community, compost, and the celebration of the self against the twentieth-century African American poet Lucille Clifton's treatment of these same topics. I argue that Clifton, a poet self-consciously in dialogue with Walt Whitman, develops an ecopoetics that insists upon mortality and loss, scarcity and endings, as essential to the production of real ethical and ecological community. Clifton's rich ecopoetry articulates the difficulties and dangers of Whitman's (and often, our own) uncritical embrace of consumption and compost.

Ultimately, Whitman helps make visible how recycling authorizes consumption without limits and yields a fundamentally static and therefore nonegalitarian, antiecological vision of community. By demonstrating that material recycling is the linchpin of Whitman's indiscriminate appetite, I argue that wealthy resource omnivores[24] in the United States should reexamine the relationship between their own runaway consumerism and a corresponding intellectual and affective investment in the idea of recycling. While environmentally minded critics and theorists including Serpil Oppermann[25] and Donna Haraway have recently turned to compost to theorize "building a habitable earth in sustained troubled times,"[26] Whitman speaks a word of caution about how we incorporate principles of recycling and compost into our vision of biotic community.

Digesting the Nation: Whitman's Appetite

In one of the more famous passages of *Leaves of Grass*, "Walt Whitman, an American," described as "fleshy and sensual. . . . eating drinking and breeding," remarks, "I believe in the flesh and the appetites," and the poems certainly reflect it.[27] In "Song of Myself," in particular, Whitman incorporates—makes part of his body of work—everything from humans, described as "ever the eaters and drinkers"; to work, the process whereby men "feed the greed of the belly [by] the brains liberally spooning"; to beef; chowder; tea; shortcake; and other literal consumables.[28] In fact, even the poem is characterized as food, "true sustenance" for its readers.[29] "Sit awhile wayfarer," the speaker commands. "Here are biscuits to eat and here is milk to drink."[30] Whether we're talking about food, drink, bodies, sex, work, pain, the sun, or the air, Whitman's speaker is hungry for it all. "All this I swallow and it tastes good," he tells us, "I like it well, and it becomes mine."[31] "I know perfectly well my own egotism, / And know my omnivorous words, and cannot say less," Whitman's speaker trumpets, and a voracious omnivorousness is indeed an apt characterization of his poetic stance.[32] If Emerson's evocative bodily image for the poet is a "transparent eyeball," the more appropriate metonymy for Whitman's speaker is a gaping mouth.

Whitman expressed a deep interest in food and in physical culture in his private journals, his journalism, and his poetry and fiction. Before writing *Leaves of Grass*, Whitman contemplated a career as a kind of lecturing health guru: "His programme for attaining and preserving health was variously projected as a series of popular lectures, a manual of instructions, and a group of weekly magazine articles."[33] In 1849, Whitman even "signed a note 'to pay $25 as rent of store in Granada Hall,' apparently in connection with an abortive plan to deliver a series of lectures on physical culture and thus supplement his meager earnings from journalism."[34] By 1858, Whitman was publishing these physiological convictions in the *New York Daily Atlas* as a series of articles on "Manly Health and Training, with Off-

Hand Hints toward Their Conditions."[35] The key features of Whitman's philosophy of health around this period, according to his journals and journalism, were "frequent bathing, temperance in eating, and abstinence from medicine," alongside "a plentiful supply of fresh air." Whitman, like many of his contemporaries, was especially fixated on "the stomach as the key to health" and advocated for a plain if hearty diet: "beef, rice, fruit[,] potatoes, bread—these in plenty become a man, twice a day—perhaps even thrice a day; they are to be plain and rude."[36]

Whitman's first two editions of *Leaves of Grass* in particular bear the traces of his dietary enthusiasms during their gestation. Eating is especially central to Whitman's poetic project in *Leaves of Grass* because Whitman imagines the work of the poet as ingesting—and digesting—the people, animals, objects, and environments of the United States in order to transform them into a poem appropriately representative of the nation.[37] In his reliance on this organic metaphor for literary production, Whitman is not alone, even among his contemporaries. Henry David Thoreau, for instance, uses digestion as a recurring metaphor for reading and writing in *Walden*; for Thoreau, discrimination and limits are keys to physical or intellectual health.[38] Far from advocating rigid consumptive discipline, Whitman's poetry valorizes an unlimited, omnivorous appetite; eating and drinking, ingesting and digesting, play a central role in Whitman's literary *and* political projects in the first few editions of *Leaves of Grass*. This is in part because, as one scholar has argued, for Whitman, "democracy begins with the body, which is the link with nature and the common denominator among all classes, races, divided groups."[39] Whitman, like Thoreau,[40] draws on the linkage made by classical republicanism between the health of the body of the citizen and the health of the body politic. In "Manly Health and Training," he claims,

> The young men of Athens, and other Greek cities, were trained in
> their bodily, mental, and moral developments and perfections together,
> and this, as we have before intimated, is the only way, indeed, in
> which training can be just to the whole man . . . from such a foundation alone, he will be more apt to become good, upright, friendly, and
> self-respected.[41]

The political significance of healthy or unhealthy bodies becomes clear when we recognize that Whitman confronts the midcentury US political crisis precisely as a bodily crisis. In his 1856 polemical essay "The Eighteenth Presidency!," Whitman claims, "At present, the personnel of the government . . . in executives and elsewhere, is drawn from limber-tongued lawyers, very fluent but empty, feeble old men, professional politicians, dandies, dyspeptics, and so forth, and rarely drawn from the solid body of the people."[42] Whitman critiques the "feeble," emasculated, and dyspeptic bodies that fill the government, as opposed to the solid bodies of the people, and then turns to a renewed emphasis on the American body as a solution to the crisis of antebellum democracy he observes.

Leaves of Grass addresses the fracturing of the union, framing the crisis as a crisis of political representation—as a failure of the elected representatives to reflect the citizenry they are supposed to represent. Mark Maslan has argued that Whitman's model for perfect democratic representation is poetic possession, a state in which the will of the poet-representative is overwhelmed by a force larger than himself. In this state, the poet attempts to "*redeem* the notion of representative authority from the forces of self-interest that he sees as its ultimate enemy."[43] Whitman's naturalized, poetic democracy doesn't just repair the political formulation, "out of many, one"; it also revises it through the speaker's voracious consumption: *Into one—one speaker, one body, one poem—go many*. In this sense, the "many" become "one" by being consumed by the speaker: "And these one and all tend inward to me," explains the poet.[44] Taking the nation to—and *into*—the body of the poem helps Whitman produce the expansive sympathy *Leaves of Grass* has become known for. By ingesting the full spectrum of life in the antebellum United States, the poet achieves the bodily and emotional "merge," or "fusion," through which "he calls up a sociality of cohesion."[45] The political crisis of representation is solved through wholesale ingestion of the American populace and landscape, human and nonhuman alike. The poet doesn't just mirror the people; he ingests and incorporates them into the body of the poem, poetically perfecting the failures of democratic representation that Whitman criticizes in the public sphere.

The poetic republic that emerges from Whitman's voracious ingestion has been credited as more radically inclusive than the political republic Whitman sought to critique and improve.[46] It has become almost cliché to ascribe revolutionary, reformatory intent to the consumptive catalogues and other representational strategies of "merge" in the 1855 *Leaves of Grass*. The critics who make such claims see a radical egalitarianism and sympathy for African Americans at work in this first edition, although almost everyone admits the supposed "egalitarianism" has all but disappeared by the second, 1856 edition, which promulgates a much more typical for its time eugenicist perspective.[47] Even if we uncritically accept this reading, we might wonder at a vision of equality that can barely be maintained for a single year. But we do not have to accept egalitarianism as the only explanation for, or effect of, the famously voracious sympathy of the 1855 edition of *Leaves of Grass*.

Of the scenes of sympathy frequently cited in support of the egalitarianism or antislavery politics of *Leaves of Grass*, two stand out: first, the scene in which the speaker comforts a runaway slave, and second, the portrait of the "negro dray driver" in section 13 of "Song of Myself."[48] The first of these scenes, which occurs early in the poem, in section 10, begins when the speaker encounters "the runaway slave" who "comes to [his house] and stop[s] outside": "I heard his motions crackling the twigs of the woodpile, / Through the swung half-door of the kitchen I saw him limpsey and weak."[49] Transparently a scene of opposition to the Fugitive Slave Law, which was widely reviled because it forced more Northerners to get directly involved in enforcing slavery, we see the "Me Myself" of the poem comforting a representative *type* rather than an individual runaway slave ("*The* runaway slave came to my house," the speaker says, rather than "*A*"). The representative slave in this passage never speaks, so the speaker's portrait of him as an injured body, "limpsey and weak," with "revolving eyes" and a distinct "awkwardness," goes uncontested.[50]

Moreover, the larger context of the runaway-slave scene undermines the speaker's sympathy; it occurs at the end of a section otherwise representing scenes of hunting as integral to American identity. Beginning with the line "Alone far in the wilds and mountains I hunt," the section celebrates the different forms of community that arise through hunting, including solitary frontier hunting, the marriage of a trapper to a Native woman ("a red girl"), boatmen and clamdiggers who share a joyful meal "round the chowder-kettle," and so on.[51] Arguably, the runaway-slave episode functions as a foil that counterbalances the "celebrated" forms of hunting, yet Whitman makes no mention of the slave hunters and no more condemns this form of hunting than he condemns either hunting or slavery as a whole. That the scene is grouped with other scenes of hunting celebrated for their ability to produce US community and identity finally suggests that Whitman cares more about the Northerner's negative participation in the hunt than about the slave "quarry."

The egalitarian claims for this passage are made on the basis of the speaker's physical intimacy with the runaway slave—he gives the runaway "a room that entered from my own" and proclaims, "I had him sit next me

at table. . . . My firelock leaned in the corner."[52] From a first encounter in
the kitchen to the protective shared meal, the speaker seeks to illustrate
his hospitality and companionship in this scene, the extent to which he is
"the mate and companion of people," as he puts it in line 128. After all, as
Donna Haraway remarks in *When Species Meet*, "companion" comes from
"the Latin *cum panis*, 'with bread.' Messmates at table are companions."[53]
Yet one need only consult antebellum slave narratives such as Harriet Ja-
cobs's harrowing account of sexual harassment in *Incidents in the Life of a
Slave Girl* to realize that scenes of intimacy between Black and white bodies were not always perceived as "egalitarian" by enslaved persons.[54] Even
critics dedicated to the claim that "*Leaves of Grass* portrays African Americans as equal partners with whites in a democratic future" are forced to
admit that in this passage, the depiction of the fugitive person "in some
ways rehearses the romantic racialist notion of blacks as helpless, docile
children" and that "moreover, the slave's identity is elided: he is no longer
an actor but rather a body acted upon, objectified and [finally] consumed
by the speaker's passion to assert his own humanitarianism."[55] In this way,
Whitman replicates the problem of sympathy Saidiya Hartman outlines
in *Scenes of Subjection*: "In making the other's suffering one's own, this suffering is occluded by the other's obliteration."[56] There is finally little in
this scene to challenge or make more inclusive Whitman's claim in "The
Eighteenth Presidency!" that the "millions of white citizens" who labor are
the "true people" of the United States.

The celebration of the "negro that drives the huge dray of the stoneyard" in section 13 of "Song of Myself" is more complicated. This could
be a portrait of a free black laborer, although the grammar of the first few
lines peculiarly reverses the relationship between the man and the chained
piece of stone he is involved in moving: "The negro holds firmly the reins of
his four horses. . . . the block swags underneath on its tied-over chain, /
The negro that drives the huge dray of the stoneyard. . . ."[57] The juxtaposi-
tion of the image of the "chain" at the end of line 219 and "the negro" at the
beginning of 220 ensures that whatever type of labor is being represented,
a specter of slavery haunts the passage. Moreover, the ellipses that arrive
in the middle of each of these lines create caesuras that encourage the reader
to hear "the block swags underneath on its tied-over chain, / The negro
that drives the huge dray of the stoneyard" as a sentence that connects and
in fact subordinates "negro" to the chained "block," which seems syntac-
tically to be the phrase's primary subject. Nevertheless, this section does
offer a positive picture of Black labor, one in which the "steady and tall"
laborer "stands poised on one leg on the stringpiece":

His blue shirt exposes his ample neck and breast and loosens over his
  hipband,
His glance is calm and commanding. . . . he tosses the slouch of his hat
  away from his forehead,
The sun falls on his crispy hair and moustache. . . . falls on the back of his
  polish'd and perfect limbs.[58]

As Karen Sánchez-Eppler has observed, this description in many ways
matches the stylized portrait of Whitman that proceeded the 1855 edition
of *Leaves of Grass*.[59] Given Whitman's free-soil idealization of labor, this
positive celebration of a Black laborer stands as one of the more inclusive
moments in "Song of Myself." Yet critics who read the scene this way generally fail to note that the respectful description is immediately undercut
by the lines that follow it: "I behold the picturesque giant and love him. . . .
and I do not stop there, / I go with the team also."[60] In this context, both
"picturesque" and "giant" are familiar terms in the mid-nineteenth-century
racial vocabulary that work to dehumanize the laborer who has just been
so humanly described.

Just as important to note, however, is that the speaker's sympathetic investment does not stop with the drayman but extends to his horses as
well—"I go with the team also"—in a line that initiates the catalogue of
animal images and bodies that fills out the remainder of the section and
extends through most of the next. Just as in the runaway-slave passage,
where the hunted Black body is situated between the hunted nonhuman
animals that precede it and the famous scene of the twenty-nine bathers
that follows it, here the drayman passage follows the celebration of presumably white laboring bodies and leads into the celebration of nonhuman
animal bodies. In both passages, the "celebrations" of Black bodies are con-
textually linked to nonhuman animal bodies, an observation that should
affect the measure we take of these portraits, given the common racist use
to which such supposed linkages were put in the eighteenth and nineteenth
centuries.[61]

What does it actually mean for Whitman's sympathy to "go with the
team also"? What can this broadening of his sympathy to the nonhuman tell
us about his expressions of sympathy for humans, marginalized or otherwise? The celebratory catalogue of animal bodies in *Leaves of Grass* in
general, and in these sections in particular, is extensive. Horses, oxen,
geese, dogs, wood-drakes, mocking birds, panthers, rattlesnakes, black
bears, mice, whales, buffalo: "[I] am stucco'd with quadrupeds and birds
all over," the speaker remarks in line 671, and it is apt. Yet in Whitman's

poem, although a wide variety of American animals may be represented, and although the speaker may even occasionally imaginatively identify with them, such sympathetic representation has no effect on the material realities or social position of the animals in question. Unlike the many eighteenth- and nineteenth-century writers who begin with sympathy and end by considering animals as subjects with at least some natural rights, Whitmanian sympathy never leads to questions about how animals may be used by human beings or whether they have something like a right to live without pain and suffering.[62]

Animals are, perhaps inevitably, valued in Whitman's omnivorous epic as food, since ruminants are the necessary intermediary step between humans and the all-important grass: Animals eat the grass, and then humans eat the animals. The symbolic significance of animal flesh in the poem is clear in scenes when we see the speaker wonder, "How is it I extract strength from the beef I eat?," as he does in section 20, and the question leads directly back to the open mystery of the grass, the mystery of being: "What is a man anyhow? What am I? and what are you?"[63] Highlighting the role of ruminants as intermediaries is part of the uniquely appetitive spin Whitman is placing on the biblical source for his central symbol; when in Isaiah the prophet is told to "cry" that "all flesh is grass," we don't necessarily think of the food chain, but in Whitman, we do. Hay is called "the dried grass of the harvest-time," and Whitman devotes a section of "Song of Myself" to haying, the process whereby grass literally becomes part of human bodies by becoming fodder for food animals.[64]

Yet it is not only as food that animals receive consideration; occasionally, they are also considered as fellow sentient beings. "Oxen that rattle the yoke or halt in the shade, what is that you express in your eyes? / It seems to me more than all the print I have read in my life," the speaker says in section 13, seemingly recognizing animals as fellow laborers and perhaps even as bodies in pain.[65] But while Whitman's speaker may "think [he] could turn and live awhile with the animals. . . . they are so placid and self-contained," and while he does celebrate qualities in animals that humans seem to lack ("They do not sweat and whine about their condition," etc.), nonhuman animals are finally, like everything else in the poem, reflections of the speaker: "They show their relations to me and I accept them; / They bring me tokens of myself," Whitman writes.[66] Ultimately, none of the speaker's sympathy translates into change, into a vision of limitations on animal labor, for example, let alone a claim that animals have an absolute right to "to life, liberty, and the pursuit of happiness," as Whitman's acquaintance Bronson Alcott put it.[67] Despite recognizing that ani-

mal perspectives may occasionally have something valuable to contribute
to "Myself" and his poetic democracy, *Leaves of Grass* never fundamentally
shifts the place of animals in the nation in a way that challenges or revises
the species hierarchy. Again, context helps us take the measure of Whitman's sympathy; the long catalogue of animal bodies that comes after "I
go with the team also" is immediately preceded by celebrations of a butcher-
boy, blacksmith, and drayman. Observing this progression limits the
radical nature of all of those portraits insofar as Whitman still seems to
be operating within a hierarchy of being that becomes explicitly eugenicist and white supremacist by the 1856 edition.

Unlike other nineteenth-century perspectives on the same topic, the
sympathy expressed for the animals in the 1855 *Leaves of Grass* is thus essentially without effect, something that should lead us to reconsider other
forms of sympathy expressed in the poems. Whitmanian sympathy in the
1855 *Leaves of Grass* is an appetitive, "omnivorous sympathy" based on the
speaker's ability to consume, and thereby appropriate, all forms of life and
experience, human or otherwise. "All this I swallow and it tastes good. . . .
I like it well, and it becomes mine, / I am the man. . . . I suffered. . . . I was
there," he tells us in section 33.[68] As Whitman's "Myself" incorporates into
himself diverse forms of suffering or experience, he becomes them: "All
these I feel or am," he assures us.[69] "I do not ask the wounded person how
he feels. . . . I myself become the wounded person."[70] D. H. Lawrence famously critiques this model of sympathy, lamenting, "Whitman said Sympathy. If only he had stuck to it! Because Sympathy means feeling with,
not feeling for."[71] The distinction is critical because in "merging" with the
"negro slave," in feeling "for" rather than "with," Whitman assimilates,
or imagines himself to assimilate, the experience of the enslaved man's suffering rather than entering into the spirit of his reaction to his suffering.
This model of feeling *for* rather than *with* emerges from the speaker's zeal-
ously appetitive stance, and in this sense, it is integral to the poem's design. Yet such sympathy is ethically bankrupt because it creates aesthetic
spectacles of suffering that have no political effect. This is clear because
despite occasionally representing some of the more painful realities of slavery, emotive expressions of Black suffering in *Leaves of Grass* fail to disrupt
the political systems or social organizations that structure such suffering,
even within the poetic republic of the poem.

That Whitman erases and elides rather than remakes or reimagines
power relations is evident in a famously symbolic instance of Whitman's
"egalitarianism," the image of the geographic universality of the grass:
"Sprouting alike in broad zones and narrow zones, / Growing among black

folks as among white, / Kanuck, Tuckahoe, Congressman, Cuff, I give them the same, I receive them the same."[72] The grass here grows "among" "black folks as among white," connecting them, surely, but through a kind of natural unity that is imagined to exist between prepolitical subjects. The grass stands as an affecting natural image that unites all citizens of the republic, but because it relies on a nature/culture divide to do so, this image pictures such national unity taking place in a natural space outside of culture, rather than remaking or reimagining the political structures that organize the lives of the Black and white "folks."[73] Whitman thus never fundamentally reimagines the body politic because while he may create an expansive picture of all the things his poem, and thus the United States, can contain, he doesn't write the diverse people he represents into any new relation to one another.

In the absence of a reimagined political process, the sympathy professed in the 1855 *Leaves of Grass* coexists remarkably peacefully with racial and social hierarchies, even in cases where it initially claims to be overturning them. In a scene of carnivorous communion, the speaker shares a meal with social outcasts, proclaiming,

> This is the meal pleasantly set. . . . this is the meat and drink for natural
>   hunger,
> It is for the wicked just the same as the righteous. . . . I make appointments
>   with all,
> I will not have a single person slighted or left away,
> The keptwoman and sponger and thief are hereby invited. . . . the
>   heavy-lipped slave is invited. . . . the venerealee is invited;
> There shall be no difference between them and the rest.[74]

In subsequent editions, Whitman would revise "This is the meal pleasantly set" to "This is the meal equally set," playing up the intended equality of the scene.[75] This image of even the most ostracized inhabitants of the United States coming together over a meal "pleasantly" or "equally set . . . for natural hunger" is meant to be an image of radical inclusion in which "there shall be no difference between them and the rest." Yet by enumerating these outcasts separately, by singling them out by name for "inclusion," the speaker differentiates them, creating the "difference between them and the rest" he claims to be undoing. The inclusion of "the heavy-lipped slave" in the list, a racially coded figure to begin with, is of course especially disturbing in light of the inevitable moral coding of the "keptwoman and sponger and thief" and "venerealee" who make up the other diners. Unable to erase the divisions and problems of status that trouble the bodies that he consumes—eats and eats with—the speaker can only declare by fiat that they do not exist, even as he replicates them in his poetry.

For all their focus on America's great future, Whitman's celebratory poetics in *Leaves of Grass* finally remain locked in a present frequently represented as inevitable. The famous Whitmanian poetic catalogues are not so much acts of reimagining the possible as they are acts of naming, invoking, and ultimately reinstantiating social and political realities.[76] Whitman celebrates the body in ways that do recast Victorian social mores about natural bodily functions, including sex, but he never reimagines the body in civic terms. As the extension of Whitmanian sympathy to nonhuman animals demonstrates, sympathy *can* exist in the poem without challenging hierarchies of inequality.

Because Whitman's primary rhetorical mode in *Leaves of Grass* is characterized by aggressive consumption, this mode focuses him on representation, celebration, and preservation of what is already extant—more conservative political and aesthetic goals than those that drive literary reformers like Alcott or Thoreau. "You shall stand by my side and look in the mirror with me," the 1855 "Preface" proclaims, and the poems that follow bear out this mimetic aspiration.[77] "Knowing the perfect fitness and equanimity of things, while they discuss I am silent, and go bathe and admire myself," the speaker of "Song of Myself" brags.[78] No partisan reformer, this speaker encloses all sides rather than choosing one: "Evil propels me, and reform of evil propels me. . . . I stand indifferent."[79] In what sense, then, are we to take assertions such as "all the men ever born are my brothers. . . . and the women my sisters and lovers"?[80] Similar to the image of the grass, this statement seems to posit prepolitical or extrapolitical subjects, and these subjects are united through sympathetic familial bonds apparently unrelated to the otherwise constitutive web of power relations in which the "men" and "women" must actually live.

Whitman's poetic republic, by design, mimetically replicates the state of the midcentury US republic, in which perspectives sympathetic to the suffering of free and enslaved Black people did of course actually exist. The poetic representative who speaks in Whitman's poem is proven superior to elected political representatives partially because he manages to voice, or represent, the undeniably extant antislavery perspectives. But the fact is that since Whitman considers free white laborers as the only real citizens or "true people," he sees no need to fundamentally reimagine the human bodies he represents in *Leaves of Grass*.[81]

The point of this reading of the civic possibilities occasioned by the omnivorous sympathy of the 1855 *Leaves of Grass* is not somehow to shame the book for reflecting racial attitudes common in the antebellum United States. Rather, I wish to point out that the very reflection is essential to Walt Whitman's literary and political project. The mimetic aspiration of *Leaves of Grass* emerges from Whitman's political analysis. Whitman's words and his poetics consume the nation as a whole in order provide a *digest* of extant American bodies and character. However artful, inspired, and in some ways even democratic that digest may be, his representational strategy means that the poet of *Leaves of Grass* celebrates the status quo rather than dreaming of politically utopian futures.

Compost and the Ethics of Recycling

Stasis is not how we typically think of *Leaves of Grass*, in part because the poem so consistently pairs its quietist celebration of the social status quo with buoyant celebrations of movement and transformation. "In me the caresser of life wherever moving. . . . backward as well as forward slue-ing," he writes in one representative passage.[82] To move backward and forward at once would be to stay in the same place, of course, and careful attention to Whitman's valorization of movement reveals that the "Me Myself" frequently arrests motion even in these seemingly most dynamic moments. "To me the converging objects of the universe perpetually flow," writes Whitman, and this "me" seems to stop movement, to be the static center of a universe otherwise characterized by "flow."[83] Lines such as "Through me the afflatus surging and surging. . . . through me the current and index" are consistently preceded by or paired with things like "whatever is done or said returns at last to me, / And whatever I do or say I also return."[84] Images of great motion are thus undercut by adjacent representations of the self as the site of temporal or spatial stagnation. "I teach straying from me, yet who can stray from me?" the speaker asks, casting the "me" as a paralyzing or immobilizing force for all who are not "me."[85]

Perversely, Whitman's celebration of compost amplifies the sense of timelessness and changelessness in the poem, at the very moment that Whitman is celebrating the dynamic transformation of matter. Just how compost operates as a trope can be seen most strikingly at the conclusion of the poem eventually entitled "Song of Myself," when Whitman's 1855 speaker decomposes, becomes literal and literary compost:

> I depart as air. . . . I shake my white locks at the runaway sun,
> I effuse my flesh in eddies and drift it in lacy jags.

I bequeath myself to the dirt to grow from the grass I love,
If you want me again look for me under your bootsoles.

You will hardly know who I am or what I mean,
But I shall be good health to you nevertheless,
And filter and fibre your blood.[86]

The lush, even gorgeous description of decomposition in line 1328 renders physical dissolution and chemical recombination as a kind of willed, material generosity; flesh is purposively broken down, "effuse[d]" and "drift[ed]" into the air and earth by the aged, white-locked speaker. This elemental transformation of flesh into liquids and gases, "eddies" and "lacy jags," gives way to the more famous, fertilizing "bequeathal" of the speaker's corpse—and Whitman's corpus—to the earth, to "the grass [he] love[s]" and to future literary production: "If you want me again look for me under your bootsoles."

Whitman's 1855 speaker is figured as "departing" in the language of nineteenth-century chemistry. As David Reynolds has written, "If Liebig envisaged an exchange of life-forms through decomposition and regrowth, so Whitman fashioned metaphors that vivified the idea of the ceaseless springing of life from death."[87] Thus the famous "Song of Myself" images of the "curling grass" that "transpire[s] from the breasts of young men," "from old people and from women, and from offspring."[88] By figuring grass in relation to the cycle of compost, Whitman also implies that his poetry, his *Leaves of Grass*, is a space where matter is being recycled and renewed— new life and new poetry grows from the manifold consumed images, sounds, and thoughts that "contribute toward" the speaker and the poems.[89] Formally, the way that the poem remixes and recycles its elements through repetition and anaphora also partakes of the logic of decomposition and the cycle of death and rebirth ("And as to you corpse I think you are good manure"); when Whitman says, "it is not chaos or death. . . . it is form and union and plan," he might well be talking about his own catalogues in addition to the material universe.[90]

By the 1856 edition of *Leaves of Grass*, Whitman elaborates his recurring interest in compost and decomposition into the "Poem of Wonder at The Resurrection of The Wheat." This poem, which would be retitled "This Compost" by the 1867 edition, celebrates the recycling of organic material and seeks to convey the sublimity of "the summer growth . . . innocent and disdainful above all those strata of sour dead."[91] The poem begins with an expression of fear unusual in the emotional register of *Leaves of Grass*: "Something startles me where I thought I was safest."[92] This is a moment of doubt, rational and foresighted in Whitman's industrializing era, that the earth cannot absorb all the waste, filth, and decay of human life and lifeways. The speaker expresses a fear that earth can't "renew me," that it might "sicken," die, lose itself, or fail to provide humans with "health" because humans are "continually" polluting the earth with their own organic waste:

> Are they not continually putting distempered corpses in the earth?
> Is not every continent worked over and over with sour dead?
> Where have you disposed of those carcasses of the drunkards and
>   gluttons of so many generations?
> Where have you drawn off all the foul liquid and meat?[93]

Whitman here employs a language of soil exhaustion ("worked over with the sour dead") that figures grave digging as a kind of antifarming that depletes the earth. The frantic questioning is heightened by the anaphoric "where have you," and the whole passage hinges upon the spatial imaginary of waste disposal: The speaker suspects that there must be a space outside of or apart from life for the safe quarantine of waste and death. The speaker fears both that there's no more room for such disposal—that human waste might be overrunning the earth—and that the earth can't actually safely absorb "the foul liquid and meat" of "the sour dead." This is an almost unique instance in *Leaves of Grass* where the speaker suspects that there might indeed be limits to what can be consumed, absorbed, or recycled.

By line 16, however, the fear that the earth could be exhausted gives way to the celebration of compost—of "chemistry" and the endless recycling of waste back into useable matter, without consequence to the earth or the humans who inhabit it. Compost ensures "that all is clean, forever and forever!"[94] Chemistry explains how the earth "grows such sweet things out of such corruptions" and "renews with such unwitting looks, its prodigal, annual, sumptuous crops."[95] Whitman's celebration of matter as endlessly renewable is taken directly from antebellum scientific accounts of compost. In an 1831 essay called "A Discourse on the Burial of the Dead" (which has recently been rediscovered and embraced by the twenty-first-century "green burial" movement), Jacob Bigelow, scientist, physician, and one of the founders of Mt. Auburn cemetery, frames compost as the process that ensures that "elements which have once moved and circulated in living frames, do not become extinct or useless after death—they offer themselves as the materials from which other living frames are to be constructed."[96] This oddly voluntary ("they offer themselves") transformation of matter from "extinct or useless" back to useful material is critical to the survival of life on the earth: "Were it not for this law of nature, the soil would soon become exhausted, the earth's surface would become a barren waste, and the whole race of organized beings, for want of sustenance, would become extinct."[97] The cyclical and inexhaustible nature of the compost process is central to Whitman's optimism in *Leaves of Grass*; it is what allows for the transformation of human life from singular and linear to multiple and cyclical: "And as to you life, I reckon you are the leavings of many deaths, / No doubt I have died myself ten thousand times before."[98] The effect of this is not simply narcissism but a kind of radical anthropocentrism. The human becomes inescapable, and even death is no limit to its drive to consume: "I fly the flight of the fluid and swallowing soul," "I help myself to material and immaterial, / No guard can shut me off, no law can prevent me."[99] The law of organic recycling enables consumption on a godlike scale: "The swallowing soul" consumes everything ("material and immaterial") forever, without limit.

Somewhat counterintuitively, Whitman's celebration of the figure of compost is what ensures that, in his poetic cosmology, everything can ultimately be consumed and incorporated without limit or consequence. The cycle of composition and decomposition is thus the necessary compliment and corollary to Whitman's vision of unrestrained appetite. It purifies appetite and produces a kind of ecological justification for unrestrained poetic consumption: Just as the earth may incorporate everything and in the process of decomposition purify it, so may Whitman's speaker consume bodies of all varieties, landscapes, and objects. As a poet, Whitman can never consume too much or too grossly; any potential consequences of unrestrained appetite are circumvented through the figure of compost. Through compost, Whitman makes voracious omnivorousness ecologically sound and makes it seem natural if not also ethical.

In "Song of the Redwood Tree," compost also ultimately helps Whitman envision a settler-colonial fantasy of resource extraction that is authorized by no less than "Nature" itself. First published in *Harper's Magazine* in 1874, "Song of the Redwood Tree" has become one of the poems upon which Whitman's ecocritical reputation rests.[100] Yet Whitman described his poem about the felling of a redwood tree as a paean to Manifest Destiny: "The spinal idea of the poem I (the tree) have fill'd my time and fill'd it grandly All is prepared for you—my termination comes prophecy [*sic*] a great race—great as the mountains and the trees."[101] In this poem, in other words, a speaking redwood tree explains that it is resigned to being chopped down because its life will serve "the new culminating man" and his "empire new."[102] By the second section of the poem,

compost too is celebrated for having prepared Western American nature
for white possession:

> The fields of Nature long prepared and fallow, the silent, cyclic
>   chemistry,
> The slow and steady ages plodding, the unoccupied surface ripening, the
>   rich ores forming beneath;
> At last the New arriving, assuming, taking possession,
> A swarming and busy race settling and organizing everywhere.[103]

Compost, or "cyclic chemistry," is credited in this poem as the source of a
renewable, extractable wealth that has been lying "fallow," waiting for "the
New" whites who will "settl[e]" and "tak[e] possession." By representing
the land as having been "long prepared" yet "fallow," Whitman's compost
aids in the poem's complete erasure of the Indigenous peoples who lived
in the Western lands enumerated in the poem before the arrival of the
"swarming and busy race" of whites. In its final stanza, "Song of the Redwood Tree" returns to the language of compost's "preparation" in its triumphant naturalization of the United States' imperial destiny:

> Fresh come, to a new world indeed, yet long prepared,
> I see the genius of the modern, child of the real and ideal,
> Clearing the ground for broad humanity, the true America, heir of the
>   past so grand,
> To build a grander future.[104]

This vision politicizes compost's relation to unfettered consumption, but
it is finally only a more explicit version of the role Whitman assigns compost elsewhere in his oeuvre.

Whitman's compost makes visible the critical problem with recycling
as an environmental paradigm: It creates communities in which some are
allowed to use without limit, while others bear the embodied burden of
that use. At its most extreme, such unlimited use has been characterized
as anthropocentric domination or as the Christian idea of dominion, a
theological interpretation that licenses humankind to use the planet and
all nonhuman forms of life in whatever manner, to whatever degree we see
fit.[105] The idea, or attitude, of dominion is no relic of a benighted past; it
is very much still with us. Take William Carlos Williams's 1943 poem "The
Bare Tree," for instance:

> The bare cherry tree
> higher than the roof

last year produced
abundant fruit. But how
speak of fruit confronted
by that skeleton?
Though live it may be
there is no fruit on it.
Therefore chop it down
and use the wood
against this biting cold.[106]

The pathos of this poem comes from the sense of human need: the cold-
ness of winter, the life-or-death scenario. That need is weighed not against
the tree's life—which seems not to enter into the equation—but against
the tree's ability to bear future fruit. In both cases, it's a question of human
sustenance, comfort, and survival. The tree as a living thing to which the
human might bear some form of ethical responsibility or care is unimagi-
nable in the terms of this short, bleak poem. The cycle of the seasons and
the brevity of the poem give the poem's argument a kind of allegoric heft
that extends beyond this one tree and this one winter, into a maxim, a
principle for human relations with the rest of life: It may be very well to
tend the nonhuman world so long as the rewards are immediate, but in moments of exigency or discomfort, "chop it down."

Whether Williams is critiquing or endorsing the principle of expedi-
ency he represents in "The Bare Tree" is undecidable. What is clear from
the poem is that this attitude toward nature rests in part on human confidence in the cycle of the seasons, of nature—and trees'—ability to be
reborn every year with spring. For Whitman, that the earth endlessly
"renews" itself and the "prodigal, annual, sumptuous crops" humans
need to survive produces an almost orgiastic universe of plenty; for Williams, who is representing scarcity and human vulnerability, it is nevertheless a similar faith in yearly renewal and the recycling of matter that
enables disrespect for the "live" but "bare cherry tree." If a tree's wood is
more valuable in winter than its "abundant fruit" will be in summer,
then the unexpressed assumption is Whitman's faith in the earth's
bountiful renewal.

It might shift our perspective if we had less, or less easy, confidence in
such cyclical natural renewal. Jacques Derrida has suggestively argued that
"the moral question" is not what or whether to eat but what it means to
"*eat well* [*bien manger*]," to eat with "respect for the other at the very moment when . . . one must begin to identify with the other, who is to be

assimilated, interiorized, understood ideally."[107] We cannot refuse to live on and off of the earth, but what does it mean to consume responsibly? We might begin by refusing to celebrate unlimited appetite and refusing to "wonder" at the earth's symbolic, supposedly endless ability to "resurrect" itself, to recycle human waste, to "giv[e] such divine materials to men, and accep[t] such leavings from them at last," as Whitman concludes his "Poem of Wonder at The Resurrection of The Wheat."[108]

Philip Larkin's representation of the process of natural renewal in "The Trees," one of the great springtime poems in the English language, provides one suggestive alternative. While Larkin begins the poem in the familiar mode of representing spring as a period of possibility and renewal—"The trees are coming into leaf / Like something almost being said"—he quickly unsettles the clichéd, carefree optimism of the season by declaring that "Their greenness is a kind of grief."[109] "Is it that they are born again / And we grow old? No, they die too," Larkin insists, using enjambment to move as quickly as possible to the "no" that undercuts a reader's ability to imagine spring as a cyclical rebirth (or "resurrection") that contrasts with human mortality.[110]

For Larkin, spring growth is simply a "yearly trick of looking new" belied by the body of the tree, which is marked by its many yearly deaths "written down in rings of grain."[111] The poem's form—the regular iambs and the abba stanza structure organizing Larkin's lines—convey a confident rhythm and comfortingly cyclical completion ultimately undermined as a "trick" by the elegiac tone. In this poem, trees are mortal sufferers; nonhuman nature's ability to renew, regrow, or transform is not without cost or consequence, and even pain. Writing in 1967, Larkin represents human and tree life as intimately related, and both are equally vulnerable. By the end of the poem Larkin figures the choice or ability to "Begin afresh, afresh, afresh" as a heroic struggle forward to slough off the past, or perhaps simply despair, in periodic bursts of growth that may be rejuvenating but that can never be divorced from or outside of linear time, mortality, and death. The ethical realm, in other words.

Even more than the British Larkin, the US poet Lucille Clifton exposes the ethical and environmental stakes of Whitman's central tropes of compost, cyclicality, appetite, and celebration. In her poem "grief" (2000), one of many poems in which she self-consciously rewrites Walt Whitman,[112] Clifton amplifies and extends Larkin's sense of "greenness" as a "kind of grief." "grief" meditates on "the grass" and "the myth of America"— meditates in part[113] on Whitman's *Leaves of Grass*, in other words—but rewrites his "song" as a dirge.[114] Clifton's "grief" decenters the human, giving equal weight to "grief for what is born human/grief for what is not."[115] The poem begins by instructing readers, or the poet herself, to "begin with the pain," and the line break allows readers to assume it will be a human pain before the second line unexpectedly completes the injunction with "of the grass."[116] This is not just any grass but "the grass/that bore the weight/of adam."[117] By "begin[ning]" in this way, Clifton recasts man's biblical beginning as a moment of pain for both human and nonhuman nature. As in Larkin's poem, the suffering is shared, but Clifton does not represent human and nonhuman nature as equally innocent victims of pain and mortality; instead, humans seem to be the cause of nonhuman nature's pain. True human suffering may only begin with the Fall, with expulsion from Eden, but the suffering of nature begins with the inception of the human. Yet in Clifton's suggestive rendering, the scene of human creation produces a sympathetic "lamentation" from the grass and leads, ultimately, "to now, to here,/to grief for the upright/animal, to grief for the/horizontal world."[118] In placing a line break between "upright" and "animal," Clifton isolates each word from the other, implicating the "upright" (vertically inclined but also morally correct) human in the tragedy that must be grieved but again emphasizing the human as an animal entangled with other, nonhuman animals.

Clifton finally asks readers to grieve for the myths that helped produce our contemporary tragedy, myths that we must let go of but that are painful to relinquish: human exceptionalism, human innocence, the invulnerability of nature, and "the myth of America." The "pause for the myth of America" is particularly drawn out by being repeated twice and by being set off on the page with additional white space, as if readers need extra time and space to let go of that myth.[119] Ultimately, "grief" demands that we grieve even our inability to grieve adequately for these things and "for the disregarded planet," "for the grass." The injunction to grieve is a revision of Whitman's injunction to "assume" and consume in *Leaves of Grass*, one that demands humans accept a new affective relationship to the grass, and to the nonhuman more generally, as we come to recognize that the earth cannot in fact withstand our limitless appetites and continue to thrive on "such leavings" as we give it. The poem's emphasis on limitation is an implicit critique of capitalism and its effects on the natural world, just as Whitman's poetry is an implicit celebration of these things.

Jennifer James has compellingly termed Clifton's recognition of the earth's limitations "ecomelancholia," arguing that "ecomelancholia disavows mourning's 'renewable' economy. . . . There will be no 'fresh' objects to replace the natural world, and certainly none 'more precious.'" For

this reason, "ecomelancholia refuses to take consolation in fantasies of rec-
tification while destruction occurs unabated."[120] James aptly describes the
central feature of Clifton's rewriting of Whitman. If, in Whitman's omnivorous poetics, "all flesh is grass," and if "the grass is the people" because
humans consume ruminants, for Clifton, these biblical tropes seem instead
to gesture toward the basic liveliness of the grass and the essential similitude of all forms of life. In Clifton's hands, grass is valuable in itself—not
an object but a subject.

Despite that we end "grief" as we began, in a garden, nature here is not
cyclical or outside of linear time, and it does not seem capable of the kind
of easy regeneration that Whitman is comforted to imagine. Instead, we're
in "the garden of regret/with time's bell tolling grief/and pain."[121] Writing in a prophetic voice in "the message from the Ones (received in the
late 70s)" in 2004's *Mercy*, Clifton amplifies her critique, sounding a Whitmanian note of material recycling and reincarnation in order to drive
home the limits of regeneration:

the air
you have polluted
you will breathe

the waters
you have poisoned
you will drink

when you come again
and you will come again

the air
you have polluted
you will breathe

the waters
you have poisoned
you will drink[122]

When forced to live amid the consequences of human waste and pollution,
the assurance that "you will come again" is not so much a promise as a
threat. The cyclical nature of the mirrored stanzas does not release humans
from the impacts of their bodies and lives on nonhuman nature; in fact, it
redoubles it. Even the second-person address, which most often has an
ebullient effect in Whitman's work, where it is used to multiply the possibilities for readerly identity and identification, works differently here. In

Clifton's hands, "you" terrifyingly delimits readers to a universal and elemental fate: breathing air and drinking water that cannot be made safe and clean.

Even in her treatment of compost, Clifton rewrites Whitman back into human and environmental history. In Clifton's "mulberry fields" (2004), the speaker refuses Whitman's claim that "the summer growth is innocent and disdainful above all those strata of sour dead." In "This Compost," much space is given over to describing the delicious edibles that grow from "carcasses," and the poem's grammar grants the agency for this conversion entirely to the "bean [that] bursts noiselessly through the mould in the garden," the "apple-buds [that] cluster together on the apple-branches," and so on.[123] In Clifton's poem, however, the compost of corpses does not simply "become" crops; instead, she represents the attempted conversion of an enslaved community's graveyard to a productive and profitable agricultural use.[124] "They thought the field was wasting/and so they gathered the marker rocks and stones and/piled them into a barn," the poem begins.[125] Capitalism and social power drive the compost cycle here; the judgment that the field is "wasting" initiates the removal of the marker stones, which are repurposed "to build that wall there guarding the manor and/some few were used for the state house."[126] But in this field, compost doesn't work—"crops refused to grow."[127] Bodies in Clifton's poem aren't simply raw material to be consumed for the production of new life, and they remain marked by history and politics after death. The corpses of enslaved people can't simply be appropriated by those with power (nothing will grow). Yet the poem shows that this is how the state and capitalism operate—they consume these bodies. In this way, Clifton suggests that the workings of compost are the workings of power; the reconscription of matter to utility is not simply a neutral, natural process that takes place outside of human social hierarchies. Unlike in Whitman, it is also not cause for celebration. Compost may be unavoidable, but it is another act of violence against the remains in the field: "wild/berries warm a field of bones/bloom how you must i say," Clifton writes.[128]

Clifton is certainly not all grief. She does engage in Whitmanian "celebration," as in an untitled poem that begins, "won't you celebrate with me/what i have shaped into/a kind of life?"[129] This rewriting of the opening to "Song of Myself" lacks the egotism and insularity of Whitman's "I celebrate myself/and what I assume you shall assume."[130] The self in *Leaves of Grass* suffocates, consumes, and overtakes the reader—there is no space or identity outside of it; its thoughts and feelings become yours, and yours become its. In Clifton's poem, however, celebration is an invitation, and identity between the "you" and the "i" or "me" is neither expected nor offered. Instead, the speaker's celebration of herself invites into being a collectivity willing to join in celebrating the survival of someone "both nonwhite and woman."[131] This speaker asks us to celebrate her self-invention ("what did i see to be except myself? / i made it up") in the face of violence, her survival in a world stacked against her.[132] Such survival isn't mastery or transcendence, and the speaker doesn't seem able to imaginatively inhabit other bodies or to take on their pain. Nor does she need to, living as she does in a world where "everyday / something has tried to kill me / and has failed."[133] Yet readers are not being invited or asked to imaginatively take on the speaker's pain, either. Such pain goes unspoken, and the reader is offered only an image of insular self-sufficiency: "my one hand holding tight / my other hand."[134] The celebration is instead for her self-taught ("i had no model") artistry in inventing "a kind of life." The literal and symbolic heart of the poem is "i made it up." Creative work is crucial to survival under violent and unjust conditions, and it is finally the source of Clifton's environmental optimism as well. "What has been made / can be unmade," she reminds us in another poem from "the message from the Ones."[135]

That such creative work is also done by nonhuman nature becomes a source of tempered environmental optimism in Jane Hirshfield's "Optimism."

> More and more I have come to admire resilience.
> Not the simple resistance of a pillow, whose foam
> returns over and over to the same shape, but the sinuous
> tenacity of a tree: finding the light newly blocked on one side,
> it turns in another. A blind intelligence, true.
> But out of such persistence arose turtles, rivers,
> mitochondria, figs—all this resinous, unretractable earth.[136]

Unlike Whitman's celebrations of compost, "resilience" celebrates a distinct kind of renewal, one that coexists with consequences and limits. Resilience also implies a respect for the creative, "sinuous tenacity" it takes to produce that renewal or regrowth. This poem doesn't credit nonhuman life with the same kind of "intelligence" that humans possess—resilience is evidence of "a blind intelligence, true"—but it doesn't need to do so in order to undermine the anthropocentric vision of one-sided, unlimited use or for respect, close observation, and a sense of mutuality and care to exist between the human and the nonhuman.

Whitman's triumphant recycling—the fantastic purification and renewal of chemistry, compost, and natural cycles—is not possible in Clifton's, or

Larkin's, or even Hirshfield's poems. But the possibility of change, of a "final chance," is there, if in muted form.[137] Clifton offers only "not the end of the world/of a world."[138] Life may go on, but endings matter, and death is consequential in ways not captured by Whitman's vision of death in "Song of Myself" as "different from what any one supposed, and luckier."[139] The contrast between Whitman and Clifton suggests that a belief in endings, death, and finality as well as a refusal to celebrate nature as endlessly cyclical and renewable may finally be a sine qua non of ethical community and of transformative poetry. Larkin's and Clifton's refusal to "celebrate" nature as something outside of human time and mortality makes possible a form of ecological community in which nature can be injured by human actions, where irreversible consequences—pain, death—are possible for all.

Clifton, Larkin, and Hirshfield, in their different ways, resist the dream of cyclical, effortless material recycling. Yet nineteenth-century Whitman's twinned investment in appetite and compost remains far more characteristic of contemporary life and of the petroleum era as a whole. In fact, the logic of our petroleum era, from one perspective, is that of compost and material recycling: Our contemporary, oil-addicted world is built on the consumption of the dead, fossilized life that the earth has "recycled" for us. As the devastating reach of our environmental impact has become clear, this economy has come to seem more like cannibalism than compost or recycling. The human conviction, widespread until the late twentieth century but in evidence even now, that the earth could absorb endless amounts of coal, petroleum, and other emissions—endless amounts of our Whitmanian "leavings"—and somehow recycle and purify them, this is the conviction that Whitman so perfectly captures in his 1856 "Poem of Wonder at The Resurrection of The Wheat." From this perspective, compost and recycling become a disturbing apologia for appetite, a greenwashing fantasy that makes voracious omnivorousness seem ethical and ecologically viable. As we teeter on the brink of apocalyptic environmental scenarios, the time has come to release our grip on this detrimental paradigm.

Compost in the Capitalocene

Whitman's twinned celebration of recycling and limitless consumption captures the zeitgeist of the Capitalocene, of the conflict between our planet and our economies of unending accumulation. In recent decades, specific occasions of recycling have increasingly been called into question;

Americans now know that their batteries, electronics, plastics, and clothing are not recycled without significant human and ecological costs. Yet recycling remains among the most commonly touted environmental practices, enshrined as one of the "three R's" drilled into each new generation of US children. Whitman, Clifton, and the other figures I have discussed might help us consider how the ethical failures of individual recycling practices might relate to an ethical failure of the paradigm itself. Recycling allows some communities to imagine that they may consume without limit while others in fact bear the embodied burden of imperfectly and sometimes dangerously converting "recyclable" matter back into some more useful form. Of course, in some cases recycling is better than the other alternatives, but Whitman might provoke us to relinquish recycling not as an environmental practice but as an aspirational environmental paradigm that authorizes thoughtless consumerism.

Linking the nineteenth-century context in which recycling's appeal as an environmental ethic began to take hold—scientifically and culturally—together with our twenty-first-century state of crisis, we can begin to see not only the problematic nature of recycling as an environmental paradigm but also that recycling's problems are not simply problems of scale: They do not originate in the changing scope of consumption and recycling in the twentieth or twenty-first century but are present from the inception of the paradigm. Whitman might remind us to pay closer attention to the forms of community that particular environmental practices and paradigms call into being in the world and on the page. Donna Haraway has recently embraced compost as a community practice that could charge collectives to understand "their task to be to cultivate and invent the arts of living with and for damaged worlds in place . . . as and for those living and dying in ruined places."[140] For Haraway, compost is valuable as a principle precisely because it discourages reimagining community "from the premises of starting over and beginning anew, instead of learning to inherit without denial and stay with the trouble of damaged worlds."[141] Whitman helps make visible how critical Haraway's rejection of "beginning anew" is to the utility of compost as a community principle. Unlike Haraway's "staying with the trouble," Whitmanian compost ties recycling to the ecstatic fantasy that all matter is endlessly renewable, a fantasy that disallows real ethical community. Haraway and other theorists and critics increasingly turning to compost are not simply recovering an overlooked topos; they are envisioning more radical theoretical and literary uses of compost and recycling than have heretofore existed. Moving forward, the

Environmental Humanities would do well to learn from the earlier failures of these tropes.

It should be said that recycling and compost are seductive not only as environmental paradigms but as literary principles as well. When it comes to artistic representation, we, too, want to "believe in the flesh and the appetites," in poetic ingestion's ability to transform. We want *Leaves of Grass* to act as Whitman imagines compost to do: We hope the book might take in the disturbingly unequal elements of antebellum US culture and somehow purify them in its bowels. But the book doesn't, and it can't. It isn't only the postbellum editions, with nakedly racist poems such as "Ethiopia Saluting the Colors," or Whitman's jingoistic and white-supremacist statements in his political writings and journalism; there are failures of sympathy everywhere in *Leaves of Grass*, and Whitman's statements of equality coexist too easily with representations of both human and nonhuman life fundamentally incompatible with genuinely equitable human, let alone biotic, community.

American readers in particular need to continue to strive for more complex ways of consuming Whitman, of reading and teaching him, if we want anything like the ecstatically inclusive, antihierarchical, even protoecological community so tantalizingly promised in many of his poems. At issue is the kind of meal Whitman's readers make of Whitman's digest. The democratic aspirations of Whitman's omnivorous poem succeed, to the extent that they do succeed, because of the invitation to dine. "You will hardly know who I am or what I mean,/But I shall be good health to you nevertheless,/And filter and fibre your blood," he writes near the end of "Song of Myself."[142] By eating together of Whitman's poetic meal, there is the possibility that readers might create something of the "living union" Whitman was after.

Langston Hughes, another twentieth-century poet who digests Whitman in profound ways, might speak a word of caution here; whereas his oft-reproduced "I, Too" rests on the faith that merely sitting down together at the same table will produce equality, by the time he writes the lesser-known "Dinner Guest, Me," Hughes is deeply cynical about that possibility. Clifton, again, points the way forward here: Our consumption of Whitman's meal cannot be omnivorous.[143] Clifton's digestion of Whitman is not uncritical, despite her obvious love for his work, and she neither purifies his representations nor renews his tropes. In making American flesh out of the meat of the poem, Whitman helps produce an American cultural body: an American readership and an American poetic tradition. And

of course, finally much more than an American poetic tradition, as Whitman is taken up and taken in by poets from Chile to China. This is the
democratic work his omnivorous poetics can do, but not unless they're
transformed—"filtered"—in and through his readers. In "The Whitman
Legacy and the Harlem Renaissance," George Hutchinson has argued that
the "paradox that, overall, the effects of [Whitman's] work . . . emphati-
cally contradicted the ideological 'message' that recent critics have eluci-
dated" is resolved by the fact that "the power and beauty of an artwork are
to be found . . . in the uses to which one puts it in one's life."[144] Whitman's
voracious appetite and poetic compost do not model either a poetic, political, or environmental aesthetic for the twenty-first century, but they
have helped bring into being communities, publics, and poetry more thrill-
ingly polyvocal and ecologically sound than Whitman's own.

CHAPTER 2

Joyful Frugality: Thoreau, Dickinson, and the Pleasures of Not Consuming

In his 1844 short story "Earth's Holocaust," Nathaniel Hawthorne imagines a time—"whether in the time past or time to come is a matter of little or no moment"—when "this wide world had become so overburdened with an accumulation of worn-out trumpery, that the inhabitants determined to rid themselves of it by a general bonfire."[1] As we might expect, given Hawthorne's authorial proclivities, the "worn-out trumpery" includes social constructions and cultural institutions such as organized religion and gender roles, but it also includes an awful lot of material *stuff*—books of all varieties, "bundles of perfumed letters," smoking pipes, "boxes of tea and bags of coffee," barrels of liquor, regal robes and crowns, "blazonry of coat armor," lace, ribbons, "last season's bonnets," guns and swords, guillotines, and much, much more.[2] So many of the objects burned in "Earth's Holocaust" are consumer commodities, if not also literal consumables, that the story might almost be read as a parable of anticonsumerism. Twenty-first-century Americans are inundated with advice about how to remake ourselves and our relationship to "stuff" in order to live more happy and ethical lives. When Hawthorne's story concludes with "Purify that inward sphere, and the many shapes of evil that haunt the outward, and which now seem almost our only realities, will turn to shadowy phantoms and vanish of their own accord,"[3] it might almost be a dictum from one of the dozens of bestselling contemporary guides to minimalism.

"Earth's Holocaust" suggests that social and political change is intimately bound up with personal change: We can burn our material and social "trumpery" in a revolutionary fervor, but it won't have a permanent effect unless we remake ourselves first. It might be tempting to dismiss this as Hawthorne's idiosyncratic conservatism or as transcendental naiveté, but the idea that when it comes to consumption, the personal is political—that what you privately consume (or refuse to consume) affects the public sphere—was surprisingly widespread in the nineteenth-century United States. It permeated popular domestic guidebooks and underpinned both establishment and reformist political rhetoric. The freedom of the individual, theorized as central to classical theories of republicanism and democracy, was understood by many to be endangered by the expanding capitalist marketplace, and resisting private consumerist appetites was imagined to have political effects.

It can be hard to recover this mindset today. In the twenty-first century everything from Marxist critiques to political cynicism has diminished our collective belief in the importance of the individual self to political action. Moreover, our sense of the inevitability of capitalism is so strong that, to quote Frederic Jameson, "it is easier to imagine the end of the world than to imagine the end of capitalism."[4] And in fact, we do just that—hence the ever-increasing public appetite for apocalyptic film, fiction, and other media. Such apocalyptic fictions mark in part our increasingly desperate sense that capitalism and environmentalism are in deadly conflict. The central tenet of capitalism is, as Marx put it in 1867, to "accumulate, accumulate! That is Moses and the prophets!"[5] The logic of capitalism is unlimited growth and accumulation and endless desire. There can never be enough. Yet our environmental crisis demands that the United States and other wealthy countries curb consumption. The supposed inevitability of consumerism and economic expansionism makes solving our environmental crisis seem hopeless and apocalypse inevitable. To break this impasse, our sense of the inevitability of capitalism and its imperative to consume endlessly must be disrupted. Other ways of living must be made possible. We must open up new lifeways if we are to imagine and then and bring into being new, more hopeful futures.

Frugality seems, at first glance, an unlikely environmentalism to midwife these more hopeful futures. In the first place, how can frugality support a genuinely effective, collective politics? As an environmental principle, it seems a tailor-made target for any critique of purity politics.[6] Just as importantly, for most people with economic privilege, frugality seems unrealistic, if not also unpleasant. Other worlds have to be not just possible but appealing, if they are to disrupt our sense of the inevitability of current (capitalist) arrangements.

In this chapter, I seek to reorient our conception of frugality by recovering a popular nineteenth-century US culture of frugality that understood itself as political and as connected to joy rather than deprivation. In the first part of the chapter, readings of Lydia Maria Child's *The Frugal American Housewife* and Sylvester Graham's *The Science of Human Life* explore how an antebellum culture of frugality conceived of itself as critical to democracy in the expanding United States. In the second part of the chapter, I turn to Henry David Thoreau's experiments in frugal living at Walden Pond. By restoring Thoreau's connection to Grahamite vegetarianism and linking that with his democratic and artistic *Walden* projects, I demonstrate that Thoreau's radical minimalism links reducing consumption and curbing appetite with both political freedom and personal fulfillment. Writing against the "killjoy" Thoreau of popular US imagination, I show that Thoreau's frugality promotes joy and even justice by challenging the consumerist status quo.

The last section of the chapter explores the relationship between happiness, desire, consumption, and possession in the poetry of Emily Dickinson. To the extent that Dickinson's poetic interest in consumption has been attended to at all, it has been pathologized as "abnormal" or anorexic. Reading Dickinson back into her nineteenth-century context, a context that must include Child, Graham, Thoreau, Edward Hitchcock, and others, can help us see past familiar gendered scripts about "the myth of Amherst." In fact, Dickinson is a captivating theorist of consumer desire, and her emphasis on the pleasures of anticipation and the disappointments of consumption have much to teach all of us living in the Capitalocene. Ultimately, I argue that Dickinson and Thoreau, by shifting the sites of pleasure away from consumption, might help us envision some of the other possible and attractive lifeways we might embrace—individually and politically, for ourselves and for the planet.

A Frugal Republic: Lydia Maria Child, Sylvester Graham, and the Tyranny of Appetite

The politicization of private consumption has deep roots in Anglophone culture. During the eighteenth century, the rise of widespread consumerism in England and America was opposed by reformers who drew on the language and values of classical republicanism, which opposed "luxury" to independence and thus civic virtue.[7] Such tendencies intensified in the United States during the first third of the nineteenth century, as the country underwent an uneven transition from a rural subsistence economy into an urban-focused capitalist marketplace, a shift that was disturbing to a nation that had been grounding its ideas of national virtue in independence from the marketplace since at least Thomas Jefferson.[8] Jeffersonian agrarianism famously took a classical model of citizenship as its ideological template, making "the small-scale farmer the bastion of freedom and independence, the vanguard of American democracy," because such farmers "willfully sought to avoid commercial agriculture and preferred a 'moral economy' in which they produced for subsistence purposes rather than the market and economic gain."[9] Like the Greek *oikodespotes*, "yeoman farmers" were Jefferson's ideal American citizens because the economic independence of their small farms made them fit for participation in civic and political life.[10] Unlike a wage earner, the yeoman's mind and ultimately his vote could not be controlled by an employer—or even community opinion—thanks to his aloofness from the market. Freed from necessity by his successful management of the *oikos*, Jefferson's yeoman farmer was able to be politically independent and was therefore worthy of the responsibilities of republican citizenship.

Agrarianism in American history turns out to be symbolic, "more fiction than fact, a classic example of the intrusion of myth into history," since even colonial farmers were characterized by "commercial *mentalité*."[11] Yet the association between economic independence and republican virtue in the early United States was nevertheless powerful. By the antebellum period, the citizenship model behind Jeffersonian agrarianism was pervasive. In a nation where "freedom, democracy, and economic security" were popularly imagined to be "based on landowning small-scale subsistence farmers," the economic developments associated with industrialization were deeply troubling.[12] These changes occurred initially and most pervasively in the antebellum period in New England and the mid-Atlantic seaboard but ultimately spread to nearly every region but the South by the dawn of the Civil War. Although most Americans accepted the Market Revolution as inevitable—even Jefferson admitted "experience has taught me . . . manufactures are now as necessary to our independence as to our comfort" in 1816—the tenets of civic humanism demanded that a replacement market-based haven for republican virtue be found.[13]

Because the same economic developments that decreased subsistence farming simultaneously decreased and ultimately eliminated the home as a site of economic production for many middle- and upper-class Americans, the new seat of cultural virtue and the economic independence necessary to maintain it were increasingly located in the sentimentalized home.[14] The idea of the market independence of the home, already in play in the eighteenth century, became even more plausible a fiction in light of the newly unproductive home at the heart of the antebellum period's "cult of domesticity."[15] Building on the tradition of "republican motherhood" popular during the early national period, which emphasized the important role of mothers in the education of future republican citizens, the feminized home naturally became for many the new seat of republican virtue.[16]

A prophylactic distance between home and market may have been ideologically desirable during the antebellum period, but it was difficult to achieve. One of the period's most popular (and populist) guides to homemaking, Lydia Maria Child's *The American Frugal Housewife*, provides a useful case study for how domestic literature tied both individual and national happiness and virtue to economical practices designed to insulate the domestic sphere from capitalism. First published in 1829, Child's book is "dedicated to those who are not ashamed of economy" and offers two moralizing epigrams printed on both the cover and the title page. The first, by the flexitarian Founding Father Benjamin Franklin, explicitly ties household economy to individual virtue: "A fat kitchen maketh a lean will." Child's guidebook follows the spirit of this epigram throughout, as recommendations for home economy are spiked with moralizing cautionary tales about the practical and moral dangers of "extravagance." Child diagnoses extravagance as "the prevailing evil of the present day," claiming that an extravagant lifestyle in anyone but the very rich is immoral because people of moderate fortune should be saving money with which to confront "any unforeseen calamity" of the sort that capitalism's boom-and-bust cycle of "crash after crash" had made not just possible but increasingly likely.[17] Home economy was a sound response to the uncertainties of antebellum economic life; frugal practices enabled urban families to amass surplus wealth, and it was surplus wealth that allowed the home to seem insulated from the market.[18]

In *The American Frugal Housewife*, surplus wealth is not merely the basis for economic security; for Child, it is also a foundation of moral behavior: "True economy is a careful treasurer in the service of benevolence," she writes. "The man who is economical, is laying up for himself the permanent power of being useful and generous."[19] Charity, one of the most important Christian social values, is impossible without financial stability. More importantly, however, a refusal to save one's money indicates participation in the extravagant, market-oriented society, where "a man's cloth is of more consequence than his character."[20] In direct opposition to the civic humanist's ideal republican, such citizens are utterly dominated by "Fashion," and the excessive and unnecessary consumption fashion entails. Throughout much of her book, Child details how the form of consumption Thorsten Veblen would deem "conspicuous" at the end of the nineteenth century corrupts antebellum domestic life. For instance, the last third of Child's *The American Frugal Housewife*, entitled "Hints to Persons of Moderate Fortune," contains little more than a series of anecdotes designed to illustrate how thoroughly and inevitably a neglect of frugality poisons the domestic happiness of such "Persons." Child describes marriage after marriage ruined for lack of the "*home education*" that would have taught women how to live within their means and still create a barrier between their family and the insecurities of economic life in the form of "a few thousands in the bank."[21]

This call for "economy" by Child and so many other authors of nineteenth-century domestic manuals remains linked etymologically to the Hellenic model of republican citizenship, since it comes from the Greek word *oikonomia*, meaning the proper management of the *oikos* or household. In this sense, "economy" was always an essential part of republican citizenship. Child emphasizes one of the meanings of "economy" that arose alongside market capitalism in the seventeenth century, however—frugality.[22] In her account, frugality is at the heart of proper household management because a refusal to economize makes the home vulnerable to the market forces that are always threatening its destruction. In keeping with the emphasis civic humanism places on freedom from necessity and independence from the market, Child explicitly ties lavish consumption and a concomitant rage for leisure travel and "public amusements" to a decline in republican virtue:

> The good old home habits of our ancestors are breaking up—it will be well if our virtue and our freedom do not follow them! It is easy to laugh at such prognostics,—and we are well aware that the virtue we preach is considered almost obsolete,—but let any reflecting mind inquire how decay has begun in all republics, and then let them calmly ask themselves whether we are in no danger, in departing thus rapidly

from the simplicity and industry of our forefathers. . . . A republic
without industry, economy, and integrity, is Samson shorn of his locks.
A luxurious and idle *republic!* Look at the phrase!—The words were
never made to be married together; every body sees it would be death
to one of them.[23]

In other words, after innumerable parables about marriages where luxury
and idleness ruins the happiness and security of the relationship, we find
out that another "marriage," another union, is also threatened by the luxury Child is decrying—the nation. The antebellum fad of middle-class
tourism is merely the particular development that crystallizes the more en-
demic problem of market capitalism: It pulls citizens of every income level
out of the sanctuary of the home and into the cash nexus, destabilizing the
basis of republican virtue. Tellingly, Child ends her book with an anecdote
that shows that even farmers, the ideal citizens of civic humanism, are being touched by the mania for excessive consumption. Influenced by the
example of borders and friends, and feeling that they have "a right" as citizens of the republic to enjoy what everyone else is enjoying, Child's exem-
plary farmer and farmer's wife set off on a trip for Quebec that catalyzes
their near financial ruin. Child leaves her readers with this final admon-
ishment: "We make a great deal of talk about being republicans; if we are
so in reality, we shall stay at home, to mind our business, and educate our
children."[24] Child was a novelist and reformer who worked in the abolitionist, women's rights, and Indian rights movements, and her domestic
guidebook also becomes legible as political activism once "stay[ing] at home"
is linked to the maintenance of a sound nation.

Child's guidebook makes visible the politicization of private, domestic
consumption during the early part of the antebellum period. The space of
the home was given a kind of political content that allowed Americans increasingly to imagine that domestic arrangements could have real effects
on civic life. Yet there was a problem with making the home carry this
heavy burden: Economic downturns—any "unforeseen calamity," as Child
puts it—could destabilize domestic life. Child advocates for home economy, but even she does not promise that this will be enough; everyone living in her rapidly changing America must be prepared for financial ruin.
The last three pages of *The American Frugal Housewife*, entitled "How to
Endure Poverty," suggest that riches of character must maintain one "when
poverty comes (as it sometimes will)." "A mind full of piety and knowledge
is always rich," Child promises. "It is a bank that never fails; it yields a per-
petual dividend of happiness."[25] Because the volatility of the market makes

the home unstable, Child finally suggests that individual, internal resources must maintain one when financial resources fail.

The antebellum vegetarian reform movement, headed by Sylvester Graham, picks up where Child and other domestic-advice authors leave off. The most famous health reformer of the antebellum period, Sylvester Graham (1794–1851), is now only slightly remembered, if at all, as the name source of the graham cracker—a commercial product that bears merely an ironic resemblance to Graham's anticommercial philosophy. Denigrated as "the prophet of sawdust" by antebellum newsmen and "the poet of bran bread and pumpkins" by Ralph Waldo Emerson,[26] Graham lived an obscure life until the early 1830s, when he began his popular-lecture series. These lectures evolved during the 1830s to encompass not only temperance but a more general theory of health that included chastity and a collection of dietary and hygienic recommendations that Graham referred to as "The Science of Human Life."

As Graham saw it, American bodies were threatened by food that was increasingly mechanized and commercially produced, symbolized most acutely for Graham by animal products and the newly popular white bread being sold by urban bakeries. A key component of Graham's vegetarian diet was therefore "Graham bread," a bread made from unrefined flour and baked in the home by a loving wife or mother; only such bread, according to Graham, was capable of providing proper physiological but also spiritual nourishment. In 1839, Graham's authority and popularity was consolidated with the publication of his magnum opus, *Lectures on the Science of Human Life*, a collection of his physiological and lifestyle recommendations that ran more than 1,200 pages.[27] Fully established as a leading reform movement of the antebellum period, at the height of their enthusiasm Graham's followers established the nation's first vegetarian society, set up Grahamite boarding houses, opened the nation's first health-food stores where products such as "Graham flour"[28] were bought and sold, and even ran the student commons at Oberlin College on Grahamite principles. The Grahamites established their own journal, *The Graham Journal of Health and Longevity*, in 1837, and friendly articles were printed about the health system in many other journals during the antebellum period, including Fowler and Wells's popular *Life Illustrated*.[29]

Like Child, Graham responds to the challenge of an irrational economy with a call for frugality, but his economy comes in the form of a diet that tames an internal "vital economy" that Graham substitutes for the market economy. Graham's "vital economy" demands similar management techniques to the market economy; runaway consumption is his culprit, and appetite control is his solution. "A stern simplicity of diet commenced in childhood and rigidly adhered to through life" is the only way to curb the depraved, voracious appetite that Graham believes dominates his contemporaries,[30] and such a simple diet is also calculated to avoid taxing the body's "vital economy."[31] According to Graham, "every human being comes into existence with a determinate amount of constitutional stamina, an unreplenishable fund of life. This fund . . . can be profligately squandered in one-fourth or one-tenth part of the time which it might be made to last," or it can be managed with thrifty care through the consumption of nonstimulating vegetable foods.[32] Graham rejects capitalism's ideals of surplus and accumulation; all "stimulation" to Graham's internal "vital economy" is harmful because unlike the unlimited amount of capital and resources that characterize the external market economy, the internal "vital economy" has a precisely delimited fund of life that may be spent before it collapses.

Graham's call for frugality, like Child's, is so vehement because it is theorized as the only means of attaining autonomy in the face of an irrational economy. By advocating for a dietetic "economy" that would help vegetarians achieve mastery over an out-of-control appetite, Graham's vegetarian diet granted a more achievable form of economic self-sufficiency. The hunger of a "flesh-eater," Graham insists to his readers again and again, is fundamentally "imperious," "despotic, vehement, impatient . . . [and] craving."[33] Those who convert to vegetarianism, Graham promises, will oust such controlling and immoral appetites through adherence to the "constitutional laws" of the "permanently established constitutional economy" and thereby preserve their health.[34] Indeed, not merely the health of individual Americans but of the nation. Graham's system, conceived in the language of republicanism and shot through with the problems of capitalism, actually aimed at the reform of what Graham calls "civic life."[35] Explicitly connecting the care of the individual constitution with the care of social and political constitutions, antebellum vegetarianism offered Graham and many of his converts a way of thinking about individual human "constitutions" and their proper form of "government" at the same moment that political crises caused these questions to be debated at the national level in the United States.

As Michel Foucault observes in *The Use of Pleasure*, politicizing bodily appetites was a standard feature of classical republican political theory. Appetite took on a political role because private life was theorized as the training ground for civic participation; virtuous citizens constituted themselves as such precisely through the regulation of individual appetite.[36]

Eileen Joy has argued that "for Foucault . . . ethics is a practice (an ascetics, or set of *exercises*) of freedom that revolves around the fundamental imperative: 'Take care of yourself.'"[37] Foucault's emphasis on the importance of appetite regulation—in Hellenic citizenship theory and to radical forms of freedom—helps illuminate the political work Graham and his nineteenth-century vegetarian followers imagined attention to regimen could achieve. According to Graham, "the dangers of the table" are primarily that improper indulgence runs the risk of "multiplying and pampering" "appetites" until they threaten to make people "perfect slaves" who are "led captives by their lusts to their destruction."[38] As Michael Warner has observed, nineteenth-century temperance movements more broadly conceived of desire as an external, controlling force and bodily discipline as the path to freedom.[39] Graham's vegetarian system explicitly politicizes these assumptions, promoting civic virtue by exchanging the body politic for individual "political bodies" who could be liberated through a vegetarian diet. In shifting the site of market insulation from the family farm or domestic home to the human body and then providing a regimen that weaponized diet and appetite control against industrial capitalism, Grahamite vegetarianism politicized the human body by giving it a role in the maintenance of a virtuous public sphere.

Because it made diet an explicitly political problem, with ramifications for the safety and security of the nation, vegetarian politics denominated the human body as a site of direct civic engagement. Graham can posit the human constitution as a useful substitute for an irreparably flawed political constitution because he theorized a human body that had one more crucial characteristic: a universal constitution. Unlike the "compromised" US Constitution described by Graham in his "Letter to the Hon. Daniel Webster" as unable to unite the American population,[40] Graham's *Lectures on the Science of Human Life* paints a picture of a human constitution so uniform as to demand the identical management of every body. "We have been told," he scoffs, "that . . . what is best for one man, is not for another . . . different constitutions require different treatment."[41] These "erroneous dogmas," he continues, are propagated primarily by those "willing to observe no other rules of life than the leadings of their appetites."[42] According to Graham, such slaves to appetite miss the "incontrovertible truth" that

> the human constitution is ONE, and there are no constitutional
> differences in the human race which will not readily yield to a correct
> regimen . . . and consequently, there are no constitutional differences

in the human race which stand in the way of adapting one general
regimen to the whole family of man; but, on the contrary . . . what is
best for one, is best for all; and therefore, all general reasonings
concerning the human constitution, are equally applicable to each and
every member of the human family, in all ages of the world, and in all
conditions of the race, and in all the various circumstances of
individuals.[43]

Echoing the claims of self-evidence and universality that Lynn Hunt's *Inventing Human Rights* has shown to characterize eighteenth-century
human rights theory,[44] Graham posits a new, physiological basis for the
Declaration of Independence's claim that "all men are created equal," one
that expands the implied subject of that phrase to include "each and every
member of the human family . . . in all conditions of the race" and, presumably, "all conditions" of gender, since Graham's regimen makes no distinction between the needs and constitutions of male and female bodies.

Of course, the universal human constitution Graham posits could not
literally deliver social or political equality to free Blacks or enslaved persons (or any other disenfranchised group). Yet theorizing a universal human
constitution was an important step toward such equality, since activists on
both sides of the slavery question framed physiological homogeneity as one
of the most significant gatekeepers on the path leading African Americans
to freedom and equality. Proslavery scientists conducted unthinkably cruel
medical experiments and ethnological research into supposed "African"
and primate biological similitude in an effort to prove the incommensurable physical difference of Black bodies from white, while abolitionist literature and lectures retorted with displays of suffering Black bodies
designed to demonstrate that Blacks felt physical and emotional pain as
keenly as whites.[45] Physiological homogeneity was an active site of cultural contestation during the antebellum period; in this cultural milieu,
Graham's argument for physiological universality, framed in the explicit
context of the slavery question, offered a trenchant polemic aid to those
working toward abolition and racial equality—an observation that perhaps helps explain William Lloyd Garrison's supportive interest in Graham's work.[46]

Lydia Maria Child and Sylvester Graham share a conviction that consumption has a public, political effect. Ultimately, each struck a nerve with
many of their contemporaries because both taught a form of frugality
designed to subdue privately ruinous, publicly antisocial and antidemocratic appetites. Rather than a simple turn to the individual away from

the collective, dietary and domestic frugality practices attempted to mediate a perceived conflict between individual, private desires and national, political goods. Amid rising consumer appetites and deeply unpredictable financial cycles, Child guided her readers to an anticonsumerist frugality that promised both private and public happiness and virtue. At a moment when internecine war seemed to be the increasingly inevitable outcome of a disunified body politic, Graham contributed a universal theory of diet and physiology that bound Americans together in the most intimate way possible and tied physiological consumption to political virtue. In their different ways, Child and Graham popularized the idea that personal and political freedom and happiness were linked with frugal consumption. As the rest of the chapter will show, Henry David Thoreau and Emily Dickinson's rich literary engagements with the popular idealization of frugal consumption extends frugality into even more complex—and anticapitalist—territory.

Radical Minimalism: Walden *in the Capitalocene*

> There is a certain class of unbelievers who sometimes ask me
> such questions as, if I think that I can live on vegetable food alone;
> and to strike at the root of the matter at once,—for the root is
> faith,—I am accustomed to answer such, that I can live on board nails.
> If they cannot understand that, they cannot understand much that
> I have to say.
>
> THOREAU, *Walden*

Henry David Thoreau famously "began to occupy [his] house" at Walden "on the 4th of July," 1845, and the implications and effects of this declaration of personal, political, and economic independence have been discussed and debated almost ever since.[47] In his own time, Thoreau's gesture was seen as everything from a sincere attempt at utopian living, to the misguided gesture of a harmless crank, to the hypocritical invention of a Barnumesque humbug.[48] Among contemporary critics, there is little agreement as well. To some, Thoreau is a tongue-in-cheek parodist whose main aim is to provoke; to others, he is a sincere lover of nature, working out one of the earliest-articulated ecological perspectives in the United States. Among those critics inclined to engage the more political aspects of Thoreau's thinking in *Walden*, there is, if possible, even less agreement. Although some critics have read *Walden* as a work of serious political import based on its confrontation of some of the most serious economic or political issues facing antebellum US society,[49] many others, including Michael

Gilmore and Sacvan Bercovitch, have dismissed *Walden*'s ability to reform its society on the grounds that despite his vocal critique of the economic and political status quo, Thoreau merely replicated the conditions of his society while at Walden, rather than imagining a substantive alternative.[50] Despite recognizing *Walden*'s reformist ambitions, such critics read Thoreau's text as a "defeated book,"[51] one ultimately guilty of "a forsaking of civic aspirations for an exclusive concern with 'the art of living well.'"[52]

Perhaps Thoreau's *Walden* investigation of modes of living is difficult to recognize as political because it is seldom read in the context of the eighteenth- and nineteenth-century British and American reformers who opposed "luxury" to independence and thus civic virtue.[53] Yet such republican, anticonsumerist, reformist rhetoric was widespread; in fact, Joanna Cohen has recently argued that two distinct models of citizenship vied for primacy in the early United States, models distinguished from each other precisely through their opposed attitudes to consumerism. In *Luxurious Citizens*, Cohen demonstrates that a Revolutionary-era model of "patriot-consumers," whose duty as citizens was "tied to self-sacrifice and withdrawal from the marketplace," was gradually eclipsed by "citizen-consumers." Once taxation power had been transferred to the federal government through Article 1, Section 8 of the Constitution, the "consumer's duty as a citizen was now linked to making a purchase." While these two ways of relating to citizenship and consumerism coexisted (perhaps uncomfortably, even antagonistically) through the antebellum period, Cohen argues that the ascendency of the "citizen-consumer" over the "patriot-consumer" was so complete by the close of the Civil War that most Americans now have trouble even recognizing the patriot-consumer model when they see it outside of the narrow context of the Revolutionary War and pre-Revolutionary boycotts.[54]

Certainly we have trouble recognizing it in *Walden*. For instance, when in October 2015 the journalist Kathryn Schulz published a splashy Thoreau hit piece in the *New Yorker* entitled "Pond Scum: Henry David Thoreau's Moral Myopia," her screed centered on the charge that Thoreau's account of his two-year "experiment in living" at Walden Pond is shot through with a repugnant, apolitical obsession with physiological purity and not consuming.[55] "I cannot idolize anyone who opposes coffee (especially if the objection is that it erodes great civilizations; had the man not heard of the Enlightenment?), but Thoreau never met an appetite too innocuous to denounce," Schulz writes. After many paragraphs detailing Thoreau's "adolescent" and "insufferable" views, Schulz concludes on a note of unsympathetic faux-pity:

Ultimately, it is impossible not to feel sorry for the author of
"Walden," who dedicated himself to establishing the bare necessities
of life without ever realizing that the necessary is a low, dull bar;
whose account of how to live reads less like an existential reckoning
than like a poor man's budget, with its calculations of how much to eat
and sleep crowding out questions of why we are here and how we
should treat one another.[56]

Schulz accuses Thoreau of playing at poverty for fun, apparently un-
aware that his time at Walden Pond was what we today would call a writer's retreat; after working a series of demanding jobs that left him little
time to write, his experiment in lowering his living expenses was a mostly
self-funded, two-year writing fellowship. Lacking the wealth simply to
bankroll his artistic aspirations (Schulz misrepresents Thoreau's class position as elite), Thoreau reduced his expenses in order to become a full-
time writer. In this and other respects, "Pond Scum" is oversimplified and
often misinformed, as others have pointed out.[57] Yet Schulz's essay is only
the latest in a long line of *Walden* denunciations decrying Thoreau's supposedly apolitical obsession with appetite and consumption.

The few critics who have addressed the topic of diet and consumption
in *Walden* most often ignore or dismiss it as evidence of Thoreau's unpleasant, sanctimonious side[58] and generally fail to contextualize his interest in
appetite, consumption, and consumerism in its wider, popular antebellum
context.[59] Like many other careful observers of antebellum US culture,
Thoreau expresses in *Walden* a keen awareness of the economic changes
happening around him. When Thoreau begins *Walden* with advice about
the frugal management of appetite and household affairs, he places his book
squarely in the tradition of popular domestic guidebooks and advice literature of the kind being produced by Catherine Beecher, Lydia Maria Child,
William A. Alcott, and especially Sylvester Graham.[60] Just as other antebellum domestic guidebook authors do, Thoreau devotes a great deal of
space in *Walden* to decrying his neighbors and contemporaries' marked lack
of market independence, painting them as trapped by their consumerist
desires. "Honestly think[ing] there is no choice left,"[61] such men and women
spend their lives in mistaken pursuit of luxury[62] and a lifestyle intended to
impress their neighbors,[63] losing their freedom in the process. As Lance
Newman has observed, when Thoreau "recommends a simple life, he does
so not because bodily needs are low or trivial, but because the way we fulfill them is deranged" by social conventions and pressure to consume
conspicuously.[64]

As *Walden* makes clear from the outset, one of the primary obstacles to "improving" life is that the old model for a useful and virtuous life—farming—is no longer viable. In an age of market capitalism, farming, which was for Jefferson the height of personal freedom, has become a kind of slavery; farmers, according to Thoreau, are "serfs of the soil."[65] The vision of the mythically independent, subsistence-farming yeoman has been eradicated, and in its place is a modern farmer whose commercial mentality has produced farms where "nothing grows free, whose fields bear no crops, whose meadows no flowers, whose trees no fruits, but dollars."[66] Moreover, Thoreau recasts prosperity as a burden repeatedly in "Economy," envisioning the propertied man as a radically encumbered body dragged down by "all the trumpery which he saves and will not burn."[67] Ultimately, "the more you have of such things the poorer you are"[68] because they cost so much of a person's limited stock of "life" to maintain. Thoreau agrees with Graham that "life"—time—is the real capital to be hoarded.[69]

Thoreau's philosophical alignment with Graham is signaled by the fact that he generally follows a Grahamite diet while living at Walden Pond. He takes frequent morning baths, as Graham was one of the earliest to recommend, avoids consuming most commercial food products, and eschews stimulating substances such as coffee, tea, alcohol, and, for the most part, animal products.[70] Also similar to Graham, Thoreau claims that appetite and the inappropriate consumption patterns related to appetite indulgence are the ultimate source of personal and civic subjection. Thoreau endorses Graham's central emphasis on the role of stimulation in disease and death when he offers his own theory of physiology near the beginning of *Walden*,[71] and in a passage that sounds quintessentially Grahamite, Thoreau adopts Graham's framework that equates fast living with domestic and civic degeneration:

> The nation itself, with all its so called internal improvements . . . is
> [as] . . . ruined by luxury and heedless expense, by want of calculation
> and a worthy aim, as the million households in the land; and the only
> cure for it as for them is in a rigid economy, a stern and more than
> Spartan simplicity of life and elevation of purpose. It lives too fast.[72]

Even Thoreau's famous formulation "the cost of a thing is the amount of what I will call life which is required to be exchanged for it, immediately or in the long run," when reread in light of Graham's vegetarian physiology, can be seen as drawing on Graham's theory of a limited fund of life that individuals have to "spend" throughout their lives.[73] Both Graham and

Thoreau place "life" as the central value of their economic system, and it
is the hoarding of "life" that represents "economic" success for both men.
Thoreau purports to be "treating the subject [of food] rather from an economic than a dietetic point of view," but from the vantage point of antebellum vegetarianism, the distinction is meaningless.[74]

Thoreau's primary rationale for his vegetarian diet in *Walden* turns out
to be that meat is just one more of the market luxuries that keep unimagi-
native citizens in the thrall of the market:

> One farmer says to me, "You cannot live on vegetable food solely, for it
> furnishes nothing to make bones with;" and so he religiously devotes a
> part of his day to supplying his system with the raw material of bones;
> walking all the while he talks behind his oxen, which, with vegetable-
> made bones, jerk him and his lumbering plough along in spite of every
> obstacle. Some things are really necessaries of life in some circles, the
> most helpless and diseased, which in others are luxuries merely, and in
> others still are entirely unknown.[75]

In passages such as these, Thoreau is building on the anticonsumerist, vegetarian abstemiousness of Sylvester Graham but broadening that philosophy. *Walden* presents a picture of simple living to all "circles" in order to
teach even "helpless and diseased" citizens the difference between luxury
and necessity—the precondition for real freedom, according to Thoreau.

For Thoreau, at issue in this management of appetite and consumption
is nothing short of personal freedom and the meaning of the American
dream. More than any other chapter in *Walden*, "Baker Farm"[76] makes
these stakes clear. Immediately preceding "Higher Laws," Thoreau's more
famous chapter about dietary matters, "Baker Farm" is significant for being the only moment in *Walden* where we actually see Thoreau recommend
his diet and lifestyle to any of his contemporaries. In this episode, Thoreau takes refuge from a rainstorm in what he believes to be an abandoned
cabin near Baker Farm but finds it occupied by an extremely poor family
of Irish immigrants, the Fields. As they wait out the rainstorm together,
Thoreau listens to the family patriarch, John Field, give an account of his
hard life, to which Thoreau responds by offering his own consumption patterns as a possible solution to the Field family's troubles.

Comparatively little has been written about "Baker Farm," and the pur-
pose of the chapter is often misunderstood. For instance, one critic opines:

> There is perhaps no more unpleasant chapter in *Walden* than "Baker
> Farm." . . . The sight of the celibate Thoreau airily patronizing Field
> and his family in the name of philosophy, urging him to drop his job,

change their diet, and go a-huckleberrying, is as unsettling and vaguely repellent as it would be to see Socrates persuading Phaedo and company to commit suicide.[77]

There is no doubt that Thoreau takes a patronizing tone toward Field in this chapter, but to read Thoreau's suggestions to the Field family as being simply "in the name of philosophy" is to miss the point. Thoreau sees John Field's tale of hardship as evidence of "a poor . . . bargain,"[78] and he "trie[s] to help him with [his] experience, telling him . . . that [he] too, who came a-fishing here, and looked like a loafer, was getting [his] living like himself,"[79] with the difference

> that I did not use tea, nor coffee, nor butter, nor milk, nor fresh meat, and so did not have to work to get them; . . . and when he had worked hard he had to eat hard again to repair the waste of his system. . . . He had rated it as a gain in coming to America, that here you could get tea, and coffee, and meat every day. But the only true America is that country where you are at liberty to pursue such a mode of life as may enable you to do without these, and where the state does not endeavor to compel you to sustain the slavery and war and other superfluous expenses which directly or indirectly result from the use of such things.[80]

The lesson that Thoreau is trying to teach Field here is not some abstruse philosophical point but a simple lesson in appetite management. When Thoreau says "I did not use tea, nor coffee, nor butter, nor milk, nor fresh meat, and so did not have to pay for them," he is highlighting the economy of his Grahamite diet. Field may have "rated it a gain in coming to America, that here you could get tea, and coffee, and meat every day," but Thoreau points out that indulgence in those commodities threatens the autonomy and liberty of the individual. Field's fundamental problem, in Thoreau's account, is that he mistakes freedom with the consumption of market goods when true freedom in fact inheres in the appetite management that allows one to "do without . . . such things."

For Thoreau, frugal consumption is an act of resistance to capitalism. "He that does not eat need not work," he writes in "Brute Neighbors," casting food as the ur-commodity that keeps individuals tied to the unstable and compromising capitalist system of exchange that, in the tradition of civic humanism, threatens the virtuous independence of republican citizens.[81] Thoreau devotes himself to the evaluation of man's basic needs— to finding out what are the "grossest groceries"—because such needs are the only necessary ties between an individual and a vampiric capitalist marketplace. Thoreau recognizes that the marketplace threatens individual autonomy, and he sees that it is impossible for individuals to become independent until they have learned to control their appetite. Such appetite control isn't a *part* of Thoreau's independence project, then; it *is* the project. As he puts it in "Economy," "my greatest skill has been to want but little."[82] Marx makes a similar point in volume 1 of *Capital* when he writes, "Individual consumption provides, on the one hand, the means for the workers' maintenance and reproduction; on the other hand, by the constant annihilation of the means of subsistence, it provides for their continued re-appearance on the labour-market."[83] Echoes between Thoreau and Marx are less a coincidence of their shared historical moment than they are evidence of Thoreau's attentiveness to and participation in nineteenth-century anticapitalism; as scholars have demonstrated, in his Walden experiment Thoreau "saw himself as engaged in a vitally important conversation with the utopian socialists" at Brook Farm, even if the social aspect of intentional communities remained unappealing to him.[84]

Fundamentally, Thoreau manages his body not in order to compete more effectively in the capitalist marketplace but in order to withdraw experimentally from it as far as is practicable. Thoreau's larger point in all of this is that the demands of capitalism are antithetical to both the demands of radical democracy and meaningful intellectual and personal independence; following the consumerist and acquisitive imperatives of capitalism means not only enslaving others, in the literal sense that buying the market products of slavery helps perpetuate the slave system, but also oneself, since—following Graham—an inability to manage one's appetite, one's "internal economy," means being controlled by the external market economy.

Thoreau's project in *Walden* is not, as it has sometimes been characterized, an attempt to develop a pattern book of a meaningful life that could be replicated by anyone hoping to escape a life of "quiet desperation."[85] We might think of *Walden* as something like contemporary experiments with limiting consumerism, where practitioners reduce their possessions to one hundred items or downsize their wardrobe to thirty-three items (or even a single dress) for three months or a year.[86] The idea of these experiments is not that practitioners would permanently embrace such extreme restrictions but that temporarily adopting them might remap their consumption habits, and perhaps even their personal and political imagination, in the service of more ethical and ecological modes of living.[87]

Strangely, despite the obvious resonance of Thoreau's *Walden* experiment with anticonsumerism and with the currently very trendy philosophy (or lifestyle, if you prefer) of radical minimalism, Thoreau and *Walden* are not cited as a precursor for the obsession du jour of unhappy privileged consumers in the United States, Japan, and elsewhere. Even when such works virtually parrot his system of economic reckoning in "Economy," as does the cult classic *Your Money or Your Life*,[88] the claim is that these ideas are brand new, born of the despair of late capitalism. What would it mean to acknowledge that they are not new? To recognize a homegrown, minoritarian vein of anticonsumerism that has been there all along, an integral part of US culture?

Private reform cannot substitute for political reform; Thoreau's support of John Brown and his active participation in the Underground Railroad, for example, illustrate that he understood the importance of collective action. Yet democracy entails active, collective collaboration in the classical republican tradition; as far as Thoreau is concerned, his neighbors must learn to participate actively in their *own lives* first. Rather than eating, working, reading, thinking, and consuming mechanically,[89] Thoreau wants his fellow Americans to "live deliberately,"[90] as he does—to engage in deliberation, to think, choose, and act for themselves. This is a political aspiration in a republican society because a "true form of self-government cannot exist without a critical self: when people act like machines, democracy ceases to be practiced on an everyday level."[91] Like its close contemporary *The Communist Manifesto*, *Walden* therefore frequently collapses its critique of the state and critique of the market because from Thoreau's perspective, both the "public" state and the "private" market are interfering with how one can manage the most significant "private" economy—the human body.

Thoreau casts general social reform as a private ill in *Walden*, just one more consequence of an ill-governed appetite,[92] because in most of his political writings he views society as an accretion of distinct individuals. If collectivities are mere accumulations of distinct, individualized bodies, and if these bodies have been mechanized through immersion in a capitalist marketplace, the revival of the robust independence of mind that self-government requires cannot result from *more* contact with the mechanized "mass of men."[93] Instead, in "Resistance to Civil Government," written while he was living at Walden Pond, Thoreau promotes the social utility of the well-governed individual using a bread metaphor: "It is not so important that many should be as good as you, as that there be some absolute goodness somewhere; for that will leaven the whole lump."[94] Later in this same essay, Thoreau famously calls for a "resting-place without [society]," from which he might move it.[95] Walter Benn Michaels points out that this place cannot be mere "Nature," for Thoreau repeatedly shows that when the individual gazes into nature, he merely sees himself reflected back.[96] Michaels focuses on "the empty space [Thoreau] sometimes calls wilderness" as the solution,[97] but in the context of *Walden*, Thoreau's praxis suggests that if the individual cannot disappear into nature, then the individual's body needs to become "the resting-place" outside of society. From this perspective, the reform of society depends upon the social and market autonomy of the individual that Thoreau's vegetarian and domestic lifestyle are designed to promote.

Like Sylvester Graham, Thoreau believes that abolition and significant social reform are impossible so long as the "very Constitution is the evil," as he writes in "Resistance to Civil Government,"[98] and he shifts his attention to the same human constitution as Graham for the remedy. In fact, in "Slavery in Massachusetts," Thoreau, like Graham, advocates for the substitution of a perfect physiological constitution for a flawed political constitution when he writes:

> The question is not whether you or your grandfather, seventy years
> ago, did not enter into an agreement to serve the devil, and that service
> is not accordingly now due; but whether you will not now, for once and
> at last, serve God,—in spite of your own past recreancy, or that of your
> ancestor,—by obeying that eternal and only just CONSTITUTION,
> which He, and not any Jefferson or Adams, has written in your
> being.[99]

Even more than Graham, who takes refuge in an equal-opportunity embodied constitution but who, like antislavery Constitutionalists such as Charles Sumner, attempts to imaginatively redeem the spirit of the US political constitution, Thoreau finds that the political constitution amounts to "an agreement to serve the devil" because he feels that it incontrovertibly supports slavery. The hopelessly flawed political constitution is finally irrelevant in the face of the "eternal and only just CONSTITUTION . . . written in your being," a physiological constitution theorized as decidedly universal and radically egalitarian. Obeying the "eternal and only just CONSTITUTION . . . written in your being" is clearly denominated as a political act in "Slavery in Massachusetts." If "the mass of men serve the State . . . with their bodies" and if "the State never intentionally confronts a man's sense, intellectual or moral, but only his body," as Thoreau argues in "Resistance to Civil Government," it makes sense to resist an unjust government with one's body, as well.[100]

The value of Thoreau's frugality is not that it bolsters a fantasy of self-sufficiency; the significance Thoreau gives consumption in fact reflects our interdependence with our environment and with one another. As Matthew Klingle has argued, the human body is a space where various scales, forms, and temporalities of consumption come together, and such consumption affects producers as well as consumers; it affects here and there, now and then (past as well as future). In fact, "some of our deepest and most meaningful connections to nature come through consumption," making consumption a continual reminder of our dependence on the earth.[101] Rather, the value of *Walden*'s frugality is that it refuses the correlation of consumption with freedom and happiness. In her work on Thoreau, Jane Bennett has asked, what is a "self capable of an act of conscientious dissent[?] What kind of being could be disobedient to civil authority?"[102] By focusing on Thoreau's dietary frugality, I am trying to ask: What is a self capable of resisting the lure of consumerism? What kinds of beings could be disobedient to the capitalist imperative to consume? The US economy and indeed American culture prize unlimited growth, accumulation, and the fostering of endless appetites and consumer desires. *Walden*'s celebration of frugality suggests that we might challenge the most destructive aspects of capitalism without compromising our happiness—a critical precondition for motivating political responses to runaway consumption in the twenty-first century.

Thoreau loved to renew worn-out words by going back to their roots. At its root, "frugality" contains the Latin word for "fruit," with all its sweetness, joy, and regeneration. Thoreau's Walden experiment in extreme frugality is compelling insofar as it multiplies, not reduces, possibilities, futures, and modes of living. "Nature and human life are as various as our several constitutions," *Walden* assures us. "Who shall say what prospect life offers to another?"[103] When Thoreau leaves Walden it is because "perhaps it seemed to me that I had several more lives to live."[104] The optimism of Thoreau's "several more lives" has become difficult to maintain in the Capitalocene, as we confront the reality that many of us, and Americans in particular, must drastically curb our consumption of everything from plastics to fossil fuels if we want to keep any but the most drastic futures possible for our planet. *Walden* might offer us a glimmer of hope insofar as it weds personal happiness and political possibility—the multiplication of options and futures, creative and political—to reducing consumption and curbing appetite. Thoreau may seem or even *be* a killjoy for some readers, but his frugality promotes joy and fulfillment against the world-ending "quiet desperation" of empty, unending consumerism.

The *"Banquet of Abstemiousness"*: *Dickinson's Desire and the Pleasure of Limits*

Enough is so vast a sweetness I suppose it never occurs—only pathetic counterfeits—Fabulous to me as the men of the Revelations who "shall not hunger anymore."

EMILY DICKINSON TO T. W. HIGGINSON, SEPTEMBER 26, 1870

In *Walden*, Thoreau suggests that happiness depends upon appetite and desire being managed, if not mastered. For Emily Dickinson, however, desire is an integral part of the human condition, inescapable and even to be embraced as a source of pleasure. Pleasure is not always the first thing that we think of when we think of Dickinson. She has been diagnosed by critics as depressed, repressed, agoraphobic, and anorexic, to name just a few of the more common charges. Yet as often as she writes of death, madness, or misery, she writes of pleasure, of "maddest Joy."[105] According to Thomas Wentworth Higginson, Dickinson told him, "I find ecstasy in living—the mere sense of living is joy enough," and when Higginson questioned this "ecstasy in living" by asking whether she "never felt want of employment, never going off the place & never seeing any visitor," Dickinson's rebuttal to his intimation that her life might be somewhat empty, or at least lonely, could hardly have been more straightforward, or strident: "I never thought of conceiving that I could ever have the slightest approach to such a want in all future time," adding, "I feel that I have not expressed myself strongly enough."[106] A joyful self-sufficiency is not how Dickinson is typically understood, but her self-characterization might suggest that perhaps there's more than a little paternalism in Higginson's—and our own—characterizations of Dickinson's life and literary perspective as "abnormal," unhappy, and wanting.[107]

Dickinson's expressions of happiness and her poetic explorations of joy are so easy to ignore because they're often tied to hunger, lack, and desire. "Who never wanted—maddest Joy / Remains to him unknown—," she writes in an emblematic instance.[108] Dickinson's frequent conceptualization of desire in relation to food and abstemious consumption—her many representations of food, hunger, starvation, and more general "consuming" in her poetry—stand alongside the sometimes exuberant relish with which she writes about food in her letters. For instance, an 1851 letter to Austin luxuriates in its vivid description of the family's ripening fruit: "The peaches are very large—one side a *rosy* cheek, and the other a *golden*, and that peculiar coat of velvet and of down, which makes a peach so beautiful. The grapes too are fine, juicy, and *such* a purple—I fancy the robes of kings are not a *tint* more royal."[109] It is also relatively well known that Dickinson was an accomplished baker, with bread and dessert making being her "special province" within the family.[110] Suggestively, her particular specialty was whole grain "Graham Bread," as well as puddings and desserts. Yet, when Dickinson's "poetics of food" is explored, critics such as Heather Kirk Thomas or Vivian Pollak have found her style and content to be "anorexic"[111] or her food imagery to be "transgressive" and "Gothic," as Elizabeth Andrews has it.[112]

Anorexia and pathology are not the only contexts though which we might read Dickinson's ongoing interest in food, desire, and frugal consumption.[113] As this chapter has already demonstrated, antebellum domesticity and dietary-reform literature frequently valorized extreme frugality and a refusal to consume market goods and even food in some contexts. We know that Dickinson was conversant in this feature of antebellum reform culture. David Reynolds has observed that "Dickinson, who was fully aware of antebellum popular culture in all its dimensions, seems to be intentionally playing on well-known temperance images" in many of her poems.[114] In fact, Dickinson's father gifted her Child's *The American Frugal Housewife* in 1832, and the book's worn pages testify to its status as a household staple. Sylvester Graham lived one town over in the 1840s, in Northampton, making him Dickinson's neighbor. We also know from her letters that Dickinson wrote about at least one temperance dinner,[115] discussed baking Graham bread in her letters,[116] and sometimes playfully parodied Grahamite language and principles, as she does in an 1851 letter to Austin.[117]

Even more familiar to Dickinson than Graham was Edward Hitchcock, president of Amherst College and an eminent naturalist whose botany book Dickinson quotes from in letters. Hitchcock takes up the popular subject of diet in his *Dyspepsy Forestalled and Resisted, or, Lectures on Diet, Regimen, and Employment: Delivered to the Students of Amherst College, Spring Term, 1830*. Like Graham and other self-styled diet and regimen experts, Hitchcock devotes a great deal of time to the question "How much shall we eat?" The answer, as it turns out, is not much. Hitchcock's "first rule" is "that the quantity of food at any one meal shall be very moderate."[118] In illustrating this rule, he writes approvingly of "the eastern Christians" who "allowed themselves but twelve ounces of bread per day, as their only solid food, and water alone for drink: yet they lived long and happy." He even lauds a man who ultimately "reduced his food so much, that it is said he lived several days upon the yolk of a single egg."[119] In the context of Hitchcock, Graham, Child, and a broad popular temperance and reformist culture that routinely valorized limiting food intake and managing appetite, the reoccurring imagery of starvation and lack in Dickinson's poetry hardly seems especially notable, let alone pathological.

Locating the recurring images of consumption and self-denial in Dickinson's poetry in their broader cultural context means including dietary reformers, but we might also place them alongside nineteenth-century critiques of capitalism such as those levied by Thoreau in *Walden* (or, for that matter, Marx). Elizabeth Hewett, Betsy Erkkila, Peter Stoneley, and others have established that Dickinson frequently uses economic language in her poetry and letters and that this language is not simply metaphorical.[120] "Instead, Dickinson's frequent employment of economic vocabulary signifies her abiding concern with, and study of, human need and human commerce."[121] This political and economic context might help us disarticulate Dickinson's interest in scarcity from the connotation of illness and to begin to explore the full interest and complexity of Dickinson's poetic delight in lack. The narrow pathologization of Dickinson's interest in not eating and not consuming comes to seem distinctly gendered when we notice how many of her contemporaries, male as well as female, were interested in the same subject and were theorizing modes of freedom—spiritual freedom, freedom from capitalism, and more—attendant on refusing to eat and consume.

Reading Dickinson's poetic interest in food, starvation, and lack in its nineteenth-century context invites the possibility that definitions of happiness to which critics have held Dickinson might be fruitfully neglected in pursuit of unfamiliar, even alien, pleasures. Take poem F748, "God gave a Loaf to every Bird—." Seemingly, the poem supports the critical tendency to pathologize Dickinson's speaker's curbed appetite.

> God gave a Loaf to every Bird—
> But just a Crumb—to Me—
> I dare not eat it—tho' I starve—
> My poignant luxury—[122]

The speaker here appears to revel in refusing to consume her tiny portion, "tho' [she] starve," an attitude that indeed might be characterized as disordered. But as the poem continues, it becomes clear that rather than abstinence for abstinence's sake, this poem advocates a pleasing form of frugality—what the contemporary "simple living" movement often calls "enough." Others have more, the speaker tells us, but this one "Crumb" is a treasured, "poignant luxury."

To own it—touch it—
Prove the feat—that made the Pellet mine—
Too happy—for my Sparrow's chance—
For Ampler Coveting—

It might be Famine—all around—
I could not miss an Ear—
Such Plenty smiles opon my Board—
My Garner shows so fair—[123]

The speaker compares herself to a bird, and the object in question is food, but the language of pleasurable possession ("To own it—touch it—") is so general that it could apply to any cherished material object. The affective state being described is not deprivation or depression: The speaker is "Too happy," "Plenty smiles opon" her, and her "Garner shows so fair." She can take pleasure in her "Pellet" because she has learned the trick of satisfaction—rejoicing in what one possesses rather than longing for what one does not. As a result, the speaker can conclude,

I wonder how the Rich—may feel—
An Indiaman—An Earl—
I deem that I—with but a Crumb—
Am Sovreign of them all—[124]

To be wealthy and independent in this poem is to have mastered one's appetite not in order to starve (it's a possibility, not a guarantee—"*tho'* I starve") but in order to delight in one's portion. The poem advocates against acquisitiveness in several registers. Most obviously, the poem incorporates familiar aspects of Christianity. "Ampler Coveting" weds amplitude, or having more than enough, to the most craven and even sinful form of craving and desire ("Thou shalt not covet"). On the other hand, the speaker's "Crumb" might call to mind the broken bread of the Christian sacrament, and her disregard of materialism is Christ-like. The speaker's rejection of consumption is also celebrated through imagery of democratic self-sufficiency: A pattern of diction casts the speaker as an American farmer with a full granary who measures wealth (or refuses to) in wheat and "Ear[s]" and whose frugality makes her "Sovreign"; her opposites are a British "Indiaman" and "Earl" whose riches come from colonialism, imperialism, slavery, and class exploitation—the labor of others, in other words.

One might argue that there's something antisocial about the mode of being celebrated in "God gave a Loaf to every Bird—." The crumb is a piece detached from the whole loaf, it is never consumed (which might evoke communion and community), and by the end of the poem this way of relating to her "Crumb" has transformed the speaker into a seemingly solitary "Sovreign." Perhaps this way of relating to one's portion is not so much antisocial as singular, however. To prioritize possession and inter-action ("To own it—touch it—") over acquisition and consumption goes against the way of the world—the wealth-acquisition imperative implied by all those "Rich" Indiamen and Earls.

Dickinson's celebration of freedom and satisfaction through voluntary simplicity resonates powerfully with Thoreau's similar portrait in *Walden*. When in poem F806 she writes,

> Partake as doth the Bee—
> Abstemiously—
> A Rose is an Estate
> In Sicily—[125]

Dickinson is pointing us, every bit as much as Thoreau, Graham, Child, and others, to the often co-constitutive and frequently fraught relation-ship between desire and satisfaction. Rather than an empirically determin-able constant, one's definition of "plenty" can depend upon one's habits and expectations for consumption. Instead of decreasing one's pleasure in consumption, abstemious or frugal consumption in fact increases the plea-sure of the thing consumed—the simple and highly accessible "Rose" be-comes a voluptuary "Estate/In Sicily." Rather than a difficult, externally imposed regimen, the poem suggests that this form of consumption is highly natural—it is how "the Bee" partakes. In other Dickinson poems, the bee appears as a figure for sexual and alcoholic indulgence, which re-inforces the sense of pleasure and plentitude this little poem paradoxically accords moderation.[126]

Dickinson's poems often insist that food's "Significance" is in pro-portion to its "Distance," a perspective that yields a surprisingly strong and complex theory of consumer desire. For instance, in poem F626, she observes,

> Undue Significance a starving man attaches
> To Food—
> Far off—He sighs—and therefore—Hopeless—
> And therefore—Good—
>
> Partaken—it relieves—indeed—
> But proves us

That Spices fly
In the Receipt—It was the Distance—
Was Savory—[127]

This poem offers a theorem of desire: "Far off—He sighs—and therefore—
Hopeless—/ And therefore—Good—." What the theorem "proves" is the
ability of desire to distort or magnify the qualities of things we want. Possession may bring "relie[f]," but it does not bring the full measure of delight anticipated because "It was the Distance—/ Was Savory—." Lacking
food, a "starving man" can never "attach" the correct amount of "significance" or meaning to the object of his desire.

    This failure of perception or perspective arises because in Dickinson's
poetry, states of desire, want, lack, and even "famine" (one of her favorite
terms) are relational: They are produced not on their own terms but by
the experience of plenty. As she writes in poem F870,

The fact of Famine—could not be
Except for Fact of Corn—

Want—is a meagre Art
Acquired by Reverse—[128]

The truth or experience of scarcity, even in its most material form, depends
upon the experience of harvest's plenty. It is not just that lack and plentitude depend upon one another for their meaning; in Dickinson's framing,
the ordinary value of need and possession seem almost reversed. Need, or
hunger, is the hard-won "Art" (if a "meagre," fleshless one), while "want"
is the subject of acquisition. "Reverse" suggests a loss of fortune but also
alterations of perspective that might be desirous (uncovering, or showing
the other side of something) and even the act of writing and revising poems (re-versing).[129] That Dickinson uses food to destabilize the positive
valuation of bounty is not only *not* unusual; it's precisely in keeping with
how contemporaries including Thoreau, Graham, and Child approach the
same questions of appetite and abundance.

    What is perhaps most interesting, however, is that Dickinson's "starv-
ing man" or her abstemious Bee are not the joyless figures temperance or
vegetarian caricatures would have us imagine. She writes in poem F1447,

Who never wanted—maddest Joy
Remains to him unknown—
The Banquet of Abstemiousness
Defaces that of Wine—[130]

Rather than pathology, anorexia, or masochism, Dickinson's speaker's "abstemiousness" is born of a complex understanding of the nature of desire and its often negative relationship to possession and consumption. Delight is not consumption or possession in Dickinson's account but the moment just before, and her poetry frequently seeks to dwell in that moment of "maddest Joy," to dilate it in order to linger inside of it.[131] Such forestalling is a bid *for* pleasure, not a rejection of it—it's a hedonist's ploy. In fact, one effect of Dickinson's characteristic dashes can be to render formally this dilation of desire, to defer linguistic completion or fulfillment. In poem F1447, for instance, the dash in the first line defers the delivery of "maddest Joy," leaving a reader time to "want" it.

"Who never wanted—maddest Joy" adds a new twist to the recurring theme that desire is more powerful than possession; by taking up an entire line, Dickinson's paradoxical "Banquet of Abstemiousness" makes lack look and feel expansive, like plenty, an effect reinforced by the line's extra ninth syllable. Dickinson's use of the word "abstemiousness" might put a reader in mind of the kind of chastity and temperance celebrated in Thoreau's "Higher Laws" chapter of *Walden*, but here it is not the death of an inner animal being idealized; rather, the sheer existence of that appetitive inner animal is being celebrated as the source of powerful pleasures. Without appetite, poem F1447 suggests, we could not experience the "banquet" of desire that "defaces that of wine." "Defaces" not only connotes obliteration but hints that the appeal of wine's banquet might be quite superficial (literally, on the surface); the brevity of the line and Dickinson's decision not to repeat "banquet" reinforces that wine's banquet is paltry compared to that of "abstemiousness."

The poem's second stanza offers more precise detail about the ideal relationship between "Desire" and "the Actual":

> Within it's reach, though yet ungrasped
> Desire's perfect Goal—
> No nearer—lest the Actual—
> Should disenthrall thy soul—[132]

"Within it's reach, though yet ungrasped" idealizes and abstracts the moment in time just before the fulfillment of desire into a kind of general principle, a suggestive echo of Keats's "Though winning near the goal yet, do not grieve" from the second stanza of "Ode on a Grecian Urn."[133] If for Thoreau being in the thrall of desire is a source of limitation, for Dickinson to be "disenthrall[ed]" by "the Actual" is a possibility so painful that "the Actual" must be cordoned off with dashes from the rest of the poem.

Happiness is a matter of desire, and desire, as John Locke insisted, is a matter of taste: "Though all men's desires tend to happiness, yet they are not moved by the same object."[134] Dickinson's poems describe again and again failures of taste: The feast is achieved, but it is never as delicious as the imagination promised. Dickinson's own taste is therefore for desire itself, for the feast of the imagination—for expectation, which tastes better than any actual present or future consumable. Experiencing "maddest Joy" in expectation of food, or delight, rather than its consumption or achievement is not perverse so much as a legible, contextualizable, if bold and creative, response to the "happiness scripts" available to Dickinson and to many of her female contemporaries.

Critics have become quite comfortable thinking of Dickinson as rejecting certain conventional teleologies—the clichés of heteronormative patriarchy, for instance, including traditional roles of wife and mother, as well as many of the expectations for a Victorian female poet—but what about the teleology of happiness? As Sara Ahmed argues in *The Promise of Happiness*, happiness is not something to happen upon or find; it is culturally produced and often comes with normative, regulatory power: "What is good" may "make us happy," but when we parse this we find that happiness and claims about happiness "*participat*[e] in making things good."[135] Happiness, Ahmed suggests, reifies particular "paths" or "scripts" and not others: "Happiness is not simply used to secure social relations instrumentally but works as an idea or aspiration within everyday life, shaping the very terms through which individuals share their world with others, creating 'scripts' for how to live well."[136] To be unwilling or unable to "express happiness in proximity to the right things" is to be what Ahmed calls an "affect alien,"[137] and perhaps this is one way we might imagine Dickinson—as an affect alien resisting the "happiness scripts" of gender and sexuality as well as capitalist imperatives about what it is to be a happy woman: a heterosexual wife and mother and an eager consumer of market commodities.

Dickinson does occasionally celebrate possession, but even in these cases she seems to be working against accumulation as a principle or orientation to the world. In poem F1267, she meditates on the enjoyment of "Possessions" in four deceptively simple lines:

Our own Possessions though our own
'Tis well to hoard anew
Remembering the dimensions
Of Possibility.[138]

One of the pillars of consumerism is the notion that new possessions are portals to new possibilities—new experiences, new forms of self-presentation, maybe even new lives and new selves. Here, instead, the "dimensions/Of Possibility" may best be remembered or accessed through what we already own. Perhaps also the "dimensions" of pleasure, since "Possession" in its 1844 *Webster's* definition has a sense of enjoyment built right into it, as one of its meanings is "any thing valuable possessed or enjoyed." The speaker calls for us to continually enjoy or treasure what we own ("hoard anew") even as she recognizes that treasuring what you already own is difficult ("though our own"). A great deal of the power of this poem hinges on the last line, which is simultaneously spare—just two words—and expansively polysyllabic; thus "Possibility" enacts how much might be contained in a small space. Because it is linked with "dimensions" and with cherishing "our own Possessions," "Possibility" becomes less abstract and more concrete—it seems like something that might be fathomed or even measured (the 1844 *Webster's* definition links "dimension" with geometry), and there is a specific directive for how to achieve it. Altogether, Dickinson's depiction of cherishing what we already possess goes contrary to consumerist practice and undermines the essential capitalist imperative to "accumulate."

Dickinson does at times represent desire as something unquenchable and as a source of pain. Poem F851 begins with a description that makes human life synonymous with unfulfilled, and perhaps unfulfillable, desire. "'I want'—it pleaded—All it's life—/ I want—was chief it said."[139] The poem universalizes desire into the essence of the human condition, yet, paradoxically, to experience desire in this way is to be emptied out, dehumanized, transformed into an "it." In fact, satisfaction of this kind of desire ("That single—steadfast sigh—") is possible only after "it" is "newly dead."[140] In poem F1311, Dickinson strengthens the connection between unfulfilled and unfulfillable desire and human nature when she represents freedom from this kind of desire as transformation out of, or beyond, a human state. "Art thou the thing I wanted?/ Begone—my Tooth has grown—," the poem begins.[141] In the final stanza, it becomes clear that the speaker has "grown" beyond the most elemental form of need or desire: the need for "the mystery of Food."[142] Such freedom turns out to be literally inhuman, however; moving beyond the ability to be "goad[ed]" by desire, the speaker "abjure[s]" food, "Subsisting now like God—."[143] Despite the divine comparison, such "subsistence" doesn't sound particularly sensuous or appealing, given the word's connotation of bare minimums; certainly it requires the figurative death of the human part of the speaker, which requires "Food." The dash after "God" that ends the poem further calls into question the benefits of the speaker's new state by raising but refusing to answer what God's "subsistence" is "like." Thus, the poem simultaneously invites its readers to imagine the speaker as deathless, timeless, ageless, omnipotent, and eternal—above and outside the constituent elements of mortal existence, in other words—even as it leaves open the possibility that the speaker may no more exist than God (whose existence cannot be proven, as Dickinson observes in other poems). Here and elsewhere, Dickinson renders the appeal of existing beyond desire doubtful at the very least.

Taken together, Dickinson's poems deliver consumerism a powerful one-two punch: The poems undermine the value of consumption first by suggesting that anticipation and desire might be productive of greater joy than possession and then by suggesting that it's possible to take so much pleasure in what you have that what you do not have pales in comparison, even if it is technically "more." Moreover, Dickinson disables one of the most potent myths of consumerism that keeps people buying and accumulating: that consumption can fundamentally change the consumer. If, as the anthropologist Daniel Miller has argued, most consumerism is about bridging the difference between who you are and who social norms claim you ought to be in order to diminish the "discrepancies between the normative and the actual," then consumption is something allied with social conformity, not individuality.[144] In this context, Dickinson's famed (and sometimes maligned) celebrations of insularity might in fact be helpful. For example, in poem F645, she writes,

> Exhiliration—is within—
> There can no Outer Wine
> So royally intoxicate
> As that diviner Brand
>
> The Soul achieves—Herself—
> To drink—or set away
> For Visitor—or Sacrament—
> 'Tis not of Holiday
>
> To stimulate a Man
> Who hath the Ample Rhine
> Within his Closet—Best you can
> Exhale in offering—[145]

Joy, passion, thrills, cheer: All of these and more are "within." We self-"intoxicate" to the extent that "The Soul achieves—Herself—." As the poem goes on, the boundaries of inside and outside, which seem so stable and distinct initially, are confused with stanza breaks. By the end of the poem, the "Exhiliration," so deeply interior and insular in the first stanza, does become peculiarly social; playing on the visual and aural similarities of "Exhale" and "Exhiliration," the last stanza imagines breathy, "stimulat[ing]" communion. Like the divine breath of Genesis 2:7, we might enliven one another with the life and joy we have "achieve[d]" rather than imagining we can buy a self or permanently fulfill our desires with consumption and consumerism.

Joyful Frugality for the Present

Learning to enjoy our possessions and, yes, manage desire for commodities is increasingly demanded of middle-class and wealthy Americans in particular. These Americans have become ecological debtors, in the sense that they have helped draw down the earth's resources past the point of renewal; this debt will have to be confronted in the political realm if life, human and not, is to continue to flourish on our planet. Before or alongside this work, Child, Graham, Thoreau, and Dickinson suggest that many of us in the United States must also confront our private appetites and connect them to our public, political, and ecological failings.

Dickinson and Thoreau help us imagine that curbing consumption might be joyful; Sylvia Plath, by contrast, might help us reframe consumerism as a death wish. Plath's "A Birthday Present," written in 1962, just months before her death, ridicules many of our most quintessential fantasies of commodity consumption. The poem begins,

What is this, behind this veil, is it ugly, is it beautiful?
It is shimmering, has it breasts, has it edges?

I am sure it is unique, I am sure it is just what I want.
When I am quiet at my cooking I feel it looking, I feel it thinking

"Is this the one I am to appear for,
Is this the elect one, the one with black eye-pits and a scar?

Measuring the flour, cutting off the surplus,
Adhering to rules, to rules, to rules.

Is this the one for the annunciation?
My god, what a laugh!"[146]

The poem opens with the absolute mystery of the object "behind this veil"—even its most basic features are not known—but quickly shifts into certainty about at least some of its qualities: "I am sure it is unique, I am sure it is what I want." The rapid shift in tone between lines 1–2 and line 3 amplify the absurdity of the speaker's confidence in the unknown gift's superlative nature and its ability to satisfy her. This absurdity is further heightened by the ridiculousness of the gift's self-important pronouncement in lines 5–10, especially when measured against the gift's description of the gift-receiver's human shortcomings. The gift receiver, "the elect one," clearly falls far short of deserving "the annunciation" of the gift's bestowal. Her quiet, dull domesticity and adherence "to rules, to rules, to rules" is mocked by the gift and perhaps also by the poem. The frugal housewife's "cutting off the surplus"—a necessary act in baking but also in household economy and the management of unruly desire—comes in for particular scorn.

The gift seems at first to be the antidote to a disappointing, spectacularly ordinary life, but ultimately, "A Birthday Present" interrogates the common if often unexamined sense that consumption—a lot or a little, generally or of one special item in particular—could fundamentally change the consumer, could make a consumer more attractive or happier, could make living in a painful world more bearable. In Plath's poem, this belief is violent; by the end of "A Birthday Present," desire for possession of the present blends seamlessly into a desire for death: The one seems to provoke the other. The pun of "present"—gift and temporality—is suggestive. The speaker does not want to want the temporal present, in which the gift is mysterious and unopened; she wants to circumvent desire and possess the object, a wish that the poem represents as suicidal. Perhaps more than any other single work, "A Birthday Present" represents the death drive of commodity consumption, our acquisitiveness despite (because of?) our clear-eyed understanding of its dramatically negative effect on other people, other creatures, future generations, and the planet as a whole.

Dickinson and Thoreau work against the idea that consumption will produce transformation or lasting happiness. For Thoreau, consumption is what gets in the *way* of self-transformation and joy; living as a creative and political being is only possible once appetite has been contained and controlled. For Dickinson, happiness comes from embracing desire's ever-welling permanence, and transformation happens to the extent that we find ways to cherish what we already possess. Thoreau and Dickinson, each in their different ways, disrupt normative happiness scripts that drive consumption by relocating pleasure elsewhere. Both Dickinson and Thoreau are, to return to Sara Ahmed's term, "affect aliens" unable or unwilling "to express happiness in proximity to the right things." *Walden* and Dickinson's poems each reject capitalist imperatives about what it is to be happy; neither locates happiness in being a consumer of market goods, in being a generator of surplus capital, or in performing the reproductive labor required to regenerate the workforce. They're anticapitalist killjoys, but contra the popular and even critical clichés, they are not themselves without joy.

The point is not that we all have to live in the singular modes chosen by the historical Henry David Thoreau or Emily Dickinson. Most of us cannot, for all kinds of reasons. Rather, the point is that their respective rejections of capitalist imperatives and their relocation of pleasure to sites other than consumption open up novel possibilities for living—for themselves and also for us. The solution to our consumption-driven environmental disaster will not be found in consumer choice; the source of our problems will not be its solution. Shifts in consumer choices do little to bring about the large structural changes that could mitigate economic oppression, labor exploitation, or climate change. Yet we need popular acquiescence to the economic shifts that must take place if our environmental crisis is to be addressed: Americans in particular cannot honestly or plausibly demand solutions from our politicians to climate change, pollution, and other environmental problems when we remain so collectively unwilling to modify our own consumption patterns. The value of Thoreau's and Dickinson's questioning of cultural imperatives to find pleasure in consuming is not (or not simply) that they might transform our private consumption practices but that their ideas might transform our civic selves into selves capable of working for meaningful responses to consumption-driven environmental crises.

CHAPTER 3

The Problem with Preservation: Aesthetics and Sanctuary in Catlin, Parkman, Erdrich, Melville, and Byatt

When the history of US environmentalism is being told, preservation is typically cast as a progressive development away from damaging utilitarian approaches that treated nonhuman nature as resource and raw material.[1] In histories of American attitudes toward nature such as Roderick Nash's classic *Wilderness and the American Mind*, the type of nature appreciation and preservationism that emerged during the nineteenth century has often been opposed to more "utilitarian" attitudes to nature. The usual narrative, drawn by Nash, Hans Huth in *Nature and the American*, and others, has been that the nineteenth century marked a transition away from the earlier Puritan view of America as a "howling wilderness" whose inert natural features needed cultivation into the "garden" of the middle landscape.[2] The traditional vision of nature as a passive (if hostile) repository of raw material for human use only began to give way, according to the familiar accounts, in the late nineteenth century, when visionary preservationists such as John Muir, inspired in part by Ralph Waldo Emerson's and Henry David Thoreau's Transcendentalist approaches to nature, came to conceive of a value in wild nature and to demand the protection of at least some small part of it from human development and settlement. This triumphalist narrative dominates not only scholarly but also popular environmental histories, as, for instance, Ken Burns's much-celebrated 2009 documentary series *The National Parks: America's Best Idea*, which begins its history of American nature preservation with John Muir, Theodore Roosevelt, and the formation in the 1870s of Yellowstone and Yosemite National Parks.[3]

In this chapter, I seek to tell a different story about preservation as an environmental ethic. I do so in the first place by recovering the antebellum literary and artistic origins of preservationism in the work of the painter, writer, and showman George Catlin. The first part of the chapter explores Catlin's 1844 *Letters and Notes on the Manners, Customs, and Conditions of North American Indians*, which contains the first proposal for national US wilderness preservation. I build on the work of historians such as William Cronon and Mark David Spence to interrogate critically the attitudes and ideas that led to the "revaluing" of nature supposedly captured by the preservationist movement.[4] I demonstrate that the attitudes and assumptions that led Catlin to his preservationist mission, including his call for a "nation's park" thirty years before the establishment of Yellowstone, hinge on a growing appreciation of the aesthetic value of indigenous "wild" spectacles for an increasingly "civilized" white US population.

The second part of the chapter puts Catlin's arguments for preservation into conversation with Francis Parkman Jr.'s *The Oregon Trail* (1849), in order to demonstrate one of the weaknesses of valuing nature according to aesthetic criteria, namely, that aesthetic judgments are subjective rather than universal. Whereas Catlin saw beauty in Plains peoples, bison, and their threatened landscape, Parkman saw ugliness in need of violent erasure. Together, the first two parts of this chapter consider how Easterners imagined bison extinction and preservation in order to explore the ecological stakes of nineteenth-century aesthetic judgments about the natural world. Ultimately, I argue that the material history of bison preservation—and the philosophical and cultural value judgments that underlie that history—deeply complicate preservation's relationship to extinction and disappearance and disrupt triumphalist claims about the progressiveness of American attitudes toward nature in the nineteenth century (and perhaps today).

From the flawed aesthetic logic of preservation, I turn to Herman Melville's *Moby-Dick* (1851) to explore the flawed spatial logic that characterizes preservation as an environmental concept. I show that Melville's Ishmael considers and rejects the possibility of whale extinction because of his commitment to a romantic vision of the sea and its creatures as finally unconquerable, which encourages a false confidence about oceanic and planetary resilience. I explicate the failure of this romantic notion by way of A. S. Byatt's 2013 "Sea Story," a tale of plastic pollution that plays out the consequences of *Moby-Dick*'s portrait of the sea in the Anthropocene. Altogether, the chapter suggests that preservation has been a damaging environmental ethic (if not always practice) and that the benefits of this ethic only continue to diminish as environmental degradation intensifies.

Catlin's "Living Monuments": Problematizing Artistic Preservation

No one is more closely associated with the preservation of American bison than William Temple Hornaday. Yet Hornaday's preservation began in a curious manner: In 1886, he convinced his employer, the Smithsonian Museum, to fund a hunting expedition in which he proposed to (and did) kill twenty-five of the estimated last thousand remaining buffalo still roaming the western prairie. Hornaday would go on to become the first director of the Bronx Zoo, a position he would leverage to help preserve the bison species. He is popularly remembered now primarily for displaying a Congolese man, Ota Benga, in a cage in the monkey house of the Bronx Zoo for eighteen infamous days in the autumn of 1906.[5] But in 1886, Hornaday was the chief taxidermist at the fledgling national museum, hoping to secure specimens to develop into a bison display. But why didn't the museum already have bison specimens by the late 1880s? Between five and six million buffalo were slaughtered on the southern plains in the five-year period between 1870 and 1875 alone; hides were hardly hard to come by. In fact, that is precisely the point—buffalo were considered too ordinary to mount as elaborate museum trophies until their numbers had dwindled enough to make them exotic.[6]

The devastation of the buffalo from an estimated peak of thirty million down to a few hundred individuals by the late nineteenth century was a complicated process. Bison were casualties of grazing competition from wild horses, bovine diseases introduced by settlers' cattle crossing on the Overland Trail, drought, blizzards, and other environmental factors. But it was overhunting that caused the worst of the destruction and overhunting that captured nineteenth-century Americans' imaginations.[7] Crucially, the near extinction of the bison was no accident of laissez-faire capitalism but an active campaign supported by, and in some cases waged by, the US Army—a key strategy in the frontier army's conquest of the "Far West." As Colonel Richard Dodge urged one hunter in 1867, "Kill every buffalo you can! Every buffalo dead is an Indian gone."[8]

Hornaday's 1886 "last buffalo hunt" (as he called it), far from an aberrant irony in the annals of preservation, is in fact the primal scene of pre-twentieth-century preservationism: killing to capture a representative specimen for posterity.[9] For Hornaday, bison preservation initially took the form of taxidermy; the cover of this book features one of those 1886 buffalo kills, a bull in mid-preparation for display at the Smithsonian.[10] Taxidermy preserves visual specimens for viewers' enjoyment and edification; these are also the goals of those seeking to preserve American nature in painting and literature. The works of John James Audubon, in fact, are notable for intermixing accounts of bird and other animal slaughter, taxidermy, and consumption with lush illustrations and vivid descriptions of the animals' habits and manners, at times also accompanied by explicit discussion of the creatures' increasing disappearance. For instance, Audubon's notes on the pinnated grouse describe the bird's initial abundance and consequent lack of value in Kentucky and the eastern United States and chronicle its wanton and wasteful destruction by hunters who often did not even bother picking up the bodies of grouse they had shot. By the time of Audubon's writing in the 1830s, "the Grouse have abandoned the State of Kentucky and removed (like the Indians) every season farther to the westward, to escape from the murderous white man."[11] Appreciative descriptions of the grouse's habits and habitats, mating behaviors and cries, appearance, and so on sit side by side with hunting advice for sportsmen and descriptions of the grouse's mass slaughter and increasing disappearance, including detailed accounts of Audubon's own personal participation in grouse killing.[12] At one point in his essay, Audubon describes how he collected and tamed a flock he kept like chickens before "order[ing] them to be killed" because they were becoming a garden nuisance. Throughout the entry on the pinnated grouse, Audubon reports copiously on the market prices of the birds and the taste of their flesh (the young are "most excellent eating," but the mature bird's flavor is indifferent—"I never thought much of it").[13]

The relationship between slaughter and artistic preservation is direct and intimate in Audubon's life and career. Audubon worked briefly as a taxidermist before perfecting his drawing technique, and shooting, posing, and then drawing his kills was essential to his celebrated "life-like" effect. "My drawings have all been made after individuals fresh killed, mostly by myself, and put up before me by means of wires, &c. in the precise attitude represented, and copied with a closeness of *measurement* that I hope will always correspond with *nature* when brought into contact."[14] With his *Birds of America* Audubon wished "to raise an everlasting monument, commemorating with a grand effect the history and portraits of the birds of

America," a monument particularly urgent to produce given that "as time flies Nature loses its primitiveness, and that pictures drawn in ten, or twenty, or more years, will no longer illustrate our delightful America pure from the hands of its Creator!"[15] As in his description of the pinnated grouse, Audubon is conscious just how much of the value of his represen-tations of American nature derives from its transformation, and in some cases disappearance, at the hands of man.

Distinct as Audubon and Hornaday's aims and means might seem, the painter and writer George Catlin's preservation project bridges the dis-tance between such apparently disparate artistic and material preserva-tion efforts. In the epistolary account of his 1830–1836 travels among the Native peoples of the Plains, *Letters and Notes on the Manners, Customs, and Conditions of North American Indians* (1844), Catlin details his quest to "preserv[e] by pictorial illustrations" "a literal and graphic delineation of the living manners, customs, and character of an interesting race of people, who are rapidly passing away from the face of the earth."[16] Catlin shares with many of his contemporaries the faith that Native peoples and bison are "destined" to disappear as white settlers continue to expand westward;[17] while he (not without ambivalence) laments this supposed fact, he seems most concerned with the loss of a visual spectacle. Throughout his writ-ing, Catlin primarily represents Native Americans as interesting aesthetic objects rather than human beings whose interests should (or even, could) compete ethically with whites' own.

Catlin opens his epistolary narrative with a telling account of how he conceived of his project to visit and paint the Plains Indians, an anecdote that articulates his sense of the value of his subject. Catlin writes that just as he was studying painting and searching for "some branch or enterprise of the art, on which to devote a whole life-time of enthusiasm," a delega-tion of "noble and dignified-looking Indians" arrived in his city, "arrayed and equipped in all their classic beauty,—with shield and helmet,—with tunic and manteau,—tinted and tasseled off,—exactly for the painter's pal-ette!"[18] What Catlin sees when he looks at this group of Indians is not a party of contemporaries, human beings like himself; Catlin's "enthusiasm" is for an aesthetic spectacle. The "classic beauty" he sees before him strikes him as an almost miraculous, ready-made tableau—"exactly for the paint-er's palette!" Moreover, Catlin is explicitly aware that he is not the only one who appreciates the spectacle of the Native American delegation; Cat-lin notes that the Indians attracted "the gaze and admiration of all who beheld them," making it clear that there is a large white audience eager to consume such spectacles. Even the "lords of the forest" themselves, who in Catlin's account spend their time "strut[ting] about the city . . . wrapped in their pictured robes," seem cooperatively conscious of their own picturesque qualities.[19]

What emerges from this remembered encounter is a kind of Romantic manifesto in support of painting Indians outside the purview of "civilization":

> Black and blue cloth and civilization are destined, not only to veil, but
> to obliterate the grace and beauty of Nature. Man, in the simplicity
> and loftiness of his nature, unrestrained and unfettered by the
> disguises of art, is surely the most beautiful model for the painter,—
> and the country from which he hails is unquestionably the best study
> or school of the arts in the world: such I am sure, from the models I
> have seen, is the wilderness of North America.[20]

Uncorrupted by "black and blue cloth and civilization," Native peoples of the Plains retain "the grace and beauty of Nature," making them "surely the most beautiful model for the painter," just as the "wilderness" home of these Indians "is unquestionably the best study or school of the arts in the world."

Catlin claims that this perfect, indigenous beauty is fast disappearing, a state of affairs that only heightens the value of both the spectacle and his preservation of it on canvas. It is "a subject of great interest and some importance to the civilized world; rendered more particularly so in this age, from their relative position to, and their rapid declension from, the civilized nations of the earth."[21] Catlin insists, again and again in his writings, that it is only Indians uncorrupted by Anglo-American "civilization," who hold any cultural or aesthetic interest. "Their habits (and their's [*sic*] alone)" are "native, and such as I have wished to fix and preserve for future ages."[22] Catlin's language here calls to mind Hornaday's taxidermy; there's something remarkably static and deathly about the aspiration to "fix and preserve" living peoples and their culture "for future" (presumably white) "ages." At the same time, Catlin insists that any still-living Native peoples who have had contact with whites are culturally dead: Having lost their "native simplicity and beauty," they are "as a basket of *dead game*,—harassed, chased, bleeding and dead; with their plumage and colours despoiled."[23] The slippage between Native peoples and native animals in Catlin's "basket of *dead game*" simile implies that both are aspects of "wild" nature destined for one of two fates: They may be treated as a mere (natural, cultural) resource, to be hunted out of existence, or they may be valued for their wild and beautiful properties and preserved as an aesthetic and spiritual commons for white Americans.

It is his conviction that Indigenous human and nonhuman beauty is in danger of extinction that leads to Catlin's famously prescient call for a national park. Catlin, in his last letter of volume 1 of *Letters and Notes*, laments that

> many are the rudenesses and wilds in Nature's works, which are destined to fall before the deadly axe and desolating hands of cultivating man; and so amongst her ranks of *living*, of beast and human, we often find noble stamps, or beautiful colours, to which our admiration clings; and even in the overwhelming march of civilized improvements and refinements do we love to cherish their existence, and lend our efforts to preserve them in their primitive rudeness. Such of Nature's works are always worthy of our preservation and protection; and the further we become separated (and the face of the country) from that pristine wildness and beauty, the more pleasure does the mind of enlightened man feel in recurring to those scenes, when he can have them preserved for his eyes and his mind to dwell upon.[24]

Little resembling the broadly humanitarian impulse that is often explicitly or implicitly read into Catlin's proposal for a "nation's park,"[25] this is an argument for preservation that emerges from a Romantic appreciation of the aesthetic value of "Nature's works." Similar to many of his contemporaries during the nineteenth century, Catlin is arguing that some of the "noble stamps, or beautiful colours" that are being lost to the transformation of the American landscape wrought by expansion, settlement, and industrializing development should be set aside and protected for the leisured consumption of "the mind of enlightened man." The "wilds in Nature's works" become pleasurable and "worthy of our preservation and protection" in direct proportion to how far "civilized" man separates himself from them. Although Catlin's respect for nature is often represented as protoenvironmental, it is closer to the popular, alienating aesthetic Rochelle Johnson has argued was characteristic of antebellum US culture: an anthropocentric form of nature appreciation that centers or even magnifies the significance of the human viewer rather than decentering or diminishing humanity.[26]

Catlin's call for a national park turns out to be rather different than the visionary precursor to the subsequent US national park system that it is often represented to be.[27] When critics, historians, and anthologists highlight Catlin's vision for a national park, they typically ignore the fact that it is preceded by a "melancholy contemplation" that inflects how Catlin's vision of a "magnificent Park" should be read. The two paragraphs read in full:

> It is a melancholy contemplation for one who has travelled as I have, through these realms, and seen this noble animal in all its pride and glory, to contemplate it so rapidly wasting from the world, drawing the irresistible conclusion too, which one must do, that its species is soon to be extinguished, and with it the peace and happiness (if not the actual existence) of the tribes of Indians who are joint tenants with them, in the occupancy of these vast and idle plains.[28]
>
> And what a splendid contemplation, too, when one (who has travelled these realms, and can duly appreciate them) imagines them as they *might* in future be seen, (by some great protecting policy of government) preserved in their pristine beauty and wildness, in a *magnificent park*, where the world could see for ages to come, the native Indian in his classic attire, galloping his wild horse, with sinewy bow, and shield and lance, amid the fleeting herds of elks and buffaloes. What a beautiful and thrilling specimen for America to preserve and hold up to the view of her refined citizens and the world, in future ages! A *nation's Park*, containing man and beast, in all the wild and freshness of nature's beauty![29]

Catlin's "melancholy contemplation" of disappearance not only precedes the "splendid contemplation" of preservation narratively but also temporally, since the melancholy contemplation is grounded in the present, in things as they currently, actually exist.[30] Bison extinction and the end of the Indian way of life are "irresistible conclusion[s]" that one "must" arrive at, while the "magnificent park" Catlin proposes is a tentatively imagined future, what "*might*" be—and Catlin's italics lay heavy stress on the "might." The park dream here represents a hope, not entirely original in an era when whites were widely convinced that any contact at all between whites and Native peoples must result in the extermination of the Native peoples, that "a system of non-intercourse could be established and preserved," as Catlin put it.[31]

What *is* rather original about Catlin's "contemplation" is his desire to have the bison and Native Americans "preserved" for civilized (that is, white) Americans to view in "future ages," but he almost immediately undercuts the plausibility of his park vision by sadly concluding:

> But such is not to be the case—the buffalo's doom is sealed, and with their extinction must assuredly sink into real despair and starvation,

the inhabitants of these vast plains, which afford for the Indians, no other possible means of subsistence; and they must at last fall a prey to wolves and buzzards, who will have no other bones to pick.[32]

The "magnificent park" is a brief interlude in a larger fantasy of extinction that turns out in any case to be as much a dream of preserving the bison and Indians as it is a dream of preserving the memory of Catlin, who modestly assures readers that he would "ask no other monument to my memory, nor any other enrolment of my name amongst the famous dead, than the reputation of having been the founder of such an institution."[33]

The "institution" Catlin wishes to found resembles not so much a park as a museum diorama: "What a beautiful and thrilling specimen for America to preserve and hold up to the view of her refined citizens and the world, in future ages!"[34] Even when Catlin describes the plains' currently existing biotic community, it sounds like a carefully managed museum display, "stocked" with "specimens": "It is on these plains, which are stocked with buffaloes, that the finest specimens of the Indian race are to be seen."[35] The emphasis in Catlin's vision, as in Hornaday's later quest to collect bison specimens for the national museum and in antebellum natural science collecting more broadly, is to preserve representative "specimens" of non-human nature and indigenous humans for the edification and "pleasure" of "the mind of enlightened [white] man." This vision of literal preservation is continuous with Catlin's artistic preservation aims; both idealize stasis and seek to capture representative specimens of wild nature for the cultural benefit of white Americans increasingly distanced from the beauty of nature's "primitive rudeness."

For all its ambivalence, Catlin's vision of a national park is only a single reverie in one of his many letters; by far the greater part of his *Letters and Notes* supports the idea that literal preservation of Indigenous peoples and wild nature is not possible or even necessary. "I have, for many years past, contemplated the noble races of red men, who are now spread over these trackless forests and boundless prairies, melting away at the approach of civilization," Catlin writes in a typically lachrymose mode.

I have flown to their rescue—not of their lives or of their race (for they are "*doomed*" and must perish), but to the rescue of their looks and their modes, at which the acquisitive world may hurl their poison and every besom of destruction, and trample them down and crush them to death; yet, phoenix-like, they may rise from the "stain on a painter's palette," and live again upon the canvass, and stand forth for centuries yet to come, the living monuments of a noble race.[36]

Rather than the literal scheme of Indian and bison preservation for which he is remembered, Catlin primarily mounts an aesthetic argument for preservation, and this call is best answered by his own work; by capturing the looks and decorative objects of representative human and animal "specimens" in his "Indian Gallery," Catlin has preserved what really matters to him—and to the many ardent admirers of his "Museum" who eventually mounted a successful national heritage argument for Catlin's painting collection and succeeded in having it purchased for the national Smithsonian Museum (where parts of the collection remain on display to this day).

The ethical complexities of Catlin's preservationism are suggested by Susan Sontag in *On Photography*, when she writes that "although the camera is an observation station, the act of photographing is more than passive observing." Sontag continues:

> Like sexual voyeurism, it is a way of at least tacitly, often explicitly,
> encouraging whatever is going on to keep on happening. To take a
> picture is to have an interest in things as they are, in the status quo
> remaining unchanged (at least for as long as it takes to get a "good"
> picture), to be in complicity with whatever makes a subject interesting,
> worth photographing—including, when that is the interest, another
> person's pain or misfortune.[37]

The complicity Sontag assigns to photography also fits Catlin's nineteenth-century documentary painting project; Catlin has an interest in the "status quo" of endangerment and disappearance "remaining unchanged," since that is precisely what gives his work its value. At times, his complicity with bison disappearance and destruction—what makes his subject interesting, worth painting—is quite literal. Early in his first visit to the "Far West," Catlin describes a buffalo hunt he conducted with other white men, in which he wounds a buffalo bull. Since, as he puts it, "I went not for 'meat,' but for a *trophy*," once Catlin is sure that the bull is too wounded to harm him, he begins to "preserve" the animal after his wonted manner:

> I drew from my pocket my sketch-book, laid my gun across my lap,
> and commenced taking his likeness. He stood stiffened up, and
> swelling with awful vengeance, which was sublime for a picture, but
> which he could not vent upon me. I rode around him and sketched him
> in numerous attitudes, sometimes he would lie down, and I would then
> sketch him; then throw my cap at him, and rousing him on his legs,
> rally a new expression, and sketch him again.

> In this way I added to my sketch-book some invaluable sketches of
> this grim-visaged monster, who knew not that he was standing for his
> likeness.[38]

Having first shot the buffalo bull, Catlin draws him as he expires, torment-
ing the creature as he sketches a slow and painful death he finds "sublime
for a picture." Later, in letter 31, when Catlin laments at length the disappearance of the buffalo from the plains, it is to this and a similar portrait
of a female buffalo that he directs his readers for "faithful traces of the male
and female of this huge animal, in their proud and free state of nature."[39]
While the buffalo traces that mark the land may be overlaid with railroad
tracks or converted into emigrant highways and thus forgotten, this material erasure is offset for whites who accept Catlin's assurance that his
"faithful traces" on canvas have preserved the wild spectacle for all time.[40]
Catlin's Indian project thus privileges art as the enduring medium through
which to preserve what it frames as the ephemeral, disappearing material
reality of Indian life and culture beyond the bounds of white "civilization."
The violence of Catlin's approach is literal—as with Hornaday, even as he
laments their extinction Catlin participates in buffalo slaughter in order
to faithfully capture the animals' "traces" on canvas. But this violence is
also of course cultural—by creating artistic "living monuments" to the
Plains Indians he insists *must* disappear, Catlin's preservation helps license
that very disappearance.

Catlin's approach to Indian and bison preservation crystallizes one of
the problems with preservation as an environmental approach. "Keeping
alive, or unchanged" (as in, preserving one's beauty, or preserving a corpse)
is a key part of the meaning of the word "preservation," an ideal of unchanging inanimateness epitomized by taxidermy, whose definition, lest
we forget, really is "the *art* of preservation," as the *OED* has it. Taxidermy,
artistic preservation, zoos, and national parks are related practices on a con-
tinuum, and they share a logic. Figures such as Catlin or William Temple
Hornaday engaged in multiple forms of preservation over the course of
their careers, and literal and artistic preservation, like taxidermy, have a
kind of stasis or deadness necessarily embedded in them. The prairie was
a polyculture, and white settlers didn't only exterminate the bison and dis-
place the Plains peoples; they also plowed up the roots of the prairie grass,
chopped down the prairie's trees, and so on. It was an ecosystem being ex-
terminated, and that ecosystem was not "preserved" in the paintings of
Catlin's "Indian Museum" or in the Smithsonian's taxidermy displays. Nor

even in the zoos, wildlife preserves, and national parks that subsequently preserved some of the Plains' live animals.

"*You Are Too Ugly to Live*": Aesthetics and Violence *in* The Oregon Trail

Part of the reason why Catlin's aesthetic argument for Indian preservation is ineffective is that the aesthetic value of the "wild" spectacles he paints is in the eye of the beholder, and there was not agreement among antebellum elites that these human and nonhuman subjects were, or could be, beautiful, picturesque, or sublime. For instance, *Roughing It* (1872), Mark Twain's account of a six-year visit to the "Far West," records a vicious portrait of the "Goshoot Indians" (the Kusiutta), who strike Twain as "small, lean, 'scrawny' creatures; in complexion a dull black like the ordinary American negro . . . a silent, sneaking, treacherous looking race" who "inhabit one of the most rocky, wintry, repulsive wastes that our country or any other can exhibit."[41] This glancing encounter with the unpicturesque Kusiutta and their "repulsive" landscape convinces Twain, formerly "a disciple of Cooper and a worshipper of the Red Man," that the good qualities he had previously imputed to the noble savages of his imagination were simply "paint and tinsel," which, as they "fell away," revealed Indians to be "treacherous, filthy, repulsive."[42]

More obviously parallel to Catlin's book than *Roughing It* is Francis Parkman Jr.'s *The Oregon Trail* (1849). Parkman, a wealthy easterner reflecting on his ethnographically interested adventures among the Plains Indians during the summer of 1846, travels through some of the identical territory Catlin visited nearly a decade earlier, but Parkman writes after the first phase of Indian removal has been completed in the United States, and his attitude toward the Plains peoples he encounters differs markedly from Catlin's. Published in the early period of the watershed westward expansion justified as Manifest Destiny, Parkman does express the requisite confidence in the inevitable "dwindl[ing] away" of both the Indians and the buffalo along the Oregon Trail, yet his confidence is far shakier than Catlin's. For this reason, Parkman's narrative abounds in anxious, angry, even murderous scenes that bespeak an uneasy relationship to western conquest and the Native peoples who pose a significant obstacle to westward emigration and white expansion. Parkman frequently paints the Native peoples he describes with a dehumanizing brush by associating Plains Indians with degraded forms of animal life, and these negative comparisons to snakes, wolves, vultures, and especially buffalo are used to sanction Native human eradication. But what is especially significant in the context of Catlin's work is how consistently Parkman's murderous fantasies rely for their justification on aesthetic pronouncements about the "ugliness" of the wild animals and the Indians he encounters.

According to his own account, Parkman travels to the West "almost exclusively with a view of observing the Indian character,"[43] but unlike Catlin, Parkman remains remarkably incurious about "Indian character" throughout his narrative. In fact, he tells his readers at one point, "such a narrative as this is hardly the place for portraying the mental features of the Indians. The same picture, slightly changed in shade and coloring, would serve with very few exceptions for all the tribes that lie north of the Mexican territories."[44] Instead, early in *The Oregon Trail*, Parkman editorializes on the real reason he has come west in a "wild and striking scene" that juxtaposes a Native encampment with a passing emigrant wagon train:

> For several acres, the ground was covered with a temporary encampment; men, women, and children swarmed like bees; hundreds of dogs, of all sizes and colors, ran restlessly about; and close at hand, the wide shallow stream was alive with boys, girls and young squaws, splashing, screaming, and laughing in the water. At the same time a long train of emigrant wagons were crossing the creek, and dragging on in their slow, heavy procession, passed the encampment of the people whom they and their descendants, in the space of a century, are to sweep from the face of the earth.[45]

Parkman's early, contrasting description of Native and white colonial cultures works to establish distinct temporalities for their lives in order to naturalize settler ascendancy. The Native people are associated with short-lived bees and dogs and depicted as individuals full of activity and vitality; the glacial, undifferentiated emigrant wagons are marked not by the temporality of an individual human (or nonhuman animal) life but in the multigenerational terms of an enduring civilization measured in centuries. Apparently having made up his mind about the monolith he calls "Indian character" before his first horse was ever saddled in Missouri, Parkman's true subject in *The Oregon Trail* is the displacement and eventual disappearance of Indians by whites emigrating from the east to the west—in short, Manifest Destiny, a term that first gained currency in July 1845, one year before Parkman set out on his western excursion.

Adventuring on the Oregon Trail in the summer of 1846, Parkman's journey, if not the hunt for "Indian character" Parkman proclaims it, is nevertheless a hunt for Indians. By 1840, Indian removal east of the Mississippi had been effected, and starting out on the trail from Missouri, this absence is signified by the whitened animal bones that litter the trail and signify scenes of past slaughter and removal: "As [the traveler] advances, indeed, he will see, mouldering in the grass by his path, the vast antlers of the elk, and farther on, the whitened skulls of the buffalo, once swarming over this now deserted region."[46] This opening image of travel on the Oregon Trail signals a metonymic link between Native peoples and native animals that will drive Parkman's entire narrative. Bison and other animals are "clearly felt as partners to and surrogates for the Indians" in Parkman's narrative,[47] an association Parkman consciously fosters throughout his book with passages that emphasize the absolute dependence of Plains Indians on the buffalo:

> The buffalo supplies them with almost all the necessaries of life; with habitations, food, clothing, and fuel; with strings for their bows, with thread, cordage, and trail-ropes for their horses, with coverings for their saddles, with vessels to hold water, with boats to cross streams, with glue, and with the means of purchasing all that they desire from the traders. When the buffalo are extinct, they too must dwindle away.[48]

Parkman ties the fate of Plains peoples inextricably to that of the buffalo: "When the buffalo are extinct," Plains Indians "too must dwindle away."

The association of Indians and buffalo in the nineteenth-century Anglo-American mind may not surprise us, but in *The Oregon Trail* this familiar synecdoche takes on especially murderous overtones because Parkman's book is first and foremost a chronicle of buffalo slaughter. Richard Slotkin has argued that during the 1840s and 1850s, "the chosen myth"[49] of the western writer was the self-sufficient hunter; despite being an easterner, Parkman takes this as the model for his own literary character in the west as well. Over the course of *The Oregon Trail*, Parkman extensively details the multiple buffalo hunts he and the other white men in his group conduct on their trip across the plains. Eventually Parkman also accompanies a Lakota group on its own buffalo hunt, before giving over the last seventy pages of his book to a senselessly extended account of the wasteful slaughter of scores of buffalo bulls that Parkman and his party shoot only for entertainment. Yet Parkman appears to turn to buffalo primarily because he dares not hunt the game he truly desires: Indians.

Parkman circles around his desire to "hunt Indians" in *The Oregon Trail* in subtle and less subtle ways, with the least subtle being his thirteenth chapter, which is bluntly entitled "Hunting Indians." At this point in the text, Parkman is on the "hunt" for a Lakota village whose buffalo-hunting expedition he wishes to join, but lest readers suppose the chapter title is simply an unfortunate pun, Parkman spells out its meaning in a passage marked by naked racism and a shockingly casual approach to murder. Parkman describes one of his Native traveling companions as

> the old conjurer, who with his hard, emaciated face and gaunt ribs was perched aloft like a turkey-buzzard, among the dead branches of an old tree, constantly on the look-out for enemies. He would have made a capital shot. A rifle bullet, skillfully planted, would have brought him tumbling to the ground. Surely, I thought, there could be no more harm in shooting such a hideous old villain, to see how ugly he would look when he was dead, than in shooting the detestable vulture which he resembled.[50]

The "conjurer" Parkman imagines shooting with so little compunction is a guide accompanying his party, prudently protecting Parkman as well as himself by scanning the horizon for "enemies." That Parkman makes no attempt to justify his sense that the man is a "hideous old villain" is typical for *The Oregon Trail*, since Parkman repeatedly asserts that almost every Native person he meets on the prairie is some variety of "villain," despite never reporting anything but respectful and hospitable treatment from the Plains peoples he encounters. It is notable that Parkman allows himself to imagine using "a rifle bullet, skillfully planted" to murder his guide by framing the conflict in aesthetic terms: The man's supposed "ugliness" means that he does not need to be preserved. "Hideous" and resembling a "detestable vulture" or "turkey-buzzard" in life, Parkman's repellant curiosity wishes to "see how ugly he would look when he was dead," an aesthetic spectacle whose interest Parkman never bothers to explain, apparently little doubting his white audience would readily comprehend its interest. As much as any moral or practical consideration, it may finally be a fear of an identification between himself and the Plains peoples, what Philip Terrie and others have called "indianization,"[51] that prevents Parkman from acting on his perpetually submerged and occasionally overtly expressed desire to "hunt Indians" on the Oregon Trail.[52]

Instead, Parkman focuses his energy on a single-minded, brutal slaughter of the buffalo who stand in for Plains Indians in his text. While extended depictions of buffalo slaughter occur everywhere in the book, they are nowhere as pervasive as the last seventy pages, which consist of little besides loosely connected and oddly uneventful anecdotes of senseless buffalo killing (senseless because Parkman and his companions have no intention of eating or otherwise using the buffalo bulls they kill in such abundance). Parkman is clear that this slaughter is deeply satisfying, writing, "at first sight of him every feeling of sympathy vanishes; no man who has not experienced it, can understand with what keen relish one inflicts [the buffalo's] death wound, with what profound contentment of mind he beholds him fall."[53] Parkman revels in the spectacle of buffalo slaughter both because he claims it is just punishment for the buffalo's "blindness and stupidity" in not knowing an enemy is near and also because, as with his earlier Indian traveling companion, the buffalo are supposedly too "ugly" to deserve to survive. In one typical instance, Parkman, after watching buffalo bulls divert themselves with playful head butting and dust baths, responds by leveling his rifle as punishment for their "puerile conduct": "'You are too ugly to live,' thought I; and aiming at the ugliest, I shot three of them in succession."[54] What we get in *The Oregon Trail* is finally Plains peoples represented as utterly bound to their ecosystem, and both humans and that ecosystem are shown to be on the verge of a manufactured extinction crisis. Parkman's relentless "savagism"[55] means that he not only views this extinction crisis with evident satisfaction but also actively participates in the violence through extended scenes of senseless buffalo slaughter.

For every Catlin who saw something of aesthetic worth in an "untamed" Native American population beyond the white frontier, there were Parkmans and Twains whose sense of the Indians' "ugliness" was an argument for their eradication; in each case, it is simply a difference in the viewer's "taste." Significantly, this difference in taste—whether one experienced beauty or ugliness in looking at Native peoples—is tied to whether a viewer believes the Indians in question can be mastered by whites; Twain connects his claims about the "filthy" "repulsive[ness]" of his "Goshoot Indians" to their supposedly unprovoked predations against white stagecoach drivers and travelers, while Parkman similarly justifies the extinction of his "ugly" Indians with the claim that they are simply "a troublesome and dangerous species of wild beast."[56]

Whatever their aesthetic pronouncements, for Catlin, Parkman, Twain, and other white writers and artists, the act of representing Native people and cultures was itself a fantasy of mastery, a fantasy that art can continue to enable. In her 2010 novel *Shadow Tag*, Louise Erdrich meditates on Catlin's legacy and on the intimate violence of representation. The novel captures the disintegration of a marriage between a painter, Gil (Klamath/Cree/Montana Chippewa), and the muse/wife he obsessively paints, Irene America (Ojibwe). Irene, a graduate student in history, is writing a dissertation on George Catlin that she can never seem to finish.

Throughout the novel, Irene meditates on how her serial and not wholly voluntary representation in her husband's paintings has damaged her sense of self: "She had to shed the weight of Gil's eyes. Exist unobserved. That way she could gradually soothe the ache of self-awareness."[57] Gil's portraits of Irene, like Catlin's of the Plains peoples he paints, are powerful because they are "mythic." His portraits are described as "portrayals [that] immediately evoked problems of exploitation, the indigenous body, the devouring momentum of history. More than that—he'd progressed to a technical level that allowed him an almost limitless authority."[58] It is Gil's "limitless authority" over Irene's image, in addition to (and perhaps even more than) her person, that feels so obscurely oppressive to Irene. "The image is not the person, she thought, or even the shadow of a person. So how can a person be harmed by the depiction, even appropriation, of something as intangible as one's image."[59] Erdrich casts Gil's aesthetic mastery as violence in part through a suggestive analogy with Catlin's work.

Early in the novel, Irene tells Gil an intentionally falsified anecdote about Catlin, in which the family of one of Catlin's female subjects asks for the painting to be returned. In Irene's version of the event, Catlin refuses to return the painting, instead taking it back east to display in his "Indian Gallery," whereupon the girl dies.[60] This story becomes a lens through which Gil can, at least momentarily, see the violence of his work. "Gil thought that perhaps Irene was trying to tell him something by referencing and falsifying the story. Was he stealing something from her by painting her? . . . Had he put so much of her into some image of her he'd created that he was weakening or diminishing the 'real' Irene somehow?"[61] One crucial aspect of the violence done to Irene through her image is suggested but unseen in *Shadow Tag*. In the art world, Gil is frustratingly "classified as an American Indian artist, or a Native American artist, or a tribal artist, or a Cree artist or a mixed-blood Metis or Chipewa artist or sometimes an artist of the American West, even though he lived in Minneapolis."[62] He is classified in this way, in part, because although "real Indians are so complex and various that they frustrate classification," Gil "painted Indians when he painted his wife because he couldn't help it—the ferocity between them, the need. Her blood ancestors came out in Gil's paint as he worked."[63] The novel implies that these paintings are sold and bought primarily by white collectors, and that their manner of marketing and consuming the paintings enacts the dehumanizing violence of "classification"—both Gil's and Irene's. Gil is diminished also, but he profits from the classification (his own and Irene's) as well.

Much of the public, classificatory violence of Gil's work is never explicitly represented in Erdrich's domestic portrait of a family. Instead, Erdrich uses anecdotes about Catlin to link the intimate violence of preserving certain images with the public violence of displaying those images. For instance, Catlin appears in the novel as a grave robber who "stole the skull of the horse and the skull of the chief to display back east"[64] and as a cruel profiteer who describes "with amusement" the torment of caged wild bears Catlin displays for curious European crowds.[65] Eventually, Irene notes, "[t]he bears died of the disgust of being constantly looked at."[66] Most explicitly of all, Irene tells her sister about Catlin's participation in bison slaughter to get the "dying buffalo" portrait he desired: "Irene started talking about Catlin and how he had wounded a buffalo and then sketched and painted it as it slowly died. He described the process in one of his letters. He goaded the buffalo into a fury every time it tried to lie down and die. It had broken a leg, so it couldn't charge him."[67] There is an implied analogy in *Shadow Tag* between Catlin wounding and sketching the buffalo and Gil wounding and sketching Irene. The nineteenth-century colonial violence of Catlin's act is transformed in Erdrich's twenty-first-century novel into the intimate artistic violence of Gil's paintings, but white spectatorship links both forms of representational violence. In each case, the production of an image of indigeneity for white spectators contributes to the erasure of the subjects. Irene notes that "others, disturbed that Catlin painted buffalo and took them away with him in his portfolio, tied his actions to the increasing scarcity of the herds upon which their lives depended. So it was, the shadows actually stole their subjects and, for the rest of the world, became more real, until it seemed they were the only things left."[68] By incorporating Catlin, *Shadow Tag* invites readers to consider the continuities between nineteenth-century aesthetic judgments about Indigenous people and native nature and twenty-first century representations of the same material. By novel's end, Gil has drowned himself, and Irene has drowned trying to save him, but Gil's portraits of Irene endure, the images more valuable than ever now that painter and subject are gone.

Catlin, Parkman, and Erdrich can help us see that if what we work to preserve or allow to disappear is tied to our aesthetic judgments about that material—its beauty, grace, or cuteness; its ability to move us emotionally and inspire us spiritually—then preservation's value as an environmental ethic will always be limited by the instability and subjectivity of those judgments. If the value of nonhuman nature is tethered to its threatened disappearance, then preservation participates in the supply-and-demand logic of capitalism, a reactive rather than proactive ethic. And finally, to the de-gree that preservation aspires to capture and maintain representative specimens and fragments of landscape for the cultural heritage of a con-stantly developing and expanding US population, it allows us to believe that we can offset the eradication of living ecosystems with static speci-mens preserved in paintings, literature, zoos, and bounded preserves.

"Polar Citadels": Melville, Byatt, and the Flawed Spatial Logic of Preservation

There is still one more fundamental way in which preservation has become an "unlikely" environmental solution—the very conviction that a spatial refuge will be enough to prevent nonhuman nature from disappearing has come under pressure in the twenty-first century. After "long observation" of the tremendous slaughter of passenger pigeons, Audubon puts his faith in forests: As long as there is no "diminution" of these, he writes, there can be no "end to the species."[69] Of course, there was and there was. To put it another way, and to start to move toward a conclusion, we might turn to Herman Melville's *Moby-Dick* (1855), a novel in which Melville, like Catlin, Thoreau, Audubon, and others of the early to mid–nineteenth century, considers the possibility of extinction and the social and natural costs of expansion and capitalism.

There are plenty of easy connections to be made between the nineteenth-century economies and ecologies represented in the antebellum *Moby-Dick* and our own twenty-first-century environmental predicaments. The *Pequod*, a floating factory bent on exploiting a natural resource (sperm whale oil) for profit, winds up smashed to bits by a vengeful whale. In the final paragraph of the last chapter Melville offers an ecologically contex-tualized and remarkably diminished humanity; the ship has been obliter-ated by a whirlpool, and the image we are left with is this: "Now small fowls flew screaming over the yet yawning gulf; a sullen white surf beat against its steep sides; then all collapsed, and the great shroud of the sea rolled on as it rolled five thousand years ago."[70] Read through a twenty-first-century lens, the end of *Moby-Dick* can be seen as a kind of morality-tale fantasy of deep ecology: a vision of injured nature righteously striking back.[71]

Such a reading, and any excitement over Melville's apparent prescience, breaks down a bit if we backtrack to consider chapter 105, the chapter in which Ishmael tackles the question of extinction. Melville titles this chap-ter "Does the Whale's Magnitude Diminish?—Will He Perish?" Ishma-el's answer is an unequivocal "no." "Some philosophers of the forecastle

have concluded that th[e] positive havoc" of global whale slaughter "has already very seriously diminished [whales'] battalions," Ishmael scoffs, but
such slaughter is "of little or no account."[72] After weighing what he considers the evidence, Ishmael concludes, "we account the whale immortal
in his species, however perishable in his individuality."[73]

Ishmael (and Melville, if Melville indeed endorsed this opinion) was
wrong. Whale numbers were declining in the nineteenth century, and in
the twentieth century, with the advent of diesel engines, the news got even
worse: A recent study calculated that between 1900 and 1999, almost 3 million whales were wiped out by industrial harvesting; this is likely "the
largest cull of any animal—in terms of total biomass—in human history."[74] Of course, Melville wasn't alone in his mistrust of the likelihood of
human-inflicted extinction events in the nineteenth century. Cuvier
rather controversially "discovered" extinction through his study of fossils at the beginning of the century, but there was no consensus as to how
or why species destruction might occur. Even later in the century, the
scientific wisdom from Darwin on down was that extinction, when it happened, must occur so gradually as to be imperceptible to human eyes, a
sort of natural selection in reverse. "From these several considerations I
think it inevitably follows, that as new species in the course of time are
formed through natural selection, others will become rarer and rarer,
and finally extinct," is the gradualist way Darwin describes it in *The Origin of Species.*[75]

The odd thing about Darwin's and Melville's blindness to rapidly occurring, human-caused extinction events is that both men had ample opportunity to observe them: They were occurring all around them, in some
cases widely publicized even in popular media. In fact, Ishmael raises the
most famous midcentury American example, the plight of the disappearing buffalo, as a possible point of "comparison" to the increasingly hunted
whale. The comparison between bison and whales is repeatedly made
throughout *Moby-Dick.* Ishmael likens the sea to a prairie and then,
later, a whale forehead to a prairie, calling himself a "pioneer" for attempting to read it phrenologically.[76] In "The Whiteness of the Whale," Ishmael illustrates his terror of whiteness through an extended analogy with
the fear a Virginia colt feels at the smell of a buffalo robe, concluding, "thus,
then, the muffled rollings of a milky sea; the bleak rustlings of the fes-
tooned frosts of mountains; the desolate shiftings of the windrowed snows
of prairies; all these, to Ishmael, are as the shaking of that buffalo robe to
the frightened colt!"[77] In "The Whale as a Dish," Ishmael explains the unpleasant "richness" of the whale's "hump, which would be as fine eating as

the buffalo's (which is esteemed a rare dish), were it not such a solid pyramid of fat."[78] In "Does the Whale's Magnitude Diminish?—Will He Perish?," the comparison reaches its crescendo:

> Comparing the humped herds of whales with the humped herds of buffalo, which, not forty years ago, overspread by tens of thousands the prairies of Illinois and Missouri, and shook their iron manes and scowled with their thunder-clotted brows upon the sites of populous river-capitals, where now the polite broker sells you land at a dollar an inch; in such a comparison an irresistible argument would seem furnished, to show that the hunted whale cannot now escape extinction.[79]

Melville reviewed Francis Parkman's *The Oregon Trail* for the magazine *The Literary World* in 1849 and was therefore familiar with Parkman's representations of the impact of overhunting on bison.[80] Yet, though "the cause" of the "wondrous extermination" of the buffalo "was the spear of man," Ishmael insists, "the far different nature of the whale-hunt peremptorily forbids so inglorious an end to the Leviathan." What Ishmael means is expressed simply as a question of numbers: whereas forty men on horseback might slay "forty thousand and more buffaloes," "forty men in one ship hunting the Sperm Whale for forty-eight months think they have done extremely well, and thank God, if at last they carry home the oil of forty fish." Ishmael delivers this litany of numbers with the certainty of a mathematician reciting an equation, and indeed, he concludes by promising that the difference in numerical scale between the hunts is "a fact that, if need were, could be statistically stated."[81]

Significant as the difference in numerical scale is, the spatial differences between bison and whale hunting are even more important to Ishmael. Ishmael recognizes the synergy of Manifest Destiny and capitalism that contributed a spatial dimension to bison destruction through his wry remark about the "polite broker" selling prairie land "at a dollar an inch." Large as the prairies are (or were), Ishmael argues that the sheer scale of the sea would seem to preclude the whale meeting the buffalo's fate. "Much more may the great whale outlast all hunting, since he has a pasture to expatiate in, which is precisely twice as large as all Asia, both Americas, Europe and Africa, New Holland, and all the Isles of the sea combined."[82] The "magnitude" or sheer "bulk" of the whales themselves also convinces Ishmael they cannot disappear, a bulk that is only increased by whales' tendency to "aggregat[e]" themselves into "vast but widely separated, unfrequent armies" in response to being hunted.[83]

As John Levi Barnard has pointed out, in the chapter before "Does the Whale's Magnitude Diminish?—Will He Perish?," Melville establishes the "impossibility" of whale extinction with a consideration of deep time that emphasizes the whale's permanence: The whale, "having been before all time, must needs exist after all the humane ages are over."[84] Yet it is not primarily time but space on which Ishmael's rejection of extinction rests. The problem confronting whales, as Ishmael describes it, is one of visibility: Whether whales will be hunted to extinction "owing to the almost omniscient look-outs at the mast-heads of the whaleships, now penetrating even through Behring's straits, and into the remotest secret drawers and lockers of the world."[85] Ishmael dismisses this omniscience as mere hubris; the vastness of the sea trumps man's ability to track whales. "Widely separated, unfrequent armies" are difficult for whalers to encounter and attack, a vision of whale survival that rests upon whales' ability to evade their hunters, to maintain a space apart from humankind. Concern over extinction is itself a visual mistake, a sign of human limitations rather than omniscience: Whales are not disappearing but "only being driven from promontory to cape; and if one coast is no longer enlivened with their jets, then, be sure, some other and remoter strand has been very recently startled by the unfamiliar spectacle."[86]

Even more than this, Ishmael imagines at least "whale-bone" whales as having a kind of natural wildlife sanctuary. Melville is writing during the same period that Catlin and others begin publicly calling for national parks and wildlife preserves, and Ishmael fantasizes that the polar regions might act as de facto whale preserves:

> They have two firm fortresses, which, in all human probability, will for ever remain impregnable. . . . Hunted from the savannas and glades of the middle seas, the whale-bone whales can at last resort to their Polar citadels, and diving under the ultimate glassy barriers and walls there, come up among icy fields and floes; and in a charmed circle of everlasting December, bid defiance to all pursuit from man.[87]

Our twenty-first-century eyes can easily identify one problem with this vision: the "Polar citadels'" "everlasting December" does not seem quite so "everlasting" as headlines blare "Scientists Shocked by Arctic Permafrost Thawing 70 Years Sooner Than Predicted."[88] The safety of whales' imagined retreats has been threatened, if not obliterated.

We can no longer deny that extinction occurs or doubt the swiftness with which it has been proven to occur. One of the tragic hallmarks of our current environmental predicament is the spectacle of mass extinction; the

World Wildlife Fund has estimated that Earth lost 60 percent of its wild-life in the past forty-five years, and scientists the world over argue that this is just the tip of the iceberg that is a major extinction event of our own making.[89] Relatively conservative estimations are that one-third of all reef-building corals, sharks, rays, and freshwater mollusks; a quarter of all mammals; a fifth of all reptiles; and a sixth of all birds are currently headed toward extinction.[90] Multiple major studies now confirm that Earth has entered another mass-extinction event, the sixth great mass extinction event in Earth's history but the first one caused by human beings.

In the interim since Melville wrote, our response to the plight of the buffalo, whales, and many, many other animals endangered at our hands has been a spatial response: We have created zoos, wildlife preserves, and national parks, setting aside spaces in which representative individuals could be kept alive and whole species preserved through them. One fault we might find with this approach is that there's an absence of ethical regard, perhaps not even *room* for ethical regard, for the individual lives lost when we're making a species-level calculation. Throughout his three-page consideration of the possibility of whale extinction, Ishmael slips back and forth between speaking of "the whale" singular and "whales" plural before his consideration culminates in the representative, preservationist logic already quoted: "The eternal whale" is "immortal in his species, however perishable in his individuality." Yet *Moby-Dick* is so interesting a novel to read from an environmental perspective in part because Melville asks readers at least to consider that the whale at the center of the novel may be unique, and individual, and that he and other nonhuman creatures may be due ethical consideration in consequence.[91]

For instance, in the chapter "The Whale as a Dish," Ishmael humor-ously blurs distinctions between humans and the nonhuman animal food they consume, as when he describes how "every one knows that some young bucks among the epicures, by continually dining upon calves' brains, by and by get to have a little brains of their own, so as to be able to tell a calf's head from their own heads; which, indeed, requires uncommon discrimi-nation."[92] By the last few paragraphs of the chapter, Ishmael's lightly sa-tirical comparisons give way to more serious, scathing claims about the dubious morality of consuming animal flesh: "But no doubt the first man that ever murdered an ox was regarded as a murderer; perhaps he was hung; and if he had been put on his trial by oxen, he certainly would have been; and he certainly deserved it if any murderer does."[93] The chapter begins with the supposedly "outlandish" fact "that mortal man should feed upon the creature that feeds his lamp," and by its end Ishmael decries cruel production methods of "paté-de-foie-gras" and indeed even the use of more mundane animal products such as goose-feather pens.[94] The end result, here and elsewhere, is that Melville forces his readers to confront how thoroughly their lives are enmeshed with nonhuman animal killing and to contemplate that the ethical questions that surround that killing may not be as simple or straightforward as they are ordinarily made out to be.[95]

In addition to the fact that it problematizes ethical regard for individual nonhumans, the more fundamental fault we might find with preservation is that its spatial logic is failing us, now more than ever. Since the 1970s, the theory of island biogeography has been used to demonstrate that habitat fragmentation—the process of isolating pieces of a formerly continuous ecosystem into insular pieces—will inevitably lead to a loss of biodiversity and to extinction events.[96] This means that even in the best-case scenario, wildlife preserves, national parks, and so on cannot in fact "preserve" all of the flora and fauna that flourished before habitat fragmentation occurred. Climate change has only accelerated this process; global warming does not respect the spatial boundaries that have been established as bulwarks against extinction. As climate shifts, ecologies are disrupted within wilderness preserves just as surely as they are in any other location, killing ever greater numbers of nonhuman life with each passing month.

Perhaps preservation ultimately fails because it idealizes stasis. Nothing about nonhuman nature or our relationships to it are or should be static; hoping to "preserve" a creature or even a species misses the dynamic relationships and biotic communities that really matter. To truly protect these relationships and communities we will have to shift our thinking and especially our metaphors. At the heart of Ishmael's extinction denialism is a Romantic idea of nature that defines the sea as spatially and temporally beyond humanity's ken: "Baby man may brag of his science and skill . . . yet for ever and for ever, to the crack of doom, the sea will insult and murder him, and pulverize the stateliest, stiffest frigate he can make." "No mercy, no power but its own controls it," Ishmael assures us. "Panting and snorting like a mad battle steed that has lost its rider, the masterless ocean overruns the globe."[97] A. S. Byatt's 2013 "Sea Story" meditates directly on this line from *Moby-Dick* and on how the romantic conception of a so-called masterless ocean fuels humanity's destruction of ocean creatures and environments.

Byatt's five-page short story seems at first, rather simply, to recount the life of a sea-loving young man raised on the Yorkshire coast, the son of an oceanographer (who is himself the son of an oceanographer) and an English teacher/sea poet. The young man studies English literature at Oxford, begins keeping "a kind of anthology of the sea" that includes the *Moby-Dick* line about "the masterless ocean" (indeed, this is the only extract specifically named), returns to the coast, and then falls in love with a budding oceanographer he hardly knows, Laura, who promptly deserts him for her "dream job . . . studying the life-cycle of eels" in the Caribbean.[98] Unable to forget her, the young man (still unnamed at this point in the story) writes a love letter that reads simply "Laura I love you," and then goes on to quote Robert Burns's "A Red, Red Rose":

Laura
I love you.

As fair art thou my bonnie lass,
So deep in luve am I;
And I will luve thee still, my dear,
Till a' the seas gang dry—

Till a' the seas gang dry, my dear,
And the rocks melt wi' the sun;
I will luve thee still, my dear,
While the sands of life shall run.[99]

The young man rolls up the message, seals it in a green plastic Perrier bottle (Laura's drink of choice), rows a boat offshore to where he knows that "the currents could possibly take the message as far as the Sargasso Sea," and then drops it in the water, "where it move[s], apparently purposefully, away."[100]

The bottle's departure initiates a dramatic generic shift in the story, as the human romantic love plot gives way to an inhuman tale of environmental destruction. The narrative point of view leaves behind the young man and follows the plastic Perrier bottle for long paragraphs as it travels through currents across the Atlantic Ocean and eventually south into the Caribbean, where it joins the Atlantic Gyre, which contains the Caribbean Trash Vortex, "said to be the size of Texas . . . [and] composed of human plastic waste." "It could be likened to Melville's sea of golden brit where the whales fed," the narrator tells us, "but the crustaceans, copepods and fingerling fish that composed the brit are being replaced, little by little, by nurdles, the tiny plastic spheres made by manufactured microbeads of polyethylene thermoplastic, or by rubbed fragments of plastic debris, poetically known as mermaid's tears."[101] From here, the bottle begins disintegrating, and the reader is treated to the deaths of all the sea life who eat or choke on its component parts: a mollymawk and its chicks, a green turtle, hungry fish, and so on. Some of the bits of plastic do reach their destination—on her research vessel in the Caribbean Laura looks at them "in a glass dish under a strong microscope. The message she read was the human occupation and corruption of the masterless ocean."[102] For Melville, environmental destruction depended on surveillance on a grand scale: "almost omniscient look-outs at the mast-heads of the whale-ships . . . penetrating . . . into the remotest secret drawers and lockers of the world." Barring that impossibility, the ocean and its life would be safe from human impact. Byatt's omniscient narrator allows readers to penetrate the sea's secret depths to follow the destructive progress of the Perrier bottle, but what we learn turns out to be apparent in the much more minute, localized visual register of the microscope: It is not human vision but the lack of it that currently threatens the planet. The impacts of our actions, the afterlives of our commodities, and all the things that we cannot or do not care to see are the problem.

In "Sea Story," Byatt is playing with the literary romance of the "masterless ocean" and with the effects of human perceptions of the size and scope of the sea. Harold's gesture of love, romance, and poetry has so many unintended, planetary consequences because the omnipotent image of the sea that it depends upon is wrong. By the end of her story, through the "message" Laura reads in her microscope, Byatt shifts the register from Melville's black-and-white, agonistic "mastery" to the more slippery "occupation" and "corruption" and shows that humans don't need to master or even overpower the ocean to affect it dramatically and negatively. Byatt's story moves outside the scale of human vision to demonstrate that "occupation" and "corruption," penetrating what Melville calls the "treacherously hidden," "unapparent" sea[103] in order to represent plastic as a kind of hyperobject (to use Timothy Morton's term) that makes even the relatively epic human scale of Melville's narrative space and time seem diminished.[104]

Byatt's shift in scale is critical to the shift in environmental perception her story seeks to bring about. The story's final, brief paragraph drives this connection home:

> Harold married a fellow poet, had three daughters whom he loved,
> strode along Filey Beach collecting plastic bags and debris, retired and
> died. Laura had died long ago, caught in the micromeshes of her
> netting when her boat capsized. Fires raged and floods drove through
> streets and houses as the planet became more and more inimical to
> human life. The sempiternal nurdles, indestructible, swayed on and
> under the surface of the sea.[105]

The last line of "Sea Story" is riffing on the final line of *Moby-Dick*, in which "the great shroud of the sea rolled on as it rolled five thousand years ago."[106] Ishmael's "eternal whale" and timeless sea are shown to be mortal and destructible, and Byatt leaves us instead with the "sempiternal nurdle." The quick, single-sentence resolutions of Harold's and Laura's fates, followed by the similarly rapid, even casual description of apocalyptic fires and floods emphasizes the shift in temporal scale. Melville's novel ends with an imperturbable, unchanging sea that rolls on as it has rolled for five thousand years—the scale of biblical time. Yet even in the Burns poem Harold quotes in his love letter in a bottle, a sense of geologic time (or "deep time," as Burns's contemporary James Hutton termed it) only serves to magnify the significance of human life—human love is made more significant by the claim that it lasts till until the seas go dry and the rocks melt with the sun. By contrast, Byatt clearly hopes that the destructive eternity of plastic and a planet inimical to human (and most other) life prove more difficult to romanticize.

Byatt's story illuminates the fact that the spatial, temporal, and cultural errors that allow Ishmael to deny the possibility of extinction are in fact still with us. The fantasy of preservation—of "citadels" in which nonhuman nature can repose in safety from the corrupting influence of human life—continues to animate large swaths of the twenty-first century environmental imagination. Perhaps even more significantly, Byatt's story also deeply complicates the issue of intentionality. Melville writes of "the universal cannibalism of the sea; all whose creatures prey upon each other, carrying on eternal war since the world began," but Byatt makes this sound like a more fitting description of terrestrial human life; far from the "green, gentle, and most docile earth,"[107] she chronicles the "sempiternal" violence of a single, seemingly harmless, romantic gesture in the life of an otherwise perfectly ordinary and "good" man. Byatt's Harold does not set off on a vengeance quest against nonhuman nature that "seeks [him] not";[108] he doesn't intend or understand the disastrous effects of his romantic gesture. But the story suggests that none of this matters—human environmental aims, even agency, are now beside the point. Plastic waste has occupied the oceans whether we intended it or not.

If human intentionality is not a reliable gauge for ethical outcomes in "Sea Story," neither is aesthetic value. Again and again in Byatt's story, beauty fails to correlate with ecological impact. A harmless glass bottle Harold's parents collected from the ocean is described as "sinister-looking,"[109] while the destructive plastic Perrier bottle is "lovely" in "its brilliant greenness."[110] The Caribbean Trash Vortex is a lush and alliterative "slowly swirling carpet of floating fragments." Those fragments are "jew-elled colours, emerald, opal, crimson, cobalt, ultramarine" as well as a "colourless all-colour of stained whiteness"[111] that *Moby-Dick*'s "The Whiteness of the Whale" chapter has taught us to read as metaphysically and morally overdetermined.[112] The "human plastic waste" is "like a pop painting," and the poisonous, indestructible beads of plastic are "poetically known as mermaid's tears." The "glittering" Perrier bottle floats alongside an "ethereal shopping bag" as its pieces begin their marine-life murder spree.[113] The point of all this beauty is not just that the birds, turtles, and fish who consume pieces of the bottle can hardly be faulted; more impor-tantly, "Sea Story" troubles the aesthetic as a category useful or appropri-ate for evaluating environmental impact. Byatt's depiction here answers Michael Ziser and Julie Sze's call for "an environmental justice aesthetics" that seeks to "produce narratives . . . that make palpable the largely un-graspable complexity of contemporary environmental and economic net-works."[114] Harold's poetic, romantic gesture excites readerly sympathy before Byatt demonstrates its complex, global, largely invisible destructive effects. The plastic particles and fragments are described as beautiful and pervasive to an extent that eludes ordinary human vision: They float on the surface of the ocean but also "beneath it, hidden under the movement of the sea surface, vast curtains of tiny particles hang fathoms deep."[115] Cer-tainly they are unapparent to Harold, whose love of the sea remains un-touched by them; Harold marries "a fellow poet" and spends his life "str[iding] along Filey Beach collecting plastic bags and debris" that are visible to him, blind to the plastic remnants of the youthful romantic ges-ture that will outlive him.

Thanks to decades of environmental activism, there is an increasingly prominent popular conversation about plastics in the oceans that has un-dermined what Stacy Alaimo has described as "the persistent (and conve-nient) conception of the ocean as so vast and powerful that anything dumped into it will be dispersed into oblivion."[116] Yet we have not quite made the leap from recognizing the ubiquity of human impact to letting go of the paradigm of preservation. "Sea Story" can help us bridge that gap; the combined effect of Melville and Byatt is to challenge our linger-ing collective fantasy of "preserving" nature, of setting something utterly apart from human influence. As Byatt's story suggests, the planetary im-pacts of ordinary aspects of human life—local bits of plastic, a car's car-bon emissions—mean that there are no more citadels, polar, oceanic, or otherwise. Instead, we're left with the reality of multispecies entanglements on a shared planet. One useful mode of response to the ethical demands of planetary anthropogenic climate impact comes from Alaimo, who theorizes humans' "trans-corporeality"—our material entanglement with "networks that are simultaneously economic, political, cultural, scientific, and substantial."[117] Both climate crisis and transcorporeality (and the new materialisms more generally) demand that humans refuse to indulge the belief that we are separable from the planet or that it is separable from us; citizens must instead "seek out information about how their own bodily existence—their consumption of food, fuel, and specific consumer products—affects other people, other animals, habitats, and ecosystems."[118] The next chapter will grapple more specifically with how we might begin to live in ethical multispecies community with humans and nonhumans alike.

"A Pickled World"

Byatt works against an anthropocentric gaze that is uncritically privileged in nineteenth-century preservation efforts by Hornaday, Audubon, Catlin, and others. "Sea Story" helps make visible the often unacknowledged and unexamined role that spectatorship and visual consumption continue to play in preservation as an environmental principle. In fact, the Latin root of the word "preserve" means not just to keep or keep safe but also "to observe." Recognizing the centrality of spectatorship to preservation might help us understand some of the early preservation movement's more violent episodes; William Hornaday defended his repellant 1906 caged display of Ota Benga at the Bronx Zoo, for instance, by insisting "it was done simply for the convenience of the thousands of people who wanted to see him."[119] Grappling with the complexities of preservation's uncritical embrace of Anglo-Americans' "right" to visually consume threatened US nature might also be instructive as we wrestle with the increasingly complex ethics of nonhuman-animal display in the twenty-first century, in sites as diverse as Sea World and city zoos. John Berger has compellingly compared zoos to art museums:

> A zoo is a place where as many species and varieties of animal as
> possible are collected in order that they can be seen, observed, studied.
> In principle, each cage is a frame round the animal inside it. Visitors
> visit the zoo to look at animals. They proceed from cage to cage, not
> unlike visitors in an art gallery who stop in front of one painting, and
> then move on to the next.[120]

Berger's comparison highlights zoos as a curated space designed for humans' visual pleasure. His comparison helps explain why such displays frequently privilege (some) humans' desire to look above animals' physical, psychological, and emotional needs, and perhaps also why the practice is almost universally defended with the argument that the satiation of this one-way, anthropocentric gaze is essential to human education (and thus the goal of wildlife preservation).

But what exactly are we learning about nonhuman nature when we view live animals in such artificial and static spaces as zoos or study preserved creatures in natural history museums? Thinking of the human appetite for museums, taxidermied remains, relics, and fossils, Henry David Thoreau once mused, "Men have a strange taste for death who prefer to go to museums to behold the cast off garments of life—rather than handle the life itself. . . . Would you live in a dried specimen of a world? a pickled world."[121] In his famous encounter with Mt. Ktaadn in *The Maine Woods*, Thoreau expands on this idea: "What is it to be admitted to a museum, to see a myriad of particular things, compared with being shown some star's surface, some hard matter in its home!"[122] Preservation as an environmental ethic has too often meant valuing "a pickled world" over "some hard matter in its home." It has too often meant setting aside portions of an ecosystem and curating them into visual spectacles for certain privileged human tourists. Preservation, like the trope of wilderness, has encouraged and even deepened the sense of separation most Americans feel from much of the natural world, in the sense that it valorizes "pristine" nature "untouched" by man; too often, nonhuman matter where we actually live suffers neglect or worse under this value system.[123] That our national and state parks, wilderness areas, and so on are, paradoxically, carefully constructed, managed, and tended spaces is a well-known fact that does not disrupt Americans' abilities to invest themselves in the idea of representative samples of nonhuman nature preserved from human influence.

Preservation developed as a response to Anglo-Americans' violently utilitarian relation to nonhuman nature. Yet nineteenth-century preservationism was not, as it is usually suggested, a corrective response that genuinely reckoned with expansionism's "natural" costs. Rather, it too was a transmuted utilitarian valuing of nature, a deeply ambivalent and complicit reaction to some of the effects of capitalism and settler colonialism. Preservation allowed nineteenth-century Americans to believe that they might capture literal and/or artistic representative specimens of the victims of US expansion (human and nonhuman) and that doing so was an adequate response to settler colonialism and environmental degradation. "They have made little islands for us and other little islands for the four-leggeds, and always these islands are becoming smaller" was Black Elk's indictment not of preservation but its opposite, expansion and settlement.[124] Yet such "islands" are evocative descriptions of the outcomes of nineteenth-century preservationism: Native reservations and wildlife preserves, respectively. Black Elk contrasts the "little islands" of land or habitat to a Lakota community in which "the two-leggeds and the four-leggeds lived together like relatives, and there was plenty for them and for us." This living together "like relatives" is something more difficult, more dynamic, more ecological, and finally more ethical than preservation.

Preservation cedes as its opening move the inevitability and permanence of US expansion and unilateral and utilitarian use relations between Americans and their nonhuman environment. In so doing, it has impoverished our environmental imagination and allowed environmental degradation to continue unimpeded in most spheres, even as Americans have imagined that degradation offset by the fragments of ecosystems we have set by. Of course, no reasonable person could wish that bison, or the Yosemite Valley, or any other subject of US preservation had not been preserved, given the likely alternative. But what if we stop prizing the ethic of preservation itself? What if we accept the lesson of Byatt's rewriting of Melville's oceanic romanticism: that we can no longer protect any part of the planet from ourselves—not fully? Might this be the first step to imagining real ethical coexistence with nonhuman nature? This kind of coexistence doesn't exist in any pastoral past, and it can't be appropriated wholesale from another culture. A principle and practice of ethical coexistence would have to be consciously forged, with open-eyed attention to the United States' ongoing practices of settler colonialism and imperialism and the ongoing impact of humans on nonhuman life at both the local and global scales. For such an environmental ethic to come into being, the inevitable and perhaps even continual conflicts between the interests any given human or group of humans and the rest of the living world would have to be acknowledged and consciously adjudicated; as is the case now, nonhuman interests might not often come out on top. But embracing coexistence rather than preservation as a principle might help Americans hold ourselves more accountable for how we live, where we live. It might help us reject the fantasy that we can maintain permanent sanctuaries for nonhuman life in the places we do not live, so that we can let go of our conviction that we don't (and can't) share our homes with other forms of life.

CHAPTER 4

Radical Pet Keeping: Crafts, Wilson, and Living with Others in the Anthropocene

The Anthropocene—as a name and as an idea—has by now come in for its fair share of criticism. The sociologist Jason Moore is only the most vocal critic to suggest that the term mystifies as much as it explains. For one thing, as Moore and others argue, "Global warming is not the accomplishment of an abstract humanity, the *Anthropos*. Global warming is capital's crowning achievement. Global warming is *capitalogenic*."[1] To put it another way, not all humans are equally responsible for the current planetary environmental crisis, as "the Anthropocene" implies. In its stead, Moore has argued for "the Capitalocene," a term that aims to "name the system" responsible for our crisis: capitalism. Donna Haraway has embraced "Capitalocene" while also proposing "the Plantationocene" and the "Chthulucene" as complementary alternatives meant to signal the enmeshed and entangled rather than separate or masterful way that humans coexist with other life on planet Earth, and to invoke contemporary and historical relations of power—among humans and between humans and other forms of life.[2] Still others, including the geographer Jamie Lorimer and the anthropologist Nicholas Kawa, have critiqued the anthropocentrism and Eurocentrism of "the Anthropocene."[3]

I agree with much of the criticism of the term "Anthropocene" and have used "the Capitalocene" throughout this book for that reason. Yet for all its problems, the Anthropocene—as an idea and as a name—seems here to stay. Part of its appeal has been the glimmer of hope it offers: As we fight despair about planetary systems spinning hopelessly out of control, the Anthropocene promises a return of some control. If we accept that humankind dominates the planet, we might also acknowledge that we can use our powerful impact for good as well as for ill. This is not a new idea, and those bearing the standard of the Anthropocene are not the only ones exploring it. For instance, without ever mentioning "the Anthropocene," over the last decade at least some scientists have begun arguing for an embrace of "domesticated nature"—a nature understood as fully human controlled. Once we acknowledge that "there really is no such thing as nature untainted by people," according to this position, we can begin engineering nature more thoughtfully and productively, "manag[ing] tradeoffs among ecosystem services so that nature and people simultaneously thrive."[4] More recently, in their "Ecomodernist Manifesto," a coalition of academics and environmentalists calling themselves ecomodernists and ecopragmatists have argued that human "knowledge and technology, applied with wisdom, might allow for a good, or even great, Anthropocene. A good Anthropocene demands that humans use their growing social, economic, and technological powers to make life better for people, stabilize the climate, and protect the natural world."[5] In short, the Anthropocene has been framed as "A New Epoch of Human Control over the Planet."[6] Even as the fact of humans' global impact is lamented, our technological and other accomplishments are seen as the main potential site of hope for an increasingly damaged, imperiled world. Once we acknowledge just how big the mess is and that we made it, this line of reasoning goes, we can also accept as the positive flipside the reality that we have not only the responsibility but also the capability to fix it.

Of course, humans often fail to predict correctly the outcomes of even our best intentions. As I argued in Chapter 3, we have certainly failed to predict the failures of preservation, for one. Moreover, as influential ecofeminists such as Val Plumwood have shown, a "dream of mastery" over nonhuman nature has long dogged Western science, and it has mostly proven a destructive daydream.[7] But given the amount of traction that "the Anthropocene" already has, as well as its compatibility with capitalist world systems, we may have to live with the Anthropocene paradigm whether we like it or not, at least for a while. And if we can decouple the Anthropocene from an anthropocentric and uncritical belief in human mastery of the planet, perhaps it might yet yield environmental rewards. Particularly for many in the United States, to recognize the depth of our impact on others would be a first step in acknowledging that we must coexist with responsibility to other lives. From this perspective, the Anthropocene signals just how fully we share a world with all other life. Human actions have global as well as local impacts, and humans in any given location are entangled with other lives (human and not) both where they live and where they do not.

It is simply true that the survival of many species on planet Earth increasingly hinges on their ability to "adapt to human needs and the human presence."[8] The difficulties of conceptualizing less oppressive versions of our human-dominated but multispecies communities have recently been explored by Thom van Dooren in *Flight Ways*, Cynthia Willet in *Interspecies Ethics*, Timothy Morton in *Humankind*, and many others, but seemingly always through the lens of human impact and encounters with "wild" nonhuman creatures—North American coyotes, Indian vultures, and so on. There are many excellent reasons for theorizing multispecies community through our fraught relationships with undomesticated animals, not least because, as anthropologists have suggested, living in at least partial community with wild nonhuman animals was likely a feature of our hunter-gatherer past. It is not an unthinkable or utopian dream.[9]

At the same time, however, according to the logic of the Anthropocene, it would seem that we could learn from our relationships to domesticated nonhuman animals as well, those animals who have been adapting themselves to "human needs and the human presence" the longest. When the trope of nature's "domestication" in the Anthropocene has been specified, it has generally been through the figure of the garden, as in Emma Marris's influential *Rambunctious Garden: Saving Nature in a Post-Wild World*. Recently, Ursula Heise in *Imagining Extinction* has read the Anthropocene as a speculative-fiction trope. Through the work of Orson Scott Card, Heise argues for an Anthropocene "cosmopolitanism that does not take for granted anything about humans as a biological species but instead constructs versions of the human in a careful and painstaking, cross-cultural process of assembly."[10] This chapter offers a third trope for negotiating the Anthropocene: the pet. In what follows, I explore how one particular form of domesticated animal, the pet, in one very particular context—two nineteenth-century, Black woman–authored, antiracist, antislavery novels— might help us think multispecies community in the Anthropocene.

If the nineteenth century is the period when our sense of wild nature as a distant aesthetic spectacle codified, it is also the period when Americans' most intimate way of living in proximity to nonhuman animals codified in the form of widespread pet keeping. The pet is a counterintuitive site for theorizing ethical entanglements for all kinds of reasons. Not least because, as John Berger has written, domesticated animals give up quite a lot when they enter into the pet–pet keeper relationship:

> The small family living unit lacks space, earth, other animals, seasons, natural temperatures, and so on. The pet is either sterilised or sexually isolated, extremely limited in its exercise, deprived of almost all other animal contact, and fed with artificial foods. This is the material process which lies behind the truism that pets come to resemble their masters or mistresses. They are creatures of their owner's way of life.[11]

Yet despite these and other objections, there are interesting advantages to theorizing a more just, antiracist, and even multispecies community through the figure of the pet and the site of pet keeping.

In the first place, during the nineteenth century the figure of the pet could serve as a valuable trope for figuring failures of human community. In a remarkable *Liberator* editorial written in the early moments of the Civil War, Lydia Maria Child rails against the "unlimited indulgence and submissive tenderness of the United States Government toward its pet crocodile, Slavery." During the antebellum period, she claims, the indulgent national government "continued to feed its pet with pap; it constantly widened its range, it tightly enclosed within its reach millions of men, women, and children, for it to grind in its bloody jaws."[12] In objecting to the "peculiar" or "pet" "institution" of the United States, antislavery activists like Child objected to the notion that some human beings, because of the color of their skin, should be marked out for "special" treatment, treatment different from that due to the universalized "men" who were supposedly "created equal" by the Declaration of Independence. Slavery seemed a categorical exception to the acknowledged basic rights the nation's founding documents promised were due to "all" human beings, just as pet keeping seemed a categorical exception to the acknowledged "correct treatment" of animalkind, who were otherwise fellow laborers, food, or distant, wild neighbors, not family members.

Chattel slavery as a "pet crocodile" is one of the weirder figurations of the United States' peculiar institution, but the pet-keeping metaphor arises from a constellation of slavery, animality, kinship, and violence common to the antislavery rhetoric of the antebellum period. Observations about the dehumanizing aspects of chattel slavery are commonplace—in nineteenth-century abolitionist literature[13] and in twentieth- and twenty-first-century literary scholarship—yet the complicated matrix of animality, race, gender, and personhood in American literature and culture remains poorly understood. This chapter will begin to address this lacuna by exploring the centrality of pets, beasts, and primates to both pro- and antislavery rhetoric. Animals and animal tropes were a key rhetorical battleground for the slavery question: While proslavery rhetoric sought to place enslaved peoples on the "animal" side of a human-animal dualism, antislavery rhetoric worked to shore up enslaved peoples' position on the human side of that opposition. The antislavery approach was obviously strategic—a useful and important response to virulent (and violent) racism. Yet there is a significant theoretical complication with the way that nineteenth-century abolitionists portray, and twenty-first century critics read, the dehumanizing conflation of enslaved people with animals. Namely, as I will argue, abolitionist rhetoric defends enslaved people against violence and oppression by resorting to the same form of human exceptionalism that undergirds the social construction of slaves in the first place.

Animals often serve as a limit or test case for membership in a community, an insight that drove the typical abolitionist desire to distance enslaved humans from nonhuman animals.[14] Yet there were other, riskier experiments with human-animal relationality occurring in the period's literature. In particular, Hannah Crafts's *The Bondwoman's Narrative* (c. 1853–1861) offers a remarkably different depiction of human-animal kinship, one that upends any consensus on how blurring the line between the human and the animal features in antebellum rhetoric. Apparently authored by a formerly enslaved woman and unpublished until Henry Louis Gates Jr. brought it forward in 2002, *The Bondwoman's Narrative* was "unaligned with the abolitionist movement," and perhaps as a result "Hannah Crafts eschewed the conventions that promised success to others."[15] One of the most interesting and unexamined conventions "eschewed" is the usual antislavery insistence on the distance between an enslaved person and a nonhuman animal. Early in the novel, Crafts depicts a surprising scene of human-animal kinship and care between an enslaved pet keeper and her dog. This scene of enslaved pet keeping radically critiques the logic and practice of US slavery by attacking its roots: the claim of an absolute distinction between human and nonhuman animals that structures Black oppression during the period.

A full reckoning with Crafts's scene of pet and pet keeper murder helps bring into focus Harriet Wilson's remarkable treatment of Frado's close relationship with her pet dog, Fido, in *Our Nig; or, Sketches from the Life of a Free Black* (1859). Although Frado is an indentured servant in the North and not enslaved, her mistress is "wholly imbued with *southern* principles," and the misery and racist violence Frado suffers goes unchecked by the white New England community in which she lives. Yet, like Hannah Crafts's Rose, Frado responds to her dehumanizing treatment not by foregrounding human and nonhuman difference but by treating her dog with humanizing affection and care. Throughout *The Bondwoman's Narrative* and *Our Nig*, Crafts and Wilson demonstrate that it is social treatment that produces humanized, or dehumanized, beings, and in the process, each establishes herself as a significant theorist of difference, community, and less coercive mastery. As I will argue by the end of the chapter, these are theories and practices critical to imagining a less damaging Anthropocene.

Animality, Pets, and the Rhetoric of Slavery

Important sites of antebellum human-animal theory and contact have begun to come into focus in recent scholarship. Environmental historians have demonstrated that enslaved encounters with nonhuman animals are critical to understanding life in the plantation South.[16] Activities such as animal agriculture, hunting, and fishing were opportunities for independent economic activity that allowed both enslavers and the enslaved to refine and resist the customary rights and responsibilities of US slavery. Although as "human property" enslaved people were officially stripped of property rights, there was nevertheless "a significant informal economy of property ownership and trade among enslaved people throughout the South," and much of this economy centered around nonhuman animals.[17]

Still other sites of antebellum human-animal theory and contact have come into focus through scholarship situated in "animality studies," a field described by one scholar as prioritizing "questions of human politics . . . in relation to how we have thought about human and nonhuman animality at various historical and cultural moments."[18] Leslie Ginsberg's 1998 consideration of slavery and pet keeping in Poe's "The Black Cat" has been followed more recently by work connecting animals in sentimental and children's literature to cultural negotiations of gender, race, and power.[19] Histories of nineteenth-century animal activism have further drawn attention to the overlap between reform cultures, in particular between antislavery and child- and animal-welfare activism and activists.[20] By highlighting particular human-animal encounters and their relationship to human politics, such work has advanced our understanding of the cultural formations of personhood in nineteenth-century US literature and culture more generally.

Despite such scholarship, precisely how notions of human-animal kin-ship feature in the nineteenth-century racial imagination remains under-studied. To the extent that scholars have considered animals or animality and slavery, they have tended to highlight the proslavery use of dehuman-izing animal associations. In the United States, where from the seventeenth century onward slavery had a racial component, definitions and significa-tions of slavery and animality frequently overlapped with theories of race; indeed, these categories often mutually constituted one another. The in-timate relation between matters of race, personhood, and species was made possible by new theories of racial difference that began to gain currency in the United States just as the system of African slavery formalized.[21] By the antebellum period, innate rather than environmental causes had be-come the leading explanation for racial difference, and in the face of ex-panding opposition to slavery, proslavery scientists and social theorists developed ever-more extreme accounts of just how permanent, biological, and significant racial difference supposedly was. Turning from mere sur-face traits like skin color, American racial theory from the 1830s began to focus on purported differences in "hidden depths and inner parts," includ-ing not only "the organization of bone and muscular systems, [and] the color of the blood" but also racially distinct emotional, intellectual, and spiritual capacities.[22] The permanence of the supposed differences between Blacks and whites was asserted in proslavery circles in all parts of the coun-try, but even among abolitionists in the North a "romantic racialism" that "acknowledged permanent racial differences but rejected the notion of a clearly defined racial hierarchy" prevailed.[23]

During the first half of the nineteenth century, the rapid calcification and elaboration of notions of innate racial difference enabled a broaden-ing, deepening, and literalizing of older associations between enslaved people, "Africans," and animals. Whereas earlier associations between "Af-ricans" and animals tended to be more speculative, tentative, abstract, and even metaphorical, during the antebellum period proslavery rhetoric in-creasingly denied African Americans' basic humanity by suggesting a spu-rious physiological and intellectual relatedness to primates and other "brutes" in the most literal and biological terms. This was true even in publications that shied away from claiming "the Negro" was literally sub-human, as did for instance Josiah Nott's *Types of Mankind* (1854), one of the earliest and most popular American contributions to the burgeoning fields of physical anthropology and ethnology during the nineteenth century. Nott wrote his book to promote the theory of polygenesis, or sep-arate origins for the various races of human beings, and *Types of Mankind* was influential enough for Frederick Douglass to devote an entire 1854 lecture, "The Claims of the Negro Ethnologically Considered," to refuting it. Positioning himself as a moderate on matters of race, Nott told his readers, "I belong not to those who are disposed to degrade any type of humanity to the level of the brute-creation. Nevertheless, a man must be blind not to be struck by similitudes between some of the lower races of mankind, viewed as connecting links in the animal kingdom."[24] After offering his readers this carefully worded caveat, Nott goes on to illustrate the supposed biological "similitudes" between "types" of "the Negro" and varieties of primates with illustrations that juxtapose drawings of heads and skulls of the "Creole Negro" with those of the "Young Chimpanzee" or those of the "Hottentot" with the "Orang-Outan."[25] To sympathetic white readers evaluating his racist, pseudoscientific visual "data," Nott's distinction between claiming "the Negro" *was* a member of the animal kingdom and claiming "only" that he was the "connecting link" between whites and nonhuman animals must have made very little difference.

Antislavery writers repudiated such dehumanizing claims in the most direct terms. In fact, in publications ranging from David Walker's *Appeal to the Coloured Citizens of the World* (1829), to Frederick Douglass's *Narrative of the Life of Frederick Douglass* (1845), to the masthead of William Lloyd Garrison's *The Liberator*, which was illustrated with a mixed auction of human slaves and horses, it was precisely the slippage between the human and the animal that was most often figured as the foundational violence of chattel slavery. Transforming men and women into beasts of burden, selling families piecemeal on the open market like cattle, dehumanizing enslaved people by refusing access to education and intellectual sustenance—these were among the most frequent and severe charges laid at nineteenth-century US slavery's door. As a consequence, many slave narratives and antislavery writings from the period devote abundant attention to the ways that slavery animalizes both its victims and its perpetrators, representing such instances of dehumanization as the primary obstacle to be overcome in an enslaved person's quest for freedom.

For instance, as one scholar has observed, David Walker's *Appeal to the Coloured Citizens of the World* attacks the "*insupportable insult*" that Blacks "were not of the *human family*" as the "ideological centerpiece of American racism."[26] Over and over again, in ringing tones that range from sarcasm to outrage, Walker's appeal denounces the methods by which "the whites . . . after having reduced us to the deplorable condition of slaves under their feet, h[o]ld us up as descending originally from the tribes of *Monkeys* or *Orang-Outangs*" in order to justify the perpetuation of chattel slavery.[27] "All the inhabitants of the earth, (except however the sons of Africa) are called *men*, and of course are, and ought to be free," Walker acerbically pronounces. "But we, (coloured people) and our children are *brutes!!* and of course we are, and *ought to be* SLAVES to the American people and their children forever!!"[28] Tracing the American provenance of the claim that Blacks are "naturally" inferior to whites and thus closer to nonhuman animals to Thomas Jefferson's *Notes on the State of Virginia*, Walker recognizes the influence and credibility their source has lent such notions. Yet however pervasive these racist beliefs are, Walker insists "we are men—and there is a secret monitor in [whites'] hearts that tells them we are";[29] in a masterful twist, it is to this "secret monitor," using the words of Thomas Jefferson, that Walker ultimately "appeals": "See your Declaration Americans!!! Do you understand your own language? Hear your language, proclaimed to the world, July 4th, 1776—'We hold these truths to be self evident—that ALL MEN ARE CREATED EQUAL'!!"[30] As "MEN," not "*beasts*," Walker claims the foundational protections of US personhood for free Blacks and the enslaved alike.

Such animalizing stereotypes denied universal natural rights to the enslaved by rejecting their full humanity.[31] Yet even in formulations of slavery where the enslaved are imagined (at least initially) as fully human, it is still the distinction between humans and animals that is used to construct the enslaved as such. This is the case in John Locke's influential *Second Treatise* (1689), composed at the same time that Locke was also helping write the *Fundamental Constitutions of Carolina*, which "assumed the existence of slavery and affirmed the absolute powers of life and death of slaveholders."[32] In the *Second Treatise*, Locke formulates a just-war theory of slavery that attempts to reconcile slavery with his theory of universal natural rights. Unlike many other Enlightenment thinkers,[33] and despite having significant financial investments in the slave trade and other aspects of the triangle trade,[34] Locke does not advance racist theories of human difference.[35] In fact, slavery is essentially a logical impossibility for Locke's thought; men do not have a property in themselves that they may give away to another person (such property belongs always finally to their "Creator"), and they cannot claim the right to absolute property in another person as they might an animal: "Being furnished with like Faculties, sharing all in one Community of Nature, there cannot be supposed any such *Subordination* among us, that may Authorize us to destroy one another, as if we were made for one anothers uses, as the inferior ranks of Creatures are for ours."[36] Locke's contrast between humans and "the inferior ranks of Creatures" is telling here, because it provides the tack he will ultimately take to explain the existence of slavery. In Locke's theory of slavery one "Man" may assume "Absolute, Arbitrary Power" over another only after "the Aggressor" has forfeited his own life by "put[ting] himself into the state of War with another":

> For having quitted Reason, which God hath given to be the Rule betwixt Man and Man, and the common bond whereby humane kind is united into one fellowship and societie; and having renounced the way of peace . . . and so revolting from his own kind to that of Beasts making Force which is theirs, to be his rule of right, he renders himself liable to be destroyed by the injur'd person and the rest of mankind, that will joyn with him in the execution of Justice, as any other wild beast, or noxious brute with whom Mankind can have neither Society nor Security.[37]

Locke here posits human "Reason" as the common bond, the basis for social belonging. Those entering into society on any other terms, as he says elsewhere, "are to be looked on as an Herd of inferiour Creatures, under the Dominion of a Master, who keeps them, and works them for his own Pleasure or Profit."[38] The logic of slavery put forth here depends on human exceptionalism, the perceived absolute distinction between man and other animals on the basis of "Reason": Any man who shows himself deficient enough in reason to make war against another man (the only cause of slavery Locke acknowledges) is by definition subhuman, a "Beast," and therefore deserves to be subjected to "Despotical Power" like "any other wild beast or noxious brute with whom Mankind can have neither Society nor Security." Ultimately, for Locke, slaves are those who, having behaved like "beasts" with whom no compact is possible, have been condemned to death like beasts but at the pleasure of their sentencer have had their sentence indefinitely deferred. This is no threat to universal natural rights, since the slave "whenever he finds the hardship of his Slavery out-weigh the value of his Life, 'tis in his Power . . . to draw on himself the Death he desires."[39]

In *Slavery and Social Death*, Orlando Patterson cites the broad theoretical tradition (of which Locke is a part) of viewing slaves as those "degraded" individuals who, when faced with a death sentence, chose survival despite the ignominious circumstances. Patterson views this tradition as one of the two key components in the enslaved person's "social death." He writes, "the master was essentially a ransomer. What he bought or acquired was the slave's life, and restraints on the master's capacity wantonly to destroy his slave did not undermine his claim on that life. Because the slave had no socially recognized existence outside of his master, he became a social nonperson."[40] The "second constituent element of the slave relation," for Patterson, is "the slave's natal alienation." "Alienated from all 'rights' or claims of birth, he ceased to belong in his own right to any legitimate social order. . . . He was truly a genealogical isolate."[41]

Locke's theorization of slavery (with Patterson as a useful supplement) makes visible the process of dispossession that must take place for a human being to be stripped of natural rights and constructed as a slave: Aligned with a degraded construction of "the animal" and excluded from civil society through a systemic social death, the slave is the quintessential "dead man walking," laboring ceaselessly for another man from a lifelong death row. Otherwise a logical impossibility or at least toothsome problem for liberal political theory, slavery becomes permissible once a human being ceases to be a human being: Animalized, walking corpses are outside the bounds of civil society and its politics and thus no disturbance to its functioning.

Nott, Walker, Jefferson, and Locke together illuminate the basic stakes of animality in both pro- and antislavery theory and rhetoric, but the pet in particular performed its own special rhetorical work in the debate. George Fredrickson has argued that during the antebellum period, "hard" "image[s] of 'the Negro as beast' . . . vied for supremacy in Southern propaganda with the 'soft' image of the Black slave as beloved child."[42] Frederickson schematizes the nineteenth-century models for the ideal slave into these two opposed categories—the slave as child and the slave as beast of burden—a racial dualism that has influenced many historians and literary critics examining US slavery. Yet there was in fact a third conceptual category sometimes used to theorize enslaved persons in the United States that combined elements of both "opposed" categories: that of the pet.

Pet keeping first developed as a relatively widespread phenomenon among the upper classes during the eighteenth century, but it expanded dramatically in all classes during the antebellum period as part of a trend toward leisure activities that created opportunities for self-expression and personal cultivation.[43] Thus the category of the pet was readily available to nineteenth-century Americans as a space to theorize membership in both nuclear and national families that did not rely on similitude or necessitate equal treatment or opportunities. Elizabeth Barnes has argued that from the Revolutionary period through the nineteenth century, "to be truly American one must be able to conceive of others as if they were part of one's own family."[44] Barnes convincingly demonstrates that this "familial model" used to conceptualize American democracy elided diversity, yet the category of the pet gave the sentimental family one means to incorporate a radical form of difference during the nineteenth century:

species difference. Combining features of the child and beast tropes, the pet offered a more permanent model for familial incorporation of difference. Unlike the figure of the child, who (if male) might be accorded equal status with the adult members of the family upon reaching maturity, or the figure of the beast, who by definition could not be incorporated into the human family, the pet was a category that might permanently preserve difference, and thus inequality, within the nuclear and national families.

The pet played such a key role in theorizing community-with-difference because in the United States, theories of community have often turned on forms of affinity (if not identity) that are gendered and raced. Dana Nelson, Frederickson, and others have shown that from the early national period onward US citizenship was not only implicitly but often explicitly theorized as male and as exclusively white. Even among antislavery whites, the supposed inability of the "white" nation to incorporate the Black bodies that scientific racism supposedly "confirmed" were radically distinct from a white "norm" was often seen as one of the primary practical obstacles to ending US slavery.[45] Some opponents of slavery countered this line of argument by reiterating the universalist language of the Revolutionary period's natural-rights assertions, but as Robyn Wiegman and Michael Warner have pointed out, white males were the only group ever intended to access that "universalized" subject position. Noting that the universalized form of citizenship depends upon an ability to "self-abstract" granted only to white males, this critique hinges on the observation that such citizenship is "disembodied" or "decorporealized" and so finally not bodily enough to include women and people of color, whose embodied particularity was always insisted upon in the bourgeois public sphere.[46]

In fact, during the antebellum period, antislavery and proslavery writers alike turned to the figure of the pet to make sense of racial difference, on the one hand, and African American slavery, on the other. The human-animal relationships fostered by the culture of sentimental pet keeping affected slavery debates because pet keeping produced a site within the family where kinship shaded into ownership, where economic and sentimental value were blurred,[47] and where biological differences could coexist in an "affectionate" if unequal relationship. In this sense, the logic of pet keeping reflected the proslavery defense of the affectionate inequality that supposedly characterized the patriarchal master-slave relationship.[48] In fact, contemporary observers sometimes made that connection, calling favored enslaved persons "pets" or "petted dogs,"[49] an attitude Herman Melville satirizes in *Benito Cereno* through Captain Delano's misreading of the rebel leader, Babo, as Benito Cereno's loyal pet dog. Captain Delano's first encounter with Babo is described in the terms of sentimental pet keeping: "By [Cereno's] side stood a black of small stature, in whose rude face, as occasionally, like a shepherd's dog, he mutely turned it up into the Spaniard's, sorrow and affection were equally blended." Melville implies that it is the racism signified by the pet-keeping language that produces Delano's profound misunderstanding of both the affect and power relationship between Cereno and Babo in this scene.[50]

While proslavery commentators compared "house slaves" in particular to pet dogs, usually with the intent to signify the affection and care supposedly lavished on this group, antislavery sources could use the same comparison to critique slavery's structural inequalities, as when Frederick Douglass related to an antislavery group in Belfast the story of how he first heard the Bible read "twenty years ago, while lying, not unlike a pet dog, at the feet of my mistress."[51] Antislavery writers frequently referred to slavery as the United States' "pet institution" in order to critique slavery's exceptional and protected status within the republic,[52] and the treatment of free Black men and women as "pets" was occasionally critiqued as well. In one significant example of this latter phenomenon, a journalist reflecting on the racist reception the author and activist Martin Delany received from the American ambassador in the United Kingdom (and more generally on the persistence of racial prejudice after emancipation in the British colonies) suggested that treating certain gifted and favored men or women of color as special "pets" was a way of avoiding the question of general Black equality while granting it to individual "stray" men and women of color.[53] Pets were even used in antislavery publications to test the "naturalness" of racial prejudice, as in the 1849 poem that began "The *Colorphobia*—what is that? / Does it infect the dog or cat?," although such turns to the animal could reify racial prejudice as easily as they demonstrated its unnatural character.[54] While the author of "Colorphobia" concludes that racial prejudice is not found in nature and that "colorphobia" is a mere "pretence" protecting white supremacy, in an earlier *Liberator* item submitted by a contributor and printed with Garrison's editorial endorsement of "Excellent!," a child's orphaned black kitten is rejected by a white cat intended as a foster mother. Eventually the cat "relents" and consents to nurse the black kitten, although she continues to force the kitten to remain on the other side of the box when not nursing. Apparently a morality tale for "juvenile readers" showing that "if an animal, devoid of reason," can overcome racial prejudice so might human beings, the piece naturalizes human racial prejudice and inequality along the way through an imagined interior monologue of the white cat mother that ascribes the cat's rejection of the black kitten to racial prejudice. "I do not know you, nor like you—I think you have no business here," the cat's monologue begins. "You are an ugly little black thing, and probably belong to an inferior race of cats, with whom I have no acquaintance or connexion."[55]

As these examples illustrate, the antebellum slavery debate frequently turned on human-animal distinctions and hierarchies, hierarchies that helped shape the terms of both pro- and antislavery rhetoric. Using pets, beasts, and primates, proslavery rhetoric sought to place enslaved people on the "animal" side of a human-animal dualism, while antislavery rhetoric, for its part, worked to shore up enslaved people's position on the human side of that opposition. The antislavery approach was obviously strategic—a useful and important response to anti-Black racism. However, such abolitionist rhetoric is more complicated than it might seem because it defends enslaved people against violence and economic and racial oppression by resorting to the same form of human exceptionalism in Locke and others that undergirds the social construction of slaves in the first place. In the next section, I will explore an alternative approach, one that uses pet keeping to refuse the conventional meanings of species difference in a calculated attack on antebellum racism.

A Multispecies Ethic of Care in The Bondwoman's Narrative

The stakes of combating the animalization of African Americans—as "beasts," as "pets," and as enslaved "nonpersons"—are clear, and they were clearly understood by antislavery writers and activists during the antebellum period. Yet it was possible to combat the constellation of race, animality, slavery, and violence differently, as a turn to Hannah Crafts's *The Bondwoman's Narrative* demonstrates. As Robert Levine has argued, *The Bondwoman's Narrative* should "remind us anew of the shaping impact and dehumanizing force of racial categories in the pre–Civil War United States" and is "a text that has the potential to offer new insights into racial representations and formations of the period."[56] It offers the potential for "new insights" precisely because of its willingness to depart from the conventional antislavery path in its approach to the question of animality. While Crafts's novel does take care to insist repeatedly upon the equality of all human beings,[57] such constructions of natural rights and Christian brotherhood are not pinned to a distinction between humans and nonhumans in any conventional manner. In a particularly emblematic episode, Crafts develops a disturbing vignette of pet and pet keeper torture and finally murder, representing an enslaved woman and her pet dog not to insist upon the exceptional human status of the enslaved pet keeper but to depict a surprising scene of human-animal kinship and care.

The pet in question is introduced early in *The Bondwoman's Narrative*, when the novel's enslaved narrator, Hannah, tells the story of a trauma, one that occurred at the founding of her enslaver's paternal line in the United States and that still haunts the plantation and the family. In this story Hannah's enslaver's ancestor, Sir Clifford, becomes angry with a pet-keeping slave's small dog over an unnamed minor offense, and the elderly enslaved woman, Rose, is ordered to drown her pet. Although Rose had been nurse to Sir Clifford's "son and heir" and has been "treated with unusual consideration by the family in consequence"—as "a pet," in the broadest sense[58]—she cannot convince the cruel Sir Clifford to repeal her dog's death sentence.[59] No more, however, can Rose comply with the order: The "little dog, white[60] and shaggy, with great speaking eyes, full of intelligence, and bearing a strong resemblance to those of a child," "so singularly beautiful and innocent in his helplessness," is in fact "the memorial of her lost one," a daughter Sir Clifford has sold to "the rice swamps of Alabama." The dog is for Rose "much more than a little dumb animal." "It had such winning ways, and knew so well to make its wants understood that it became to [Rose] what a grandchild is to many aged females" as well as "her treasure, and sole possession, and the only earthly thing that regarded her with fondness or to whose comfort her existence was essential."[61] Memorial, child, grandchild, treasure, sole possession, "something to love"— the dog is all of this to Rose. "It may perchance be a tree or a flower, perchance a child or domestic animal," the narrator assures us, but "the heart must have something to love" and "with poor old Rose it was her little dog."[62]

Because Rose will not execute his order, Sir Clifford, with "a refinement of cruelty," orders Rose and her dog hung up on a giant linden tree, gibbeted within sight but just out of reach of each other. In a harrowing scene of torture, Rose and her dog hang side by side on the tree for five days and nights, without food or water, taunted daily by Sir Clifford. During this time, Rose comforts her fellow victim in terms that emphasize their similarity to one another rather than their species difference:

> It was enough, they said, to have melted a heart of stone to hear her
> talk to that affectionate and equally tortured favorite so long as she
> retained the power of speech, as if she sought by such demonstrations
> of tenderness to soothe her own misery and mitigate his sufferings.
> How she seemed to consider him a being who could know; and think

and reason, and as such assured him of her undying love and regard, entreated him to be patient, and to bear with fortitude whatever the wickidness of man imposed, and strove to solace him with the certainty that a few more hours would finish all their woes, and safely confide them to the place where the weary rest.[63]

Contrary to a twenty-first-century reader's expectations and perhaps especially to the expectations of a nineteenth-century antislavery audience, Rose rejects even the most basic distinctions between the value of her own life and that of her little dog in this scene, "consider[ing] him a being who could know; and think and reason," and apparently even gain entrance to heaven, "the place where the weary rest."

Much as Simon Legree's youthful "murder" of his mother haunts the gothic plantation at the end of *Uncle Tom's Cabin*, this foundational act of human-animal murder haunts the Lindendale plantation in *The Bondwoman's Narrative*.[64] A great deal of scholarly attention has been devoted to explaining the crime against motherhood in Stowe's novel, but how do we explain why this scene of pet and pet keeper torture is the gothic crime at the back of Crafts's novel?[65] And how, especially, do we explain the tender depictions of Rose's assertions of kinship with her dog throughout the scene?

We can't simply dismiss Crafts's representation of human-animal kinship as a moment of rhetorical unawareness, since *The Bondwoman's Narrative* at other points represents the racism that allows whites to portray enslaved people as nonhuman animals. In fact, Crafts sets the scene for her portrayal of interspecies kinship with a description of slavery that blurs the line between human beings and domestic animals: "Practically he regarded them not as men and women, but in the same light as horses and other domestic animals," she writes of the narrator's enslaver.[66] Later in the novel, there is a similar passage in which the narrator laments "the false system" that "subjects others under certain circumstances to a lower link in the chain of being than that occupied by a horse."[67] Yet while Crafts acknowledges the racist slippage between enslaved people and nonhuman animals fostered by the rhetoric and practice of chattel slavery, she does not follow typical abolitionist suit by insisting on the distance between human and nonhuman animals in response.

Instead, Crafts uses Rose's refusal to drown her pet dog as an eloquent refutation of Rose's dispossession as an enslaved woman. In contrast to the totemic myth of slavery exemplified by Locke, in which slaves construct themselves as such through "bestial" acts of violence, Rose demonstrates her essential humanity by refusing to commit an act of violence, "even" against an animal. Rose's willingness to die, too, refutes her enslaved status, since according to the tautological logic of slavery, survival is supposed proof of the "naturalness" and appropriateness of the slave's slavery. Perhaps most significantly, however, Rose's refusal to kill her pet is an assertion of her ownership of and kinship with the little dog whose existence is all in all to her—"child," "grandchild," "treasure," "sole possession."

Simultaneously kin and possession, the very existence of Rose's pet dog is an attack on Rose's enslaved status, which is perhaps why her enslaver is so quick to demand the dog's extermination. As Laura Brace notes, "property is supposed to generate duties for others, and so has to involve recognition by others. . . . On this account of property, the opposite of slavery is belonging rather than freedom."[68] Pets are thus an extremely special form of property because they address both aspects of an enslaved person's social exclusion: unfreedom because as property capable of not simply recognizing but identifying the slave as their owner, pets are uniquely primed to demarcate enslaved persons as property owners, and belonging because, as beings with whom the enslaved person can form kinship and social ties, pets symbolically address the exclusion from social and genealogical community that US slaves were often forced to endure. Of course, pets could not actually restore an enslaved person's freedom or social belonging, but they could give the lie to an enslaved person's incapacity for property ownership or deep, affectionate kinship ties. Far from confirming the supposed "want of domestic affections, and insensibility to the ties of kindred" that antebellum proslavery writers insisted characterized "the African"; far from confirming "that Africans, generally speaking, betray the most perfect indifference on . . . being deprived of their relatives," a characterization used to prove that "[Africans] approach nearer to the nature of the brute relation, than any other people on the face of the globe" and thus "furnish the very material out of which slaves ought to be made";[69] far from confirming such a racist and self-serving canard, Rose's refusal to drown her pet and her conduct toward him during their torturous, extended death scene are moving and powerful testaments to an enslaved person's depth of feeling not only for her pet dog but for the lost daughter he metonymically symbolizes.

Yet Rose and her dog are martyrs to more than just liberal political theory; their protracted suffering resists the ideology of patriarchy, the logic of white supremacy, and the tradition of human exceptionalism as well, in a variety of complex ways. Sir Clifford's ability to torture Rose and her dog despite the objections of his wife and son rests on a patriarch's right to command his family, a circle that in the plantation South includes enslaved persons. His ability to murder Rose and her dog without incurring the wrath of his community (either legally or through social excommunication) rests on a system of social and jurisprudential distinctions between the value and meaning of free white versus Black, enslaved bodies, on the one hand, and human versus animal bodies, on the other.

As Crafts's novel shows us, the most radical act, the act most challenging to slavery and its logic, is *not* to emphasize the distinction between the human and the animal, the primal distinction upon which slavery finally depends, but rather to refuse the logic of such distinctions entirely and, indeed, of rights discourses in general. Instead, Rose displays toward her dog a morality that feminist theorists have called "an ethic of care," an alternative model for valuing and protecting bodies apart from rights discourses. An ethic of morality more "concerned with the activity of care," "responsibility and relationships" than "morality as fairness," as "rights and rules,"[70] Rose's ethic of care toward her dog "resists hierarchal, dominative dualisms, which establish the powerful (humans, men, whites) over the subordinate (animals, women, people of color)."[71] The advantage of this "ethic of care" model over human rights discourses becomes clear when we recognize that even when extending human rights discourses to previously excluded groups, "the same hierarchy of categories [once used to deny rights] is [frequently] presupposed, only the boundary of those included in the group with rights is extended 'downward' along the ladder, shoring up a different dichotomy as the crucial—that is, exclusionary—boundary."[72] What Rose does by recognizing common cause between herself and her little dog is identify and resist the multiple systems of oppression intersecting in Sir Clifford's torture as axes of opposition supporting "a hierarchy between the superior norm and the deviant 'other': man/woman, white/ black, adult/child . . . human/animal," and master/slave.[73]

Rose's gesture is so radical because in resisting the dualistic opposition between human and animal, she is resisting the construction of "the human" that excludes her from consideration. As Jacques Derrida has observed, human beings have constructed their notion of "Man with a capital *M*" against a construction of "Animal with a capital *A*"; they have also constructed distinctions between human beings along this same "logic of the limit," as Derrida calls it.[74] We have already seen this in Locke, and it runs all through the large body of literature that comprises modern and ancient political and philosophical discussions and definitions of slavery. This shouldn't surprise us, since "confined within this catch-all concept, within this vast encampment of the animal, in this general singular, within

the strict enclosure of this definite article ('The Animal' and not 'animals') . . . are *all the living things* that man does not recognize as his fellows, his neighbors, or his brothers."[75] *"All the living things* that man does
not recognize as his fellows, his neighbors, or his brothers" structurally
includes enslaved persons.

The act Sir Clifford asks Rose to commit in ordering her to kill her dog
is essentially a sacrificial crime, one that emphasizes the absoluteness of
Sir Clifford's power over Rose by forcing her to assert her human power
over her animal victim. For Derrida, such sacrifice is one of the three key
pillars upholding Western philosophy's claims of human exceptionalism:
The idea is "not necessarily of sacrifice as ritual sacrifice of the animal . . .
but of sacrifice as fundamental, indeed, of a founding sacrifice, within a
human space where, in any case, exercising power over the animal to the
point of being able to put it to death when necessary is not forbidden."[76]
What this means, as Donna Haraway has argued, is that "Within the logic
of sacrifice, only human beings can be murdered. . . . Every living being
except Man can be killed but not murdered. [For this reason,] to make Man
merely killable is the height of moral outrage; indeed, it is the definition
of genocide."[77] What Rose does in refusing to kill her dog—and what
Crafts does in representing the scene as one of protracted human-animal
murder rather than mere "pet killing" or "animal cruelty," is to resist this
absolute limit between the human and the animal upon which the other
axes of dualistic opposition, and ultimately oppression, are built.

Race and animality do not always mean what we expect in Crafts's novel,
yet far from confirming racist human hierarchies, the troubling of the species hierarchy in the scene of Rose's gothic martyrdom represents a complex and multilayered attack on the logic of slavery, exposing it as bankrupt
and artificial. Not only is Rose not a pet, someone to be treated as a
merely killable "animal," but her pet's animality does not mean what we
might expect—the dog is a member of the family, with "speaking eyes"
that respond to Rose's (and her daughter's before her) special treatment by
becoming much more than a dog. Rose and her little white dog are the
symbolic centerpiece of Crafts's insistence on the significance of humane
treatment to the development of humanized beings. By actively representing what Donna Haraway has called the "ontological choreography"
that turns an animal into a pet or even a "child," Crafts, through Rose,
reminds us that "actual encounters are what make beings."[78] Without undoing the species hierarchy between herself and her dog, Rose nevertheless
rejects the meaning of that hierarchy by refusing to treat her pet dog according to a speciesist logic of pet keeping: She does not make her dog

the victim of "unidirectional relations of use,"[79] and she does not treat him as merely killable—as she, in short, is treated by her enslaver. Rose's martyrdom, and the treatment of her dog that determines it, are a rejection of the inferences drawn from US slavery, racism, and speciesism about how living beings may be treated.

Rose's actions crystallize and make visible the logic whereby social value is constructed, and they are thus a dramatic prolegomenon for the rest of the novel's efforts to expose the antebellum system of racial signification as arbitrary. The novel is replete with other scenes of shared suffering that emphasize the social construction of the meanings of difference, particularly of "Black" and "white." For instance, when Hannah discovers that her mistress, Mrs. Vincent, is being persecuted by the lawyer and slave speculator Mr. Trappe, who claims to have discovered that Mrs. Vincent's mother was enslaved, Hannah says, "I cannot tell why it was that I forgot that moment the disparity in our conditions, and that I approached and spoke to her as though she had been my sister or a very dear friend, but sorrow and affliction and death make us all equal."[80] Later, when she and her mistress are "manacled together" and transported as enslaved women, all distinction between them seems to break down as Hannah writes of "our meditations," "our situation," and so on.[81] Any supposedly real racial difference between the two women disappears in the face of racist persecution.

Crafts's treatment of Mr. Trappe, a lawyer who makes his living ferreting out and exploiting secret "African blood" in others, is another important depiction of how individuals, not institutions, produce racial signification in *The Bondwoman's Narrative*. This is perhaps most clear in the dramatic interview Trappe conducts with Hannah and her "formerly white" mistress. Emphasizing the legal machinations and vagaries of fate that play such a large role in Stowe's *Uncle Tom's Cabin*, Trappe suggests that both he and the two women he has purchased are "the victim[s] of circumstances."[82] "I was not accountable," and "my conscience never troubles me," Trappe assures Hannah and her mistress. "The circumstances in which I find people are not of my making. Neither are the laws that give me an advantage over them. If a beautiful women [*sic*] is to be sold it is rather the fault of the law that permits it than of me who profits by it."[83] Trappe may insist that he bears no responsibility for the conversion of free women such as Hannah's mistress into enslaved women—that it is "the fault of the law" and the market it governs—but Crafts's novel exposes this as sophistry. In *The Bondwoman's Narrative*, each individual person chooses how they treat every other individual person, and by their actions, they *make* the meaning of legal and social categories such as Black, white, human, and animal. In Trappe's behavior toward Mrs. Vincent, we witness the transformation of a "free white woman" into an enslaved Black one through an active and purposeful dehumanization: Whereas while Mrs. Vincent was "white" Trappe treated her as a human being, now that she is "Black" Trappe treats her first as "a worm beneath his feet to be crushed or preserved" and eventually "as if she were a mere machine."[84] In *The Bondwoman's Narrative*, it is this slide down the Cartesian ladder that converts Mrs. Vincent into a commodity, and it is Trappe, not any law, who engenders the fall.

Understanding Crafts's emphasis on how particular, lived encounters make the meaning of slavery and difference sheds light on some of the novel's more singular representations. For example, the novel's relatively sympathetic depictions of a benevolent slaveholder (Mrs. Henry)[85] and an "honest" slave trader[86] follow from Crafts's approach to this question, as does Hannah's dehumanizing description of the field hands on her second enslaver's estate, which begins by blaming the dehumanization on the conditions in which the enslaved laborers live: "Degradation, neglect, and ill treatment had wrought on them its legitimate effects."[87] Crafts's emphasis on the social constructedness of race might also help explain the novel's peculiar ending, in which Hannah finds such perfect acceptance and freedom in the Black community she joins in the North. Many critics have puzzled over the historical implausibility of such an ending, dissonant as it is with other contemporary descriptions of the racism and discrimination that characterized life in the North.[88] Yet the ending, however fantastical it may be, follows logically from the rest of the novel: If slavery is socially constructed, then freedom must be as well. To be treated as enslaved is to be enslaved in *The Bondwoman's Narrative*; Hannah does not say "I did not feel a slave" but rather "I *was not* a slave" when she is in the portrait gallery at Lindendale, among the portraits of her enslaver's ancestors who "[can]not enforce drudgery."[89] According to this logic, Hannah could not be truly "free" at the end of the novel if the realities of Northern racism were acknowledged.

Humans and nonhumans are not valued equally in *The Bondwoman's Narrative*; animal comparisons and acts of dehumanization are decried in the novel, and at one point Hannah is comforted by scriptural assurance that Jesus values humans more than nonhumans (though he values nonhumans, too).[90] But the difference in value between human and nonhuman lives can't license a unidirectional use relationship and cannot make even nonhumans merely killable, as Hannah demonstrates when she inquires after the fate of the slave trader as well as his horse after an accident.[91]

Crafts's novel undermines the supposed naturalness of human racial difference, and at times even species difference, even as it represents the violent uses to which such difference is put; the end result is a sophisticated, two-pronged attack on chattel slavery and the racist ideologies supporting Black oppression in the nineteenth century.[92]

Pet Keeping and Transgressive Sympathy in Our Nig

Crafts's critique of slavery and racism in *The Bondwoman's Narrative* is original and far-reaching, but because she depicts the North as a haven from slavery and racism for her heroine, she misses an opportunity to explore some of the most significant implications of her attack on racism and human exceptionalism. To understand why, it is helpful to turn to *Our Nig* (1859), an apparently autobiographical or semiautobiographical novel penned by Crafts's close contemporary Harriet Wilson. Not only in its subject matter but in its very title, Wilson's book assures us that oppressive systems of racial signification operate on both sides of the Mason-Dixon line during the antebellum period: *Our Nig; or, Sketches from the Life of a Free Black in a Two-Story White House, North. Showing That Slavery's Shadows Fall Even There. By "Our Nig."* Although Wilson depicts the childhood of a "free Black" girl in the North, the title of her book (and the "sketches" that follow) ironize the freedom of Frado, "Our Nig." Frado, a mixed-race child, grows up an indentured servant in a "two-story white house, North," in which the "stories," or narratives, that govern Black and white lives are distinct, just as in the South. This is no coincidence, since it is racism in both cases that determines the different structures of Black and white lives; Frado tells us that her mistress, Mrs. Bellmont, was "imbued with *southern* principles," which turns out to mean a conviction that "people of color" are "incapable of elevation," an expressed disbelief in Frado's possession of a Christian soul or indeed feelings, and an apparent willingness to beat, work, and starve Frado nearly to death.[93] As one of the testifying letters Wilson appends to the end of her novel puts it, despite living in the North, Frado/Wilson "was indeed a slave, in every sense of the word; and a lonely one, too."[94]

Just as Hannah was enslaved only so long as she was treated as such in *The Bondwoman's Narrative*, Frado's unfreedom is constructed by the Bellmonts' treatment of her and overshadows her legal status as a free person. The meaning of racial identity thus turns out to be socially constructed in the North as much as in the South, a dynamic *Our Nig* devotes significant space to exploring. In fact, Wilson's attention to the construction and regulation of class and race boundaries in Frado's Northern community begins on the first pages of the novel, with the story of Frado's birth.

Frado's life originates with her white mother, Mag Smith's, transgression of first the class and then the racial boundaries that are supposed to govern her choice of a marriage partner. Not understanding the class limits of her marriage prospects as an impoverished, orphaned young woman, Mag Smith is victimized by a wealthy "charmer." Although she knows his voice "sounded far above her," "it seemed like an angel's, alluring her upward and onward." Her "crime" in this first instance is that "she thought she could ascend to him and become an equal" but is instead seduced and then abandoned.[95] After her seduction, Mag lives as an outcast from the bourgeois white community, until her extreme poverty leads her to accept a Black hooper for a husband, forming a kinship bond that violates the racial limits supposed to govern her choice of partners. Ultimately, Mag develops an "insensibility" to what Katherine Bassard has called "the societal figuration of race relations," but this "insensibility" is deeply complicated in the novel. As Bassard argues, just "as we are poised to read Mag's 'insensibility' as a liberating posture . . . the familial narrative" in which Mag knowingly abandons her mixed-race child, Frado, to the racist and abusive Mrs. Bellmont reminds us that Mag can only "jettison from her consciousness racial inscriptions that assign 'norms' of sexual propriety" by also jettisoning her biracial children, since Frado and her brother "embody the painful nexus of sexuality and race" for Mag.[96]

Although Mag Smith's flouting of antebellum class and racial hierarchies in her choice of suitors liberates neither herself nor her children, it is significant that such a transgressive history gives life to Frado, since Frado's own experiences with and theories of kinship seem decidedly unconventional. After being "given away," Frado stays with the Bellmonts rather than "wander[ing] away" because "she thought she should, by remaining, be in some relation to white people she was never favored with before."[97] One year after being abandoned by her mother with the Bellmonts, Wilson's narrator tells us this relation is explicitly a familial relation: "It was now certain Frado was to become a permanent member of the family."[98] Frado's mother, Mag, was white, so it cannot be any simple family relation, however. Indeed, what the reader sees as Wilson tells Frado's story is that Frado's "permanent member[ship]" in the Bellmont family is characterized by radical inequality, abuse, and a unidirectional use relationship. To the most abusive members of the Bellmont family, Frado is human property, but even to the kindest members of the family, Jack and James, Frado seems, at best, a kind of pet. Just as Crafts gives Rose a pet dog in order to expose and critique Rose's social construction as an enslaved person and "a pet," Wilson gives Frado a pet dog, Fido, who performs a similar office. In the novel, the fourth chapter is called "A Friend for Nig," and the "friend" is Fido. Frado is given Fido after Jack Bellmont, her mistress's son, "resolved to do what he could to protect her from Mary [his sister] and his mother" and "bought her a dog."[99] How a dog can "protect" Frado from her tormentors in the Bellmont family is initially unclear, but what the reader sees is that the pet dog is a creature with whom Frado can form social ties that powerfully critique (and somewhat mitigate) her isolation.

Fido's name is an uncanny echo of Frado's, and this echo is very much to the point, since even the kindest members of the Bellmont family treat Frado as a kind of pet. Jack, for example, amuses himself with Frado's spunky antics, rewarding her for them as he might a pet dog, and in telling bits of speech, he makes Frado and a dog seem interchangeable: "'Father is a sensible man,' argued Jack. 'He would not wrong a dog. Where *is* Frado?' he continued."[100] Jack's stream-of-consciousness association between a dog his father would not wrong and Frado, the child his father has deeply wronged by failing to protect her from his wife's abuse, exposes the limits of Jack's sympathies. Even more degrading is the occasion when Mrs. Bellmont tries to compel Frado to eat her dinner from Mrs. Bellmont's dirty plate rather than taking a clean one. Subverting Mrs. Bellmont's gesture, Frado takes the plate and "call[s] Fido to wash it, which he did to the best of his ability; then, wiping her knife and fork on the cloth, she proceeded to eat her dinner."[101] Rather than be treated like a dog, fit to clean plates after the human members of the family have dined, Frado resists with a bit of roguery that casts Mrs. Bellmont lower in the chain of being even than Fido, since it takes the dog's "washing" of the plate to make it "clean" enough for Frado to eat from. In the face of such dehumanizing treatment at the hands of the Bellmont family, we might expect Wilson to depict Frado's interactions with Fido in terms that demonstrate Frado's essential difference from her pet, asserting Frado's membership in the human family by reminding readers of her absolute difference from her dog. But as with *The Bondwoman's Narrative*'s treatment of Rose and her dog's bond, Frado's friendship with Fido is taken very seriously in *Our Nig* and depicted in terms that dampen rather than assert the species difference of the friends.

To begin with, the chapter entitled "A Friend for Nig" opens with an apparently sincerely intended epigram from Byron on friendship, which reads in part, "Friendship, the dear peculiar bond of youth,/When every artless bosom throbs with truth;/Untaught by worldly wisdom how to feign;/And check each impulse with prudential reign."[102] From one per-spective, Wilson's use of this Romantic hymn to the "artless . . . truth" of youthful friendship as a frame for Frado's friendship with her pet dog is a devastating commentary on Frado's extreme isolation and loneliness. Yet the novel depicts Frado's bond with Fido as a decidedly real friendship, not a simple substitute. "These were days when Fido was the entire confidant of Frado," the reader discovers early in the chapter. "She told him her griefs as though he were human; and he sat so still, and listened so atten-tively, she really believed he knew her sorrows."[103] As with *The Bond-woman's Narrative*, Frado's conviction that her pet understands her speech and emotional state is treated seriously by the text, not dismissed as an an-thropomorphic delusion. Indeed, other members of the Bellmont family seem able to communicate with Fido as well as Frado, as when Jack "out-wits" Fido into revealing Frado's hiding spot at one point in the novel; "tak-ing a plate from the table" and calling "Fido! Fido! Frado wants some supper. Come!," Jack "trick[s]" Fido into leading him to Frado's hiding spot, something readers are assured the dog would not otherwise have done because "he will not do what his mistress [Frado] forbids him."[104]

Just as Rose's devotion to her pet was a complex assault on the social and philosophical narratives that constructed her slavery, so Fido helps bring into relief Frado's exclusion from full membership in the Bellmont family in order to critique it. This becomes clear in scenes such as the one James Bellmont, one of the few members of the Bellmont family sympa-thetic to Frado, reports witnessing to his Aunt Abby, Frado's other primary sympathizer. James tells his aunt that he has "seen Frado's grief, because she is black, amount to agony," but what James actually reports having wit-nessed is Frado grieving not over her "blackness" but over the oppressive, exploitative *treatment* she receives because she is Black. Believing she and Fido are alone in the barn, Frado sobs, "No one cares for me only to get my work. And I feel sick; who cares for that? . . . No mother, father, brother or sister to care for me . . . all because I am black! Oh, if I could die!" James's misreading of this scene is symptomatic of the novels' white characters' inability to take responsibility for their role in constructing and uphold-ing the oppressive significations of racial difference. Frado does not real-ize James is secretly watching her as she delivers this speech to "her faithful friend Fido." Yet despite his subsequent self-reported sympathy for Frado, James does not reveal himself to Frado and does nothing to comfort her— it is Fido alone whose presence and affection palliate Frado's isolation. The scene ends with Frado turning to Fido and saying, "You love me, Fido, don't you? but we must go work in the field."[105]

James misrecognizes Frado's "grief" in this scene as a lament for "her loneliness and complexion" rather than for a loneliness that is the *effect* of how her complexion signifies within the Bellmont family and the antebellum North more generally. By characterizing Frado's "agony" as a direct result of her "complexion" rather than the meaning her complexion is given by her community, James naturalizes the effects of Frado's racial identity and particularly her exclusion from full membership in the Bellmont family. This is especially true when we notice that despite holding relatively progressive views about race and "feel[ing] like grasping time till opinions change, and thousands like [Frado] rise to noble freedom," James does not help Frado herself "rise to noble freedom," even in the moment he witnesses her "crouched down by the hay" in the barn. Instead, James allows Frado to work herself sick caring for him and confines his "sympathy" for her to small words of kindness and discussions of her tragic plight in "confidential interviews" with his Aunt Abby.

If James's sympathy is implicitly critiqued for its lack of efficacy, his treatment of Frado is nevertheless better than his mother's and sister's. Mrs. Bellmont's cruelty to Frado is so extreme that her son questions whether she is not "past feeling" entirely. While racist propaganda of the antebellum period would suggest that those with "African blood" are deficient in family-feeling and affection compared with whites, it is not Frado but the white, antislavery Bellmont family who lack family-feeling and indeed sympathy. Mrs. Bellmont consistently tries to force her children to take a mercenary view of marriage, in which the forming of new families is treated as economic exchange, and in an echo of white enslavers' selling enslaved family members away from one another, Mrs. Bellmont even sells Frado's "companion and pet," Fido, at one point in the novel, although her more compassionate husband quickly buys the dog back.[106]

Far from being deficient in sympathy, "no one has a kinder heart, one capable of loving more devotedly," than Frado, as James Bellmont testifies, and Frado's friendship with her "faithful friend Fido" is one of the novel's most important proofs of it.[107] Overlooking the species difference between them, Frado treats her dog as a "faithful friend," even as she acts with sisterly devotion to the Bellmont men most kind to her, James and his younger brother Jack. Frado's sense of kinship seems unbound by race, class, and species distinctions. True to her transgressive, mixed class and race origins, Frado is capable of imagining familial relationships between not only Blacks and whites or servants and masters but humans and animals, as well, and this capacity extends beyond her beloved Fido. For instance, when Aunt Abby chides Frado for wishing the cruel Mary Bellmont would not return from a trip by reminding her Mary "is James' sister," Frado replies, "So is our cross sheep, just as much." Frado is making a joke about the temperamental affinities between Mary Bellmont and the "cross sheep," but the grammar of her remark means that she is actually suggesting that the sheep is *James*'s sister as well as Mary's, a claim about kinship that seems to privilege both temperament and proximity over biology. Frado's sympathy is not bounded by the usual anthropocentric limitations, and her loving treatment of her pet dog is ultimately an indictment of the Bellmonts' lack of sympathy with Frado and the limits of white sympathy more generally. It is finally not just the Bellmonts but whites in the North at large who fail to allow Frado and other people of color membership into their "family." In *Our Nig*, Wilson pens a biting picture of "professed abolitionists" whose anti-Black racism prevents interracial community: "Faugh! to lodge one; to eat with one; to admit one through the front door; to sit next to one; awful!"[108] Wilson's depiction of Frado's isolation and abuse in the Bellmonts' "white house, North" finally critiques not only Frado's own suffering and abuse but the plight of Blacks living and laboring unequally in the national "white house" more generally.

Radical Pet Keeping in the Anthropocene

Instead of focusing on the legal or jurisprudential elements of antebellum Black oppression, Crafts and Wilson depict the ways in which slavery and racism are socially constructed by particular people in local encounters. While slavery and racism are decried as powerful systems of injustice, the typical source of their power in *The Bondwoman's Narrative* and *Our Nig* is not primarily the Fugitive Slave Law, the Constitution, or the Declaration of Independence but the dehumanizing treatment white characters repeatedly inflict on the novels' Black characters. Crafts's and Wilson's explorations of human exceptionalism as a tool of oppression should not be mistaken for a posthumanist rejection of the human. What they are doing is closer to Sylvia Wynter's influential critique of Western European colonial conceptions of "the Human" that exclude the enslaved and the colonized from consideration[109] or to Édouard Glissant's argument for "not merely the right to difference . . . [but] a movement, referring not to Humanity but to the exultant divergence of humanities" in which "every Other is a citizen and no longer a barbarian."[110] In fact, Crafts's and Wilson's attempts to grapple with questions of justice and equality without erasing human (or even species) difference suggestively anticipate some of the key insights about community and difference put forward by twentieth- and twenty-first-century Black feminisms. Foundational theoretical insights such as Audre Lorde's assertion that "community must not mean a shedding of our differences, nor the pathetic pretense that these differences do not exist"[111] and the Combahee River Collective's claim that "if Black women were free, it would mean that everyone else would have to be free since our freedom would necessitate the destruction of all the systems of oppression"[112] are illustrated in Crafts's and Wilson's antebellum novels.[113] Additionally, Crafts's and Wilson's vignettes of community-with-difference resonate powerfully with critiques of affinity-based models of democratic community as diverse as Elizabeth Barnes's in *States of Sympathy*, Chantal Mouffe's in *Agonistics*, and Lloyd Pratt's in *The Strangers Book*.

The examples of Crafts and Wilson suggest that we should look again and more carefully at how a broad array of nineteenth-century writers contest dominant, white-supremacist visions of community. In the cases of Crafts and Wilson, their challenges to dominant, racist, and sexist forms of community take place in part through the multispecies relation of pet and pet keeper. Diana Leong has argued "that challenges to human exceptionalism should proceed through a critique of race, or we risk reorganizing old privileges ('All Lives') under new standards of being ('Matter')."[114] This is precisely the work that Crafts and Wilson are doing as they imagine community-with-difference.

In the context of the twenty-first-century anthropogenic climate crisis, the implications of Crafts's and Wilson's theorizations of community extend far beyond human community or even humans' ability to coexist with domesticated animals. As human impact has come to delimit the survival of more and more species on planet Earth, the difference between domesticated animals whose lives depend upon our care and wild animals whose lives are lived outside the sphere of human influence becomes increasingly hazy. The conservation biologist J. Michael Scott has coined the term "conservation reliance" to describe the reality that many threatened wild species increasingly depend upon intensive human management of their habitat, breeding, food sources, predators, and so on for their very survival.[115] Once-lively environmental debates about the detriments of management practices for wild animals[116] are increasingly irrelevant; Scott and his colleagues estimate that a shocking 84 percent of the species listed under the Endangered Species Act are now conservation reliant—utterly dependent on human management and care for their survival.[117] Conservation in an era of climate change will never be finished; more and more nonhuman life will become reliant on humans for survival for the foreseeable future. The journalist Jon Mooallem's *Wild Ones* explores some of what this means in practice: the choice between hand feeding polar bears or watching them starve their way into extinction;[118] the choice between letting whooping cranes pass out of existence or supporting the now multigenerational, apparently unending, and remarkably involved interspecies collaboration to perpetuate their species.[119] Mooallem argues that humans have been reluctant to face the difficult reality of our increasingly conservation-reliant world because to do so "would mean conceding that their ecosystem is irreparably broken, and that we have to be responsible for them in perpetuity, not just step in temporarily to save them. It feels too much like playing God—even if, arguably, that's exactly what we've become."[120] God—or planetary pet keepers.

We don't have to relish the idea of planetary pet keeping to explore its possible principles or payoffs. To recognize the depth of our impact on others (human and nonhuman alike) is to recognize how fully we share a world with all other life. For all its problems, the Anthropocene signals this—that human actions have global as well as local impacts and that humans in any given location are entangled with other lives (human and not) elsewhere (where they live and where they don't). In *Wildlife in the Anthropocene*, Jamie Lorimer has argued that "the popular approaches to environmentalism emerging after the diagnosis of the Anthropocene" have tended to fall into two camps: those advocating a return to Nature and those embracing the domestication of the planet. Both of these approaches are inadequate: The "dream of mastery denies nonhuman claims on the planet, whereas the return to Nature denigrates life forms emergent from and dependent on human care; there is no place for domestic and feral species in the wilderness."[121] An antianthropocentric, antiracist pet-keeping model of relating won't work everywhere or all the time. But for those cases in which it does work, it is one alternative to "domestication" that acknowledges asymmetrical power and humans' obligation to act without presuming or privileging mastery. Radical pet keeping might be a provocative model of accepting full responsibility for just and ecological community in deeply compromised circumstances. Crafts and Wilson suggest that an ethic of care might form the basis for meaningful solidarity and community-with-difference among humans and across species, even when we are not in complete control of our circumstances or in a position of power.

Ultimately, Hannah Crafts's and Harriet Wilson's novels suggest that antebellum literary explorations of difference are more rich and diverse than we have imagined. The theoretical apparatuses that have grown up around the Anthropocene, animal studies, and Black feminisms help make legible Crafts's and Wilson's radical reframing of debates about difference, kinship, race, and community. Crafts's and Wilson's critiques of the violence authorized by animalization and human exceptionalism and of failures of solidarity across differences remain, tragically, as relevant as ever. In the United States, we continue to witness the deployment of exclusionary animal tropes, and we continue to struggle for the kind of radical democracy in which recognitions of difference coexist with political and interpersonal equality. These tremendous ethical failures are intimately related to our ongoing failure to foster just and thriving biotic community as well; as Lauret Savoy and others have suggested, they have a common source.[122] Crafts and Wilson don't represent their pet–pet keeper models as ideal but as a provisional ethic that responds effectively to violently oppressive conditions. By advocating a model of sympathy that stresses interdependence rather than independence, companionship rather than self-reliance, and kinship and affiliation despite difference, Crafts and Wilson short-circuit the white-supremacist, patriarchal, anthropocentric logic that difference can and should engender oppression.

The examples of Hannah Crafts and Harriet Wilson finally suggest that we have much to gain in revisiting and recovering the full range of writers who have sought to envision alternate, more just forms of community and from thinking community in a more holistic manner. Julietta Singh has recently written of a "dehumanist solidarity," a solidarity that seeks to imagine how we might collectively survive the racial and colonial inheritances of mastery that continue to structure violence around the globe.[123] Singh argues that we can't escape or overcome mastery but that by giving mastery our serious attention we might "envisio[n] less coercive futures among human collectivities."[124] Crafts and Wilson do just that. In *The Bondwoman's Narrative* in particular, the suffering pet dog cannot understand the source of the violence being wielded against him and his mistress, yet his mistress doesn't abandon him. The two of them suffer together, although the pet keeper does not have to do so. Might the peculiar form of mastery theorized in these nineteenth-century novels about disempowered pet keepers have something to tell us about the Anthropocene and its slow planetary violence? What would it mean for those with class, racial, gender, national, species, or other forms of privilege to commit to shared suffering and to an ethic of care in the Anthropocene? In particular, a commitment by those most insulated from the suffering engendered by the Anthropocene nevertheless to share in that suffering would foster much-needed solidarity with the human and nonhuman lives who stand to sustain the greatest share of environmental devastation, though they have done the least to cause it.

Just as importantly, for those with privilege to commit to witnessing and acting against the oppressive uses to which difference is frequently put, without seeking to erase difference by taking refuge in empty professions of universalist values ("all lives matter," etc.), would be a step in the right direction. Wilson and Crafts recognize that violence is constructed nationally and politically as well as within the family and in local, domestic places between individuals. Exploitation—of all kinds of beings and bodies— operates at both of these scales, and our responses must as well. These responses will not be effective if we cannot imagine and enact more radically ethical forms of human and biotic community. Alexander Weheliye has asked, "what different modalities of the human come to light if we do not take the liberal humanist figure of Man as the master-subject but focus on how humanity has been imagined and lived by those subjects excluded from this domain?"[125] This question, so foundational for Black studies and Black feminisms, must animate not only any study of modern humanity, as Weheliye argues, but also the environmental imagination of the Anthropocene. It is hard to think an intersectional, multispecies solidarity that could operate outside of rights models. It is especially hard to think such solidarity without diminishing the extraordinary value of natural and political rights for human subjects whose unequal ability to access those rights constitutes a major source of their oppression. The multispecies ethic of care put forward by Crafts and Wilson navigates this difficult terrain and, in so doing, points to the critical significance of Black feminisms to twenty-first-century ecotheory and US environmental thought, which must continue to theorize and practice ever more ethical and capacious forms of solidarity and community with difference during the Anthropocene.

Embracing Green Temporalities: Indigenous Sustainabilities, Anglo-American Utopias

Many mainstream US environmental ethics attempting to produce a more livable future are limited by their entanglement with and perpetuation of problematic pasts. Sustainability, recycling, and preservation support visions of current social, economic, and environmental relationships and practices persisting over time, despite the responsibility borne by these relationships and practices for our increasingly dire planetary situation. Recognizing the tendencies of these paradigms to value and maintain continuity with unjust and antiecological pasts is a first step, but embracing more transformative environmental ethics must follow. Joyful frugality and radical pet keeping are ethics that address some of the limitations of recycling and preservation, respectively, but we will need many more. More fundamentally, Americans will need to wean ourselves off pastoral fantasies about supposedly greener pasts or the future perpetuation of our carbon idyll. We can do so by confronting the US past more honestly and our future more imaginatively. I would like to conclude by illustrating these points with a comparison between an Anglo-American, manufacturing-based approach to zero waste and some indigenous American approaches to the same problem. This comparison makes visible the more profound cultural work needed to transform Anglo-American environmental ethics and practices. I argue that a utopian orientation should replace sustainability as a more radical guiding paradigm for mainstream US environmentalism in this time of crisis.

Over the last twenty years, zero waste has been popularized as a more "revolutionary" environmental ethic that responds to the reality that "recycling is not enough."[1] Although it is associated with an individualistic, self-denying lifestyle, the result of its promotion by zero-waste bloggers, Instagram influencers, and documentary stunts such as *No Impact Man*, zero waste is more broadly a manufacturing-based environmental ethic in which "zero emissions/waste represents a shift from the traditional industrial model in which wastes are considered the norm, to integrated systems in which everything has its use."[2] As an ethic, zero waste emphasizes efficiency and sustainable use, laudable goals that are nevertheless easily compatible with dominant capitalist paradigms. "Manufacturing is essential for sustaining economic growth," begins one zero-waste study, foreclosing from the start any conversation about zero growth or "degrowth" economies.[3] While zero waste initially seems like an environmental challenge to the profit imperative that drives manufacturing, it turns out to be quite compatible with traditional business aims: "Zero waste can mean greater competitiveness. . . . First came productivity of labour and capital, and now comes the productivity of raw materials—producing more from less. Zero waste in industrial networks can therefore be understood as a new standard for efficiency and integration."[4] A new standard, but perhaps an old one as well, insofar as "zero waste" might plausibly characterize the late-nineteenth- and early-twentieth-century manufacturing goals depicted in *The Jungle*.

When Upton Sinclair penned *The Jungle* (1906), he certainly didn't intend to depict Chicago's meatpacking industry as a model of zero-waste sustainability. But apart from a passing mention of industrial water pollution, overall the novel's packing plants' principle to "use everything of the pig except the squeal" sounds not just economical but environmentally sustainable. From this perspective, we might also observe that Sinclair's famous descriptions of filthy industrial food are in fact accounts of companies figuring out technological fixes that allow them to repurpose (and wrest value out of) waste: "Old and crippled and diseased cattle" are "canned"; "all the old rancid butter left over in the grocery stores of a continent" are collected, "'oxidized' . . . to take away the odor, rechurned" with fresh milk, and sold again "in bricks in the cities"; and so on and so forth.[5] The "zero-waste" efficiency of the meatpacking industry is initially nothing short of miraculous to Sinclair's hero, Jurgis, who "marveled while he listened to the tale of all the things that were made out of the carcasses of animals, and of all the lesser industries that were maintained there."[6] Marvel he should; *The Jungle* several times reminds us that the industry's commitment to zero waste goes so far as to include rendering into "Durham's Pure Leaf Lard" the bodies of unlucky workers who fall into the vats.[7] Sinclair's packing plants are engaged in food-waste reduction to the extreme.

Of course, *The Jungle* is a screed against the practices it represents, not an endorsement of them. Sinclair's socialist novel decries the brutal economic exploitation of the immigrant family laboring at the center of the novel. But the fact that it's possible to highlight the "more sustainable" approach to waste characteristic of late-nineteenth- and early-twentieth-century meatpacking practices illustrates the essential compatibility of a zero-waste ethic with the most damaging aspects of industrial capitalism, what Naomi Klein has described as "extractivism": the "nonreciprocal, dominance-based relationship with the earth, one of purely taking," that destroys the planet by treating both humans and nature as commodities.[8] Environmental ethics that tinker with the effects of growth and profit imperatives but leave capitalism as a system and a worldview unexamined cannot effectively respond to our current environmental crises, including anthropogenic climate change and the profound planetary loss of biodiversity. As Paul Wapner has argued, "climate suffering is not some effect emerging from a beneficent system, but the expression of an unjust and exploitative system. Far from resulting solely *from* climate change, suffering also fundamentally *drives* it."[9] In Wapner's formulation, climate change and its unequally distributed effects are an indictment of the failures of global capitalism, "the atmospheric expression of a system of suffering."[10]

As Klein argues, extractivism "is the opposite of stewardship, which involves taking but also taking care that regeneration and future life continue."[11] How might a zero-waste ethic grounded in stewardship, care, and reciprocity with other life differ from one compatible with extractivism? Some Indigenous approaches to zero waste demonstrate one possible answer. While it is clearly impossible to generalize across so many diverse cultural contexts, Indigenous environmental scholars such as Robin Wall Kimmerer, Kyle Whyte, Melissa K. Nelson, and others have suggested that certain general principles of reciprocity run through many (though again, not all) Indigenous knowledges, rituals, and lifeways.[12] These principles are summed up by Kimmerer as principles for "the Honorable Harvest." In outlining some of the unwritten, perhaps even unspoken "guidelines" that direct many Indigenous American peoples' practices and ethics of consumption, including but not limited to those of her own Citizen Po-tawatomi Nation and Anishinaabe people more generally, Kimmerer of-fers principles that "are based on accountability to both the physical and metaphysical worlds. The taking of another life to support your own is far more significant when you recognize the beings who are harvested as per-sons, nonhuman persons vested with awareness, intelligence, spirit."[13] When Kimmerer says "persons," she does not simply mean charismatic megafauna such as moose, bison, or deer; "persons" includes plants of all varieties, "our sweet Grandmother Earth," and everything in between.[14] Unlike the Anglo-American popular cliché of Plains peoples "using every part of the buffalo," which isolates a prohibition on waste from a larger complex of principles and relationships, in Kimmerer's telling, "Never waste what you have taken" is simply one aspect of respectful use that ac-companies guidelines such as "Never take the first. Never take the last," "Take only what you need. Take only that which is given," "Never take more than half. Leave some for others," and, finally, "Harvest in a way that minimizes harm."[15] Not wasting is only one component of what it means to look at all aspects of the world as thoroughly interrelated and to live as an ethical member of Earth's community. Achieving a zero-waste ethic in a manufacturing context requires adapting manufacturing and disposal practices and perhaps even profit models; achieving a zero-waste ethic in the context of principles and lifeways expressive of reciprocity and rela-tion with an animate world understood as kin, on the other hand, would require a profound transformation of US culture.

A manufacturing-based commitment to zero waste is certainly better than no commitment at all, but such a commitment does not fundamen-tally transform an extractivist culture into a culture that understands and practices something like just, multispecies community responsibility. This might seem to signal that Anglo-American environmental culture has much to learn from Indigenous knowledges and lifeways, and it surely does.[16] For instance, Indigenous worldviews might elaborate, enrich, and complicate one of the US environmental movement's most cherished vi-sions of broad-based, ethical biotic community, Aldo Leopold's "land ethic." Leopold's land ethic is likely the single most influential Anglo-American articulation of an interrelated world; Leopold recasts "the role of *Homo sapiens* from conqueror of the land-community to plain member and citizen of it," a shift that "implies respect for his fellow-members and also respect for the community as such."[17] Since its publication in 1949, Leopold's "A Land Ethic" has been read by generations of Americans—it is routinely taught in environmentally minded classrooms at both the high school and college level—yet it has not influenced US policies or culture as tangibly as we might hope. Perhaps this is partly due to some of the limitations of Leopold's formulation. As Lauret Savoy has observed, Leopold begins his famous essay by telling the story of Odysseus's hanging "a dozen slave-girls of his household whom he suspected of misbehavior during his absence" in *The Odyssey*.[18] For Leopold, this example is meant to signal that human judgments about who and what might be considered property, and humans' ethical obligations toward "property," have evolved from what they were in the past and should continue to evolve in the present until they include entities such as nonhuman creatures and land. Yet, as Savoy observes, it is difficult to "understand why, in a book so concerned with America's past, the only reference to slavery, to human beings as property, was about ancient Greece."[19] Reading this essay as a young woman, Savoy writes that she "so feared that his 'we' and 'us' excluded me and other Americans with ancestral roots in Africa, Asia, or Native America."[20] Savoy seeks to connect environmentalism to the questions of environmental and social justice from which it is all too often isolated. She also rejects Leopold's unpublished belief that "we shall never achieve harmony with land, any more than we shall achieve justice or liberty for people. In these higher aspirations the important thing is not to achieve, but to strive."[21] In fact, theory is not enough, as Savoy reminds us: "A democratic dream of individual liberties and rights hasn't contributed to a 'co-ordinated whole'—whether human, biotic, or the land. . . . Personal responsibility and respect for others, and for the land, can still be lost to lip-service, disingenuous manners, and legislated gestures to an ideal."[22]

US environmental culture sits alongside other cultures in which interrelation and ethical responsibility have not remained a mere "democratic dream." If Leopold's land ethic is, from one perspective, "a western interpretation of Native ecology, made understandable and palatable to a dominant culture steeped in progress, boosterism, and scientific certainty," then Anglo-American environmental culture could learn much from the cultures and contexts that have actually been living forms of its most prized ethic for many centuries.[23] Yet, as Kyle Powys Whyte has argued, this learning must be more than "supplemental" to existing US environmental culture.[24] The learning must be disruptive and deep. It also must be reciprocal—Indigenous knowledges are for Indigenous peoples, and they cannot be treated as an intellectual, cultural, or spiritual treasure trove available for neocolonial plunder.[25] Reciprocity would mean at a minimum allowing Indigenous peoples to decide how and whether Indigenous knowledges should be shared; it would also mean nonindigenous peoples supporting Indigenous sovereignty and thus Indigenous land management and knowledge practices.[26]

As much as mainstream US environmental cultures might learn from Indigenous knowledges, in the context of this book, the larger point I am making is that there is a vast difference between theorizing and enacting sustainability in relation to a history riddled with settler-colonial, capitalist, white-supremacist, and utilitarian violence and theorizing and enacting sustainability in the context of *resistance* to these forms of human, nonhuman, and environmental violence. Indigenous sustainabilities (North American and otherwise) frequently draw upon noncapitalist and precolonial lifeways and traditions and have been shaped by centuries of anticapitalist, antiracist, and anticolonial struggle. It makes sense to "sustain" such cultures, since they resist rather than perpetuate the systems responsible for our environmental degradation. By contrast, Anglo-American sustainability attempts (whether consciously or unconsciously) to maintain continuity with capitalism's profit and growth imperatives, settler-colonial human violence and resource extraction, and other values and practices inimical to just and flourishing biotic community. The Anglo-American sustainability paradigm, like the individual ethics of recycling and preservation, responds to particulars of human-inflicted environmental damage without unearthing the root causes of that damage. It also remains blind to structural inequalities of the present; the twentieth century looks like a carbon-driven social idyll from a white, middle- or upper-class, settler-colonial, US perspective, but it is a site of struggle and suffering from other perspectives and can even appear downright dystopian. Whyte has written that a friend "always reminds me that Anishinaabek already inhabit what our ancestors would have understood as a dystopian future. Indeed, settler colonial campaigns in the Great Lakes region have already depleted, degraded, or irreversibly damaged the ecosystems, plants, and animals that our ancestors had local living relationships with for hundreds of years and that are the material anchors of our contemporary customs, stories, and ceremonies."[27] The decision to "sustain" the mainstream US social, economic, and environmental status quo is not ethically neutral.

We need radical action in the United States—and soon. Such action will only come from transformative environmental ethics that help us confront our past truthfully and then imagine and act for a more just, pleasurable, and ecological present and future. One of the main obstacles to confronting our past truthfully remains our mystification of that past. For those outside its grip, the historical illogic of Donald Trump's 2016 Republican presidential slogan, "Make America Great Again," is obvious. Langston

Hughes penned a poetic unmasking of the slogan's cocktail of pastoralism and white nationalism in his 1935 "Let America Be America Again," with its powerful refrain that responds to the "again" of Trump's slogan and the poem's title by insisting, "American never was America to me."[28] Hughes transforms the nationalist's "again" from a fantasy temporal referent into an idealistic commitment to transformative equality that works against the grain of the nationalism it riffs on: "O, let America be America again—/The land that never has been yet—/And yet must be—the land where *every* man is free."[29] Pastoralism crosses party lines; the same brand of naïve ahistoricism that Hughes critiques infects the Sierra Club's 2018 "Make America Green Again" T-shirt and bumper-sticker campaign.[30] Although on the surface the sticker is a tongue-in-cheek rewriting of Trump's slogan intended to signal a depth of environmental commitment that would anger some of the MAGA crowd, its "again" nevertheless rests on a destructive pastoral fantasy that there is a greener past to which the United States can return. In fact, as Hughes's poem concludes, that greener past must be *built*:

> Out of the rack and ruin of our gangster death,
> The rape and rot of graft, and stealth, and lies,
> We, the people, must redeem
> The land, the mines, the plants, the rivers.
> The mountains and the endless plain—
> All, all the stretch of these great green states—
> And make America again![31]

The green vision Hughes describes here is one of transformation, not recovery. Not only the history and culture but also the US landscape—"all the stretch of these great green states"—must be "redeem[ed]," and that redemption comes from America being remade (made again) by a more truly democratic community that refuses ahistorical myths of the past in order to embrace transformative action in the present.

If sustainability is unlikely to prompt such radical transformation, what could? In his influential *Cruising Utopia*, José Muñoz argues for a theoretical orientation he calls "a refunctioned utopianism that is predicated on a critique of the present."[32] Muñoz draws on Ernst Bloch, Theodor Adorno, C. L. R. James, and others who have argued that, as Bloch put it, "the essential function of utopia is a critique of what is present."[33] "Utopia is essentially in the determined negation of that which merely is," Adorno writes, "and by concretizing itself as something false, it always points at the same time to what should be."[34] To articulate utopia in this manner is to focus on utopia's function rather than its content or form. Ruth Levitas describes the differences of these utopian orientations. Definitions of utopia that focus on content attempt to portray a distinct vision of the "good society." According to Levitas, the drawback of this utopianism is that "definitions in terms of content tend to be evaluative and normative, specifying what the good society would be, rather than reflecting on how it may be differently perceived."[35] Definitions that privilege form are similarly limited, as they tend to limit utopia to "a description of a good society," "an ideal commonwealth," or even "a literary genre."[36]

Rather than content or form, the mode of utopian thought that might replace sustainability as a more radically transformative orientation for mainstream environmentalism is that which has explored utopia as function. This genealogy, which includes Marxist-oriented theorists such as Levitas, Bloch, and Adorno; feminist theorists such as Lucy Sargisson and Margaret Whitford; and many others, explores "utopia as that which transforms the status quo, irrespective of its form."[37] Utopia in this mode is "a catalyst of radical change,"[38] "the expression of the desire for a better way of being." Levitas's definition recognizes that "we learn a lot about the experience of living under any set of conditions by reflecting upon the desires which those conditions generate and yet leave unfulfilled."[39] Utopia as function is flexible, changing—an adaptable critique of the present that undermines the inevitability of any status quo, no matter how powerful.

The power of a functional orientation toward utopia is that it might provide the corrective to sustainability that mainstream US environmentalism, and perhaps also some environmentally oriented scholarship, so desperately needs. Our enshrined commitment to sustainability means that we remain wedded to the perpetuation (in whole or in part) of our unjust, bleak, and environmentally damaging present. A commitment to the kind of utopian orientation I have been describing is a fundamental commitment to "meantime" environmental ethics—ethics that are attuned to justice across identities and species in the present and that enact our desire for Levitas's "better way of being." Such a utopian orientation marks a fundamental commitment to the ongoing embrace of strategic, provisional ethics—including but certainly not limited to joyful frugality and radical pet keeping—that signal better possibilities for living in the present and thus the possibility of acting for more livable futures. This utopian orientation does not "blueprint and enclose the future" but rather "stretch[es] and expand[s] our understanding of the possible, thus making a multiplicity of radically different futures not only desirable but also conceivable," as Sargisson has argued.[40]

This mode of utopia is powerful because it is not static—it unfolds in the ever-changing present, "in which you are traveling and have not arrived, in which you have cause to both celebrate and fight, in which the world is always being made and never finished," as Rebecca Solnit has written.[41] Or, as the writer Eduardo Galeano once put it, "utopia is on the horizon. When I walk two steps, it takes two steps back. I walk ten steps and it is ten steps further away. What is utopia for? It is for this, for walking."[42] Stasis is ultimately the biggest sin of sustainability, recycling, preservation, and perhaps also the Anthropocene idea itself, which risks reifying the conditions of the present and thus foreclosing possibility for action and movement against our looming disasters. Stasis limits our ability to transform the status quo and relegates us, like the protagonist of Lydia Millet's *Magnificence*, to acts of mourning and commemoration—the preservation of specimens, memories, ghosts, and remnants of lost ecologies. In *Magnificence*, Susan, Millet's protagonist, responds to the manifold ecological and human crimes of Anglo-European culture by dedicating herself to a private "museum" of the taxidermied remains of its human and nonhuman victims. She sees her dedication to the "glorious museum" of remains— her willingness to "look at them every day"—as expiation for the narcissism of a generalized "humanity" that has brought on an impending apocalypse, as well as for her own more personal moral failures.[43] From the perspective of the Anthropocene, perhaps this is moral action. From a utopian orientation, however, there is something grotesque, self-defeating, and static about clutching the taxidermied remains of the dead to our collective bosom while there is more meaningful action to be taken on behalf of the living. And there is action left to take, if we can imagine that other futures are possible. If we can believe that we are traveling and have not arrived.

I accumulated a multitude of debts as this project developed; what a pleasure it is finally to get to acknowledge the time, support, community, and love that helped midwife this book into being.

Elisa Tamarkin's genius and care profoundly shaped this project, and me. Her effortless interdisciplinarity, elegant intellect, and astonishing generosity set a scholarly standard to which I can only aspire; this book could not exist without her. Brook Thomas, Jayne Lewis, and Rodrigo Lazo were all essential guides at UC Irvine, and I benefitted enormously from their early belief in my work, their mentoring, and from their substantial feedback. I am more thankful than I can say for the time that each of them took with me and for the pedagogical and scholarly lessons I learned from each. I also thank UCI and the UCI English department more generally for early, generous funding. The rich intellectual community I found at Irvine was especially enlivened by Brandon Gordon, Adam Kaiserman, Janet Neary, Leila Mansouri, Jesse Weiner, Farida Habeeb, Jason Willwerscheid, Robert Wood, Amy Parsons, Michelle Chihara, Matt Sumell, Matt Harrison, Jessica Collier, Colby Gordon, Anna Kornbluh, Shayda Hoover, Jeff Clapp, Collier Nogues, Erin McNellis, Patrick Keller, Dennis Lopez, Jonathan Tanner, Priya Shah, Jackie Way, Robin Stewart, Mia McIver, Rei Terada, Andrea Henderson, Bob Folkenflik, Jennifer Terry, Carol Burke, Michelle Latiolais, and Michael Szalay. For five years Emma Heaney was my most important interlocutor, and I remain grateful for what her friendship and fierce intelligence taught me.

At the University of Toronto, my work was generously supported by the Jackman Humanities Institute and the Andrew W. Mellon Foundation for the Humanities. The multidisciplinary community I joined as a postdoctoral fellow at the JHI transformed my scholarship, and I am immensely grateful to Jeannine DeLombard, mentor extraordinaire, and to Andrea Most, Paul Downes, Alan Bewell, Stacy Jameson, Augustine Sedgewick, Xolchitl Ruiz, Erica Kim, Gabrielle Jackson, Ila Sheren, Robyn Clark,

Robert Gibbs, Kimberley Yates, Cheryl Pasternak, Monica Toffoli, and all of the 2012–2013 JHI Fellows.

Much of this book took shape at Connecticut College, where I have found an ideal home and exceptional colleagues. In the English department, I particularly thank Julie Rivkin and Lina Wilder for their extraordinary leadership and friendship, as well as Charles Hartman, Blanche Boyd, Denis Ferhatović, and Katie Trautlein for their support. The smarts and solidarity of my fellow junior faculty writing group members Marie Ostby, Rae Gaubinger, and Hubert Cook supported me through the last stages of this project. In Environmental Studies, I thank Jane Dawson, Peter Siver, Doug Thompson, Derek Turner, and Bob Askins for their encouragement. An Elizabeth McGuire and Anthony T. Enders Endowed Fellowship, the Judith Tindal Opatrny '72 Junior Faculty Fellows Fund, a Susan Eckert Lynch '62 Faculty Research Fellowship, and a Research Matters grant have generously funded my work. Past and present Conn colleagues and friends have offered no less crucial forms of support: Rachel Black, Ariella Rotramel, Ginny Anderson, Steve Luber, Tobias Myers, Nina Papathanasopoulou, Wendy Moy, James Lee, Courtney Baker, Liz Reich, Rijuta Mehta, Simon Feldman, Natalie Avalos, Janet Gezari, Sheetal Chhabria, Karolin Machtans, Danielle Egan, Jim Downs, Anne Bernhard, Michael Reeder, Francisco Robles, Nathalie Etoke, Jennifer Pagach, and Keleigh Baretincic. I would also like to thank my fantastic students, who have worked through many of this book's ideas with me in classes; the experience of thinking with so many smart, passionate people has made this project better. Last but not least, I thank superstar Kori Rimany for her editorial assists (and her friendship).

A portion of Chapter 2 first appeared in *American Literature* (2013) 85, no. 1, under the title "Embodied Politics: Antebellum Vegetarianism and the Dietary Economy of *Walden*." I thank Priscilla Wald and the two anonymous reviewers for their revision suggestions, as well as Brook Thomas and Elisa Tamarkin. Another portion of the same chapter appeared in *The Concord Saunterer: A Journal of Thoreau Studies* as "Radical Minimalism: *Walden* in the Capitalocene" (October 2018). I'm grateful to John Kucich for his comments on that essay.

My sincere thanks to Richard Morrison, John Garza, and Robert Fellman at Fordham University Press and to the two anonymous reviewers for the press, whose careful reading and astute and generous feedback greatly improved the manuscript. Portions of the book were presented at many conferences, but colleagues at C19 and ASLE in particular provided helpful suggestions along the way. I particularly thank the unstinting colleagues who have read and commented on portions of this book over the years: James Finley, Dominic Mastroianni, Michele Navakas, Sylvan Goldberg, Monica Huerta, Liz Reich, Rijuta Mehta, Richard King, and Derek Turner. I owe an extra, profound thanks to Michele, Dominic, James, and Rijuta for their clutch proofing assistance—I am deeply in their debt. The generosity of all these colleagues, as well as that of Kristen Case, Rochelle Johnson, Teresa Goddu, Janet Neary, Ben Reiss, Cody Marrs, Cristie Ellis, Paul Hurh, Jennifer Greiman, Lance Newman, Travis Foster, Christa Holm Vogelius, and Jamie Jones makes me glad to be part of this profession. Janet Vertesi, Kim Talley, and Brandie Taylor were a strong and supportive accountability crew throughout. Steve Rogers of the Carnegie Museum of Natural History and Heidi Stover of the Smithsonian Institution Archives helped me locate the haunting image of Hornaday's bison taxidermy manikin that graces *Against Sustainability*'s cover. Madigan Haley first brought A. S. Byatt's "Sea Story" to my attention.

Michele Navakas and Dominic Mastroianni, the funniest, smartest Book Club a person could hope for, picked me up off the floor more than once. Each has made me laugh, read drafts, challenged my thinking, mailed care packages, replied to a thousand texts, and celebrated every step of this project. I am so lucky to have their friendship. My deepest thanks also to James Finley, treasured and brilliant comrade from whom I am always learning. At every juncture James offered incisive draft feedback, innumerable pom writing sessions, endless intellectual support, and profoundly generous friendship, all of which made this book so much better. My family of friends have also discussed many of these ideas with me, and their intelligence and care have seen me through: Richard Mills, Pip Morrison, Amy Rhoades, Wendy Tronrud, Stacy Jameson, Brandon Gordon, and Adam Kaiserman. Connecticut friends Nora Lynn Leech and Jac Lahav, Hima Khoshreza, Rachel Black and Doug Cook, Mariko and Jeff Moher, and George and Cynthia Willauer helped keep the process fun. S/o also to my far-flung but encouraging pals Boback and Sarah Ziaiean, Miguel DeBaca, Sarah Palestrant, Davey Hwang, Alee Karim, and Holly Brickley.

The support of the Neely, Yates, Bryant, Swanson, and Rudholm families has been legion. I especially thank Jennifer, Mike, Paxton, and Paige Bryant; Ed Yates; Dale and Penni Neely; Carol and Gary Neely; Frank, Beverly, and Jennifer Swanson; Byron Rudholm; Sue Rudholm; and Margaret and Heinz Schu. Lenora Neely Turner, Ted Turner, and Sally Yates gave so generously of their time, love, and selves from start to finish, and I am eternally grateful to have them in my corner. This book simply could not exist without their many assists, and I cannot thank them enough.

Lenora in particular has been enthusiastically supporting this work since before it began; this project was made possible by her patience, cheerleading, and decades of care.

My greatest debt and biggest thanks are to Samuel Yates, with whom I am so lucky to pull the plow. He is my life's great good fortune, my condition of possibility, and I have been orienting by his brilliance, art, work ethic, and unfailing love and support for more than twenty years. Words cannot capture all the ways he makes my work (and my life) happen. This book is for him, for everything, for always, and for Ada Wren and Reno: my world and my reason.

INTRODUCTION. THE UNLIKELY ENVIRONMENTALISMS
OF NINETEENTH-CENTURY AMERICAN LITERATURE

1. This history will be discussed in greater depth in Chapter 3.

2. Harriet Ritvo, "At the Edge of the Garden: Nature and Domestication in Eighteenth- and Nineteenth-Century Britain," *Huntington Library Quarterly* 55, no. 3 (Summer 1992): 375.

3. See, for example, Zoe Davis and Heather Todd, "On the Importance of a Date, or Decolonizing the Anthropocene," *ACME: An International Journal for Critical Geographies* 16, no. 4 (2017): 761–80; Dana Luciano, "The Inhuman Anthropocene," *Avidly: A Channel of the Los Angeles Review of Books*, March 22, 2015; Karen Pinkus, "Thinking Diverse Futures from a Carbon Present," *symploke* 21, nos. 1–2 (2013): 195–206; Jesse Oak Taylor, *The Sky of Our Manufacture: The London Fog in British Fiction from Dickens to Woolf* (Charlottesville: University of Virginia Press, 2016); Molly Wallace, *Risk Criticism: Precautionary Reading in an Age of Environmental Uncertainty* (Ann Arbor: University of Michigan Press, 2016); and Adam Trexler, *Anthropocene Fictions: The Novel in a Time of Climate Change* (Charlottesville: University of Virginia Press, 2015).

4. Timothy Clark, *Ecocriticism on the Edge: The Anthropocene as a Threshold Concept* (London: Bloomsbury, 2015), 21.

5. This strand of ecocriticism is best captured by Laurence Buell, *The Environmental Imagination: Thoreau, Nature Writing, and the Formation of American Culture* (Cambridge, MA: Belknap, 1996), which begins by developing "a rough checklist of some of the ingredients that might be said to comprise an environmentally oriented work" (7).

6. This vein of ecocriticism has become particularly rich during the last five years, as evidenced by works such as Taylor, *The Sky of Our Manufacture*; or Stephanie LeMenager, *Living Oil: Petroleum Culture in the American Century* (Oxford: Oxford University Press, 2014).

7. For a useful summary of the strategic presentism debate, see Wai Chee Dimock, "Historicism, Presentism, Futurism," *PMLA* 133, no. 2 (2018): 257–63.

8. Taylor, *The Sky of Our Manufacture*, 9.

9. Anna Kornbluh and Benjamin Morgan, "Introduction: Presentism, Form, and the Future of History," *BO2: An Online Journal*, October 4, 2016.

10. See Donna Haraway, *Staying with the Trouble: Making Kin in the Chthulucene* (Durham, NC: Duke University Press, 2016); Anna Lowenhaupt Tsing, *The Mushroom at the End of the World: On the Possibility of Life in Capitalist Ruins* (Princeton, NJ: Princeton University Press, 2015); Zoe Todd, "Commentary: The Environmental Anthropology of Settler Colonialism, Part I," *Environment and Anthropology Society Engagement Blog*, April 11, 2017; Kim TallBear, "An Indigenous Reflection on Working beyond the Human/ Not Human," *GLQ: A Journal of Lesbian and Gay Studies* 21, nos. 2–3 (June 2015): 230–35; Maria Puig de la Bellacasa, *Matters of Care: Speculative Ethics in More Than Human Worlds* (Minneapolis: University of Minnesota Press, 2017); Alexis Shotwell, *Against Purity: Living Ethically in Compromised Times* (Minneapolis: University of Minnesota Press, 2016); Timothy Morton, *Humankind: Solidarity with Nonhuman People* (London: Verso, 2017); Thom van Dooren, *Flight Ways: Life and Loss at the Edge of Extinction* (New York: Columbia University Press, 2014); Ursula Heise, *Imagining Extinction: The Cultural Meanings of Endangered Species* (Chicago: University of Chicago Press, 2016); and Andreas Malm, *The Progress of This Storm: Nature and Society in a Warming World* (London: Verso, 2018). See also Anna Lowenhaupt Tsing, Heather Swanson, Elaine Gan, and Nils Bubandt, eds., *Arts of Living on a Damaged Planet: Monsters of the Anthropocene* (Minneapolis: University of Minnesota Press, 2017).

11. Stacy Alaimo, *Exposed: Environmental Politics and Pleasures in Posthuman Times* (Minneapolis: University of Minnesota Press, 2016), "Introduction." Nicole Seymore, *Bad Environmentalism: Irony and Irreverence in the Ecological Age* (Minneapolis: University of Minnesota, 2018), 3–7.

12. Cheryll Glotfelty, "Foreword," in *Veer Ecology: A Companion for Environmental Thinking* (Minneapolis: University of Minnesota Press, 2017), viii.

13. A recent counterexample is Christine Gerhardt, *A Place for Humility: Whitman, Dickinson, and the Natural World* (Iowa City: University of Iowa Press, 2014), which explores a single environmental principle, humility, as a nineteenth-century ethic unfolded in the oeuvres of Whitman and Dickinson.

14. The definitive account remains Ramachandra Guha, "Radical Environmentalism and Wilderness Preservation: A Third World Critique" [1997], in *The Futures of Nature*, ed. Libby Robin, Sverker Sörlin, and Paul Warde (New Haven, CT: Yale University Press, 2013), 409–31. Guha argues that "the noble, apparently disinterested motives of conservation biologists

and deep ecologists fuelled a territorial ambition—the physical control of wilderness in parts of the world other than their own—that led inevitably to the displacement and harsh treatment of their human communities who dwelt in these forests" (421). Another recent, wide-ranging exploration of American environmental paradigms being exported with detrimental effects for Indigenous peoples comes in Mark Dowie's discussion of the globalization of US models of conservation, preservation, and the ideal of wilderness. Mark Dowie, *Conservation Refugees: The Hundred-Year Conflict between Global Conservation and Native Peoples* (Cambridge, MA: MIT Press, 2009), ix–xxix.

15. Jason Moore, "Name the System! Anthropocenes and the Capitalocene Alternative," http://jasonwmoore.wordpress.com, October 9, 2016. See also Jason Moore, ed., *Anthropocene or Capitalocene: Nature, History, and the Crisis of Capitalism* (Oakland: PM, 2016).

16. See Haraway, *Staying with the Trouble*, 99–103.

17. Joni Adamson, "We Have Never Been *Anthropos*," in *Environmental Humanities: Voices from the Anthropocene*, ed. Serpil Opperman and Serenella Iovino (New York: Rowman and Littlefield, 2017), 161.

18. "Trump Quiet as the UN Warns of Climate Change Catastrophe," *Guardian*, October 9, 2018.

19. Yannis A. Phillis and Luc A. Andriantiatsaholiniaina, "Sustainability: An Ill-Defined Concept and Its Assessment Using Fuzzy Logic," *Ecological Economics* 37 (2001): 435–56.

20. Mohan Munasinghe, "Exploring the Linkages between Climate Change and Sustainable Development: A Challenge for Transdisciplinary Research," *Conservation Ecology* 5, no. 1.

21. United Nations World Commission on Environment and Development, *Our Common Future* (Oxford: Oxford University Press, 1987), 43.

22. Greg Garrard, *Ecocriticism* (New York: Routledge, 2012), 56.

23. Steve Mentz, "After Sustainability," *PMLA* 127, no. 3 (May 2012): 586.

24. Raymond Williams, *The Country and the City* (Oxford: Oxford University Press, 1973), 12–20.

25. Williams, *The Country and the City*, 12.

26. Leo Marx, *The Machine in the Garden: Technology and the Pastoral Ideal in America* (1964; Oxford: Oxford University Press, 2000), 5, 3.

27. Stacy Alaimo, "Sustainable This, Sustainable That: New Materialisms, Posthumanism, and Unknown Futures," *PMLA* 127, no. 3 (2012): 559.

28. Robin Wall Kimmerer, *Braiding Sweetgrass: Indigenous Wisdom, Scientific Knowledge, and the Teachings of Plants* (Minneapolis: Milkweed Editions, 2013), 190.

29. Bill McKibben, *Eaarth: Making Life on a Tough New Planet* (New York: St. Martin's Griffin, 2010), 102.

30. Naomi Klein, *This Changes Everything: Capitalism vs. the Climate* (New York: Simon & Schuster, 2015), 1–63, 189–290.

31. John Asafu-Adjaye et al., "An Ecomodernist Manifesto," *Ecomodernism.org*, April 2015.

32. Ashley Dawson, "Biocapitalism and Deextinction," in *After Extinction*, ed. Richard Grusin (Minneapolis: University of Minnesota Press, 2018), 182.

33. Robert Kenner, Elise Pearlstein, and Kim Roberts, *Food, Inc.*, dir. Robert Kenner (New York: Magnolia Pictures, 2008).

34. Michael Newbury, "Fast Zombie/Slow Zombie: Food Writing, Horror Movies, and Agribusiness Apocalypse," *American Literary History* 24, no. 1 (Spring 2012): 97, 96.

35. See Michael Pollan, *The Omnivore's Dilemma: A Natural History of Four Meals* (New York: Penguin, 2011); Eric Schlosser, *Fast Food Nation: The Dark Side of the All-American Meal*, rev. ed. (New York: Mariner Books, 2012); Mark Bittman, *A Bone to Pick: The Good and Bad News about Food, with Wisdom and Advice on Diets, Food Safety, GMOs, Farming, and More* (New York: Clarkson Potter, 2015); Jonathan Safran Foer, *Eating Animals* (New York: Little, Brown, 2009). Pollan explicitly calls the alternative to industrial food "the pastoral food chain," and although he is clear that he is describing "food chains that might appear to be preindustrial but in surprising ways turn out to be postindustrial," he leaves intact the notion that eating and agriculture was more wholesome and ethical before and during the lives of "our grandparents." Pollan, *The Omnivore's Dilemma*, 8. Foer pushes the shift to "two generations ago" or 1923, and he does devote two paragraphs to nineteenth century "early industrial" developments. Foer, *Eating Animals* 59, 104, 103–4.

36. Graham blames superfine white flour for the "habitual costiveness or diarrhea" that he claims "nine-tenths of the adults, and nearly as large a proportion of youth" suffer from in the antebellum United States. Sylvester Graham, *Lectures on the Science of Human Life* (New York: Fowler & Wells, 1839), 525.

37. Graham, *The Science of Human Life*, 524.

38. Graham, *The Science of Human Life*, 507.

39. Graham, *The Science of Human Life*, 498.

40. "Cows," *Connecticut Mirror*, July 12, 1824. The item was also published in newspapers across Massachusetts, New York, and Pennsylvania throughout July 1824.

41. For instance, see "A Machine for Milking Cows!" reprinted from the New York *Geneva Gazette* in *The Globe* (Washington, DC), Monday, August 5, 1833, issue 45; or "Milking Cows," in the *Rochester American*, reprinted in

Ohio's *Daily Scioto Gazette*, Friday, September 13, 1850, issue 242. That these anecdotes were being reported and reprinted throughout the Northeast, South, and Midwest testifies to their broad interest.

42. "At the Exhibition at Topsfield, Mass," *National Advocate*, November 10, 1824.

43. "Hog Slaughter in Cincinnati." *Pensacola Gazette*, issue 47 (February 23, 1839).

44. James E. McWilliams, *A Revolution in Eating: How the Quest for Food Shaped America* (New York: Columbia University Press, 2005), 73–81; Keith Stavley and Kathleen Fitzgerald, *America's Founding Food: The Story of New England Cooking* (Chapel Hill: University of North Carolina Press, 2004), 178–80.

45. Karen J. Friedmann, "Victualling Colonial Boston," *Agricultural History* 47, no. 3 (July 1973): 191.

46. Bernarde Oreste Unti, "The Quality of Mercy: Organized Animal Protection in the United States, 1866–1930," PhD diss., American University, 2002, 15–18. See also Keith Thomas, *Man and the Natural World: Changing Attitudes in England, 1500–1800* (London: Penguin, 1984), 189.

47. Stavely and Fitzgerald, *America's Founding Food*, 178–80.

48. Jacklyn Cock, "'Green Capitalism' or Environmental Justice? A Critique of the Sustainability Discourse," *Focus* 63 (November 2011): 48, 45.

1. RECYCLING FANTASIES: WHITMAN, CLIFTON, AND THE DREAM OF COMPOST

1. See, for instance, Lydia Maria Child, *The American Frugal Housewife: Dedicated to Those Who Are Not Ashamed of Economy*, 12th ed. (Boston: Carter, Hendee & Co., 1833), which begins with a section on "Odd Scraps for the Economical": "If you would avoid waste in your family, attend to the following rules, and do not despise them because they appear so unimportant: 'many a little makes a mickle'" (8). Child's influential book will be explored in detail in the next chapter.

2. Susan Strasser, *Waste and Want: A Social History of Trash* (New York: Henry Holt, 2000), 13.

3. Herman Melville, "The Paradise of Bachelors and the Tartarus of Maids," in *Tales, Poems, and Other Writings*, ed. John Bryant (New York: Modern Library, 2002), 159.

4. On e-waste, see Daniel Powell, "Finding Solutions to China's E-waste Problem," *Our World*, April 8, 2013; and Ivan Watson, "China: The Electronic Wastebasket of the World," *CNN*, May 30, 2013. On recycling batteries, see Elisabeth Rosenthal, "Lead from Old U.S. Batteries Sent to

Mexico Raises Risks," *New York Times*, December 8, 2011. On recycling clothing, see Max Bearak and David Lynch, "African Nations Are Fed Up with the West's Hand-Me-Downs. But It's Tough to Keep Them Out," *Washington Post*, May 29, 2018.

5. Dan Cancian, "Malaysia Has Started Returning Tons of Trash to the West: We Will Not Be the Dumping Ground of the World," *Newsweek*, May 28, 2019; Brittany Shoot, "China's Ban on Imported Recyclables Is Drowning U.S. Cities in Trash," *Fortune.com*, March 20, 2019.

6. Oliver Milman, "Since China's Ban, Recycling in the U.S. Has Gone Up in Flames," *Wired.com*, February 27, 2019.

7. See Susan Strasser, *Waste and Want: A Social History of Trash* (New York: Henry Holt, 2000), 229–63, 283–86, 290–93.

8. See Margaret W. Rossiter, *The Emergence of Agricultural Science: Justus Liebig and the Americans, 1840–1880* (New Haven, CT: Yale University Press, 1975), 14–22.

9. Rossiter, *The Emergence of Agricultural Science*, 35.

10. Walt Whitman, *Leaves of Grass: The First (1855) Edition* (New York: Penguin, 2005), ll. 101, 112–13.

11. Whitman, *Leaves of Grass 1855*, ll. 116–17.

12. David Reynolds, *Walt Whitman's America: A Cultural Biography* (New York: Knopf, 1995), 236–46. For a more detailed history of Liebig's influence in the United States, see Rossiter, *The Emergence of Agricultural Science*.

13. "Books," *Brooklyn Daily Eagle*, 2.

14. Mark Noble, "Whitman's Atom and the Crisis of Materiality in the Early *Leaves of Grass*," *American Literature* 81, no. 2 (June 2009): 253.

15. Paul Outka, "(De)composing Whitman," *Interdisciplinary Studies in Literature and Environment* 12, no. 1 (Winter 2005): 48.

16. M. Jimmie Killingsworth, *Walt Whitman and the Earth: A Study in Ecopoetics* (Iowa City: University of Iowa Press, 2004), 83.

17. Maria McFarland, "Decomposing City: Walt Whitman's New York and the Science of Life and Death," *ELH* 74, no. 4 (Winter 2007): 812.

18. Serpil Oppermann, "Compost," in *Veer Ecology: A Companion for Environmental Thinking*, ed. Jeffrey Jerome Cohen and Lowell Duckert (Minneapolis: University of Minnesota Press, 2017), 143.

19. Outka helpfully details the terms and implications of ecocriticism's relative disinterest in Whitman in the introduction to "(De)composing Whitman."

20. Lawrence Buell claims Whitman as a poet of urban environmental space in *Writing for an Endangered World: Literature, Culture, and Environment in the U.S.* (Cambridge, MA: Harvard University Press, 2001), while M. Jimmie Killingsworth has explored Whitman as a Long Island poet in

Walt Whitman and the Earth. Christine Gerhardt has recently traced Whitman's exploration of "nature's place in larger cultural communities" ranging from the local to the regional to the global in *A Place for Humility: Whitman, Dickinson, and the Natural World* (Iowa City: University of Iowa Press, 2014), 23; and M. Wynn Thomas explores the relationship between Whitman's conceptions of weather and his account of the progress of the Civil War in "Weathering the Storm: Whitman and the Civil War," *Walt Whitman Quarterly Review* 15, no. 2 (Fall 1997): 87–109. A number of ecocritics have taken up Whitman's prose, most notably *Specimen Days,* as for instance Daniel J. Philippon, "'I Only Seek to Put You in Rapport': Message and Method in Walt Whitman's *Specimen Days,*" in *Reading the Earth: New Directions in the Study of Literature and the Environment,* ed. Michael P. Branch et al. (Moscow: University of Idaho Press, 1998), 179–93.

21. Outka, "(De)composing Whitman," and McFarland, "Decomposing City," center compost in their evaluations of Whitman as an environmental poet. Killingsworth, *Walt Whitman and the Earth,* 83–84, and Gerhardt, *A Place for Humility,* 139–40, both treat "This Compost." See also Jed Rasula, *This Compost: Ecological Imperatives in American Poetry* (Athens: University of Georgia Press, 2002), 57–59.

22. *Walt Whitman: The Contemporary Reviews,* ed. Kenneth Price (Cambridge: Cambridge University Press, 1996), 8.

23. Angus Fletcher has argued that Whitman's poems are "not *about* the environment . . . they *are* environments." *A New Theory for American Poetry: Democracy, the Environment, and the Future of the Imagination* (Cambridge, MA: Harvard University Press, 2004). 103.

24. Madhav Gadgil and Ramachandra Guha, *Ecology and Equity: The Use and Abuse of Nature in Contemporary India* (New York: Routledge, 1995), 177–78.

25. Oppermann, "Compost."

26. Donna Haraway, *Staying with the Trouble: Making Kin in the Chthulucene* (Durham, NC: Duke University Press, 2016), 143.

27. Whitman, *Leaves of Grass 1855,* ll. 499–500, 524.

28. Whitman, *Leaves of Grass 1855,* ll. 1059, 1066.

29. Whitman, *Leaves of Grass 1855,* l. 361.

30. Whitman, *Leaves of Grass 1855,* ll. 1222–23.

31. Whitman, *Leaves of Grass 1855,* l. 826.

32. Whitman, *Leaves of Grass 1855,* l. 1080.

33. Harold Aspiz, *Walt Whitman and the Body Beautiful* (Urbana: University of Illinois Press, 1980), 49.

34. Aspiz, *Walt Whitman and the Body Beautiful,* 50.

35. Zachary Turpin, "Introduction to Walt Whitman's 'Manly Health and Training,'" *Walt Whitman Quarterly Review* 33, no. 3 (Spring 2016): 147–83.

36. Aspiz, *Walt Whitman and the Body Beautiful*, 51.

37. Ivy G. Wilson, "Organic Compacts, Form, and the Cultural Logic of Cohesion; or, Whitman Re-Bound," *ESQ* 54 (2008): 199–215.

38. Sean Ross Meeham, "'Nature's Stomach': Emerson, Whitman, and the Poetics of Digestion," *Walt Whitman Quarterly Review* 28, no. 3 (2011): 97–121, has argued that Whitman took his trope of "intellectual digestion" from Emerson; it seems likely that Thoreau took his, at least in part, from the same source, though the metaphor is older and more widespread than any of these figures.

39. M. Jimmie Killingsworth, *Whitman's Poetry of the Body: Sexuality, Politics, and the Text* (Chapel Hill: University of North Carolina Press, 1989), 8.

40. See Michelle C. Neely, "Embodied Politics: Antebellum Vegetarianism and the Dietary Economy of *Walden*," *American Literature* 85, no. 1 (2013): 33–60.

41. Walt Whitman [Mose Velsor, pseud.], "Manly Health and Training, with Off-Hand Hints toward Their Conditions," ed. Zachary Turpin, *Walt Whitman Quarterly Review* 33, no. 3 (2016): 190.

42. Walt Whitman, "The Eighteenth Presidency!" in *Walt Whitman: Complete Poetry and Collected Prose*, ed. Justin Kaplan (New York: Library of America, 1982), 1307.

43. Mark Maslan, *Whitman Possessed: Poetry, Sexuality, and Popular Authority* (Baltimore, MD: Johns Hopkins University Press, 2001), 143.

44. Whitman, *Leaves of Grass 1855*, l. 324.

45. Wilson, "Organic Compacts," 202.

46. The definitive treatment of Whitman's "radical egalitarianism and sympathy for blacks" remains Martin Klammer, *Whitman, Slavery, and the Emergence of Leaves of Grass* (University Park: Pennsylvania State University Press, 1995), 85. The more recent insistence of Rasula, *This Compost*, on the distinction between the antebellum Whitman as more radical than the postbellum celebrant of imperialism (53–56) is also typical in finding that "in its first fire Whitman's verse was magnificently tropic, a crisp, biodegradable composition of the States (not yet 'United' but cosmically chaotic) into a demonized poetic topos; a body of work that might have as its most fitting epigraph . . . 'This Compost'" (57). Most recently, Cristin Ellis has offered a more complicated account of Whitman's "egalitarian ethos," in which "the processual becomings of our permeable bodies blur the distinction between entities." Ellis concludes that this egalitarianism is finally

"politically inert," a conclusion I agree with, but I would argue that what Ellis calls the egalitarian "nonhumanism" of Whitman's representation of an enslaved person's body at auction does not fully account for his more overtly racist characterizations of Black bodies elsewhere. Cristin Ellis, *Antebellum Posthuman: Race and Materiality in the Mid–Nineteenth Century* (New York: Fordham University Press, 2018), 131–32.

47. See Aspiz, *Walt Whitman and the Body Beautiful*, chaps. 6–7. Dana Phillips, "Nineteenth-Century Racial Thought and Whitman's 'Democratic Ethnology of the Future,'" *Nineteenth-Century Literature* 49, no. 3 (December 1994): 289–320, also discusses Whitman's poetry and thought in the context of the scientific racism of the period, though Phillips's focus is primarily "Salut au Monde!"

48. Kirsten Silva Gruesz, *Ambassadors of Culture: The Transamerican Origins of Latino Writing* (Princeton, NJ: Princeton University Press, 2002), 121–36, powerfully demonstrates that by focusing exclusively on Whitman's representations of Black figures, we are missing a great deal of the picture of his vision of race, freedom, and Manifest Destiny. I choose nevertheless to focus on these famous passages because they have proven so galvanizing to Whitman criticism arguing for the 1855 edition's egalitarianism.

49. Whitman, *Leaves of Grass 1855*, ll. 183–85.

50. Whitman, *Leaves of Grass 1855*, ll. 185, 189.

51. Whitman, *Leaves of Grass 1855*, ll. 168–82.

52. Whitman, *Leaves of Grass 1855*, ll. 188, 192.

53. Donna Haraway, *When Species Meet* (Minneapolis: University of Minnesota Press, 2007), 17.

54. Gruesz, *Ambassadors of Culture*, 131–32, building on Karen Sánchez-Eppler, "'To Stand Between': A Political Perspective on Whitman's Poetics of Merger and Embodiment," *ELH* 56, no. 4 (Winter 1989): 923–49; and Karen Sánchez-Eppler, *Touching Liberty: Abolition, Feminism, and the Politics of the Body* (Berkeley: University of California Press, 1993), explores the question of political, economic, and erotic "consent" and "consensual relations" in relation to enslaved bodies and Latin American territory.

55. Klammer, *Whitman, Slavery, and the Emergence of Leaves of Grass*, 123.

56. Saidiya Hartman, *Scenes of Subjection: Terror, Slavery, and Self-Making in Nineteenth-Century America* (Oxford: Oxford University Press, 1997), 19. See also Elizabeth B. Clark, "'The Sacred Rights of the Weak': Pain, Sympathy, and the Culture of Individual Rights in Antebellum America," *Journal of American History* 82, no. 2 (September 1995): 463–93. By contrast, Jane Bennett, "Whitman's Sympathies," *Political Research Quarterly* 69, no. 3 (September 2016): 607, 616, has argued that Whitman's sympathy is a "more-than-human natural force" that allows it to transcend the limits of

sympathy based on "identification." Ellis, *Antebellum Posthuman*, 197n79, builds on Bennett's reading when she argues for Whitman's "antiracist egalitarianism" on the basis of his commitment to "an embodied ontology." While I find that new materialist and posthumanist readings such as Bennett's and Ellis's helpfully illuminate key facets of Whitman's approach to embodiment, I do not agree that they support an "antiracist egalitarianism" in Whitman's work, for the complicated reasons I argue in this chapter and for the simple reason that Whitman's "wonder of interconnected being" (Ellis, *Antebellum Posthuman*, 131) coexists so comfortably with his overtly racist representations of Black bodies, as in "Ethiopia Saluting the Colors."

57. Whitman, *Leaves of Grass 1855*, ll. 219–20.

58. Whitman, *Leaves of Grass 1855*, ll. 220–23.

59. Sánchez-Eppler, *Touching Liberty*, 55–56.

60. Whitman, *Leaves of Grass 1855*, ll. 224–25.

61. Outka's engaging and complex argument for Whitman's poetry's ability to transcend Whitman's personal racism depends upon a reading of these two scenes that highlights the adjacency of the positive portraits of white bodies. Outka does not mention the also-adjacent portraits of nonhuman animal bodies. Paul Outka, "Whitman and Race ('He's Unclear, He's Queer, Get Used to It')," *Journal of American Studies* 36, no. 2 (August 2002): 293–318. The dehumanizing linkage in nineteenth-century US racist thought between Black bodies and nonhuman animals will be discussed at length in Chapter 4.

62. See James Turner, *Reckoning with the Beast: Animals, Pain, and Humanity in the Victorian Mind* (Baltimore, MD: Johns Hopkins University Press, 1980), 175–91; or Katherine C. Grier, *Pets in America: A History* (New York: Harcourt, 2006), 160–200.

63. Whitman, *Leaves of Grass 1855*, ll. 389–90.

64. Whitman, *Leaves of Grass 1855*, ll. 161, 160–67.

65. Whitman, *Leaves of Grass 1855*, l. 228.

66. Whitman, *Leaves of Grass 1855*, ll. 684, 686–91, 693.

67. Clara Endicott Sears, *Bronson Alcott's Fruitlands* (Bedford, MA: Applewood, 2004), 130.

68. Whitman, *Leaves of Grass 1855*, ll. 826–27.

69. Whitman, *Leaves of Grass 1855*, ll. 833.

70. Whitman, *Leaves of Grass 1855*, ll. 841.

71. D. H. Lawrence, *Studies in Classic American Literature* (New York: Thomas Selzter, 1923), 259.

72. Whitman, *Leaves of Grass 1855*, ll. 98–100.

73. Outka, "(De)composing Whitman," 47, reads the operation of the grass very differently, arguing that "especially in 1855, for the hieroglyph/

grass to '*mean*' 'sprouting alike . . .' or 'growing among . . .' is to undo
definition as much as to specify it, to understand the grass ecosystemically,
as an interconnecting green force that joins what is separate, that undoes
the rigid human constructions of race and place that brought the nation to
civil war."

74. Whitman, *Leaves of Grass 1855*, ll. 372–75.

75. Walt Whitman, *Leaves of Grass: A Textual Variorum of the Printed
Poems*, vol. 1: *Poems, 1855–1856*, ed. Sculley Bradley, Harold W. Blodgett,
Arthur Golden, and William White (New York: New York University Press,
1980), l. 372. Hereafter cited as *Leaves of Grass 1856*.

76. If they don't center on the scenes of sympathy themselves, claims that
Whitman's poetics *do* resituate Black bodies on equal ground with whites, at
least within the poetic republic of the 1855 *Leaves of Grass*, generally rest on
the structure of Whitman's poetic catalogues. Betsy Erkkila, *Whitman the
Political Poet* (Oxford: Oxford University Press, 1989), 98, offers a complicated formulation of the radical grammar of *Leaves of Grass*, in which "the
conjunctive *and* . . . serves both to separate and link persons and objects in a
single nonhierarchical plane" as an "egalitarian vision of a world linked as
one loving family." Yet as Erkkila notes, "for all their poetic democracy,
Whitman's catalogues could operate paradoxically as a kind of formal
tyranny, muting the fact of inequality, race conflict, and radical difference
within a rhetorical economy of many and one" (102). This is especially true
because Whitman's conjunctive strategy never fundamentally reorders the
power relations the speaker inevitably imports along with his dialectically
opposed subjects (I am of the master as much as the slave) so much as the
strategy pretends that such power relations do not exist in the hypernatural
space of the poem. As Sánchez-Eppler, "Whitman's Poetics of Merger and
Embodiment," 924, has argued, despite Whitman's "ideals of merger and of
bodily specificity," his "poetry must remain contingent upon the very
divisions it claims to heal."

77. Whitman, Leaves of Grass 1855, 13.

78. Whitman, *Leaves of Grass 1855*, l. 48.

79. Whitman, *Leaves of Grass 1855*, l. 470.

80. Whitman, *Leaves of Grass 1855*, l. 84.

81. Whitman, "The Eighteenth Presidency!" 1311.

82. Whitman, *Leaves of Grass 1855*, l. 226.

83. Whitman, *Leaves of Grass 1855*, l. 404.

84. Whitman, *Leaves of Grass 1855*, ll. 506, 504–5.

85. Whitman, *Leaves of Grass 1855*, l. 1240.

86. Whitman, *Leaves of Grass 1855*, ll. 1327–33.

87. Reynolds, *Walt Whitman's America*, 240.

88. Whitman, *Leaves of Grass 1855*, ll. 102, 103, 105.

89. Whitman, *Leaves of Grass 1855*, l. 585.

90. Whitman, *Leaves of Grass 1855*, ll. 1285, 1308.

91. Whitman, *Leaves of Grass 1856*, line 31.

92. Whitman, *Leaves of Grass 1856*, l. 1.

93. Whitman, *Leaves of Grass 1856*, ll. 5, 6, 8, 9–12.

94. Whitman, *Leaves of Grass 1856*, ll. 32, 37.

95. Whitman, *Leaves of Grass 1856*, ll. 44, 47.

96. Qtd. in McFarland, "Decomposing City," 810.

97. Qtd. in Aaron Sachs, *Arcadian America: The Death and Life of an Environmental Tradition* (New Haven, CT: Yale University Press, 2013), 31.

98. Whitman, *Leaves of Grass 1856*, ll. 1288–89.

99. Whitman, *Leaves of Grass 1856*, ll. 799, 801–2.

100. See Killingsworth, *Walt Whitman and the Earth*; and Gerhardt, *A Place for Humility*.

101. Quoted in a footnote to Walt Whitman, "Song of the Redwood Tree," in *Leaves of Grass and Other Writings*, ed. Michael Moon (New York: Norton, 2002), 173.

102. Whitman, "Song of the Redwood Tree," l. 53.

103. Whitman, "Song of the Redwood Tree," ll. 87–90.

104. Whitman, "Song of the Redwood Tree," ll. 102–5.

105. Keith Thomas, *Man and the Natural World: Changing Attitudes in England, 1500–1800* (London: Penguin, 1984), 17–50.

106. William Carlos Williams, "The Bare Tree," in *Selected Poems*, ed. Charles Tomlinson (New York: New Directions, 1985), 157.

107. Jacques Derrida, "'Eating Well,' or the Calculation of the Subject," in *Points . . . Interviews, 1974–1994*, ed. Elisabeth Weber, trans. Peggy Kamuf et al. (Stanford, CA: Stanford University Press, 1995), 282–83.

108. Whitman, *Leaves of Grass 1856*, line 47.

109. Phillip Larkin, "The Trees," in *Collected Poems*, ed. Anthony Thwaite (New York: Noonday, 1993), 124, ll.1–2, 4.

110. Larkin, "The Trees," ll. 5–6.

111. Larkin, "The Trees," ll. 7–8.

112. While Whitman's influence on Clifton is obvious and generally acknowledged, it has only received sustained consideration in the context of Clifton's incorporation of epigraphs from "Song of Myself" in her 1976 memoir *Generations*. Edward Whitley, "'A Long Missing Part of Itself': Bringing Lucille Clifton's *Generations* into American Literature," *MELUS* 26, no. 2 (Summer 2001): 47–64.

113. Emily Lordi situates Clifton's "grief" in relation to a broader elegiac mode in Clifton's poetry that Lordi argues "create[s] an elastic black

community" that "comprises 'murdered sons' as well as imagined future members." Emily J. Lordi, "'[B]lack and Going on Women': Lucille Clifton, Elizabeth Alexander, and the Poetry of Grief," *Palimpsest: A Journal on Women, Gender, and the Black International* 6, no. 1 (2017): 45.

114. Lucille Clifton, "grief," in *The Collected Poems of Lucille Clifton, 1965–2010*, ed. Kevin Young and Michael S. Glaser (Rochester, NY: BOA Editions, 2012), 562.

115. Clifton, "grief," ll. 38–39.

116. Clifton, "grief," ll. 1–2.

117. Clifton, "grief," ll. 2–4.

118. Clifton, "grief," ll. 13–16.

119. Clifton, "grief," ll. 20–22.

120. Jennifer C. James, "Ecomelancholia: Slavery, War, and Black Ecological Imaginings," in *Environmental Criticism for the Twenty-First Century*, ed. Stephanie LeMenager, Teresa Shewry, and Ken Hiltner (New York: Routledge, 2011), 166–67. James's suggestive formulation goes on to argue that "Freud borrowed capitalist theories of human consumption to structure his concept of mourning" (166) and to read Lucille Clifton's work through the lens of ecomelancholia.

121. Clifton, "grief," ll. 33–35.

122. Lucille Clifton, "the message from the Ones (received in the late 70s)," in *The Collected Poems of Lucille Clifton*, 630, ll. 1–14.

123. Whitman, *Leaves of Grass 1856*, ll. 11, 21, 23.

124. Lucille Clifton, "mulberry fields," in *The Collected Poems of Lucille Clifton*, 582, l. 31. The title contains a suggestive echo of Whitman's lines in "Poem of Wonder at the Resurrection of the Wheat": "The resurrection of the wheat appears with pale visage out of its graves,/The tinge awakes over the willow-tree and the mulberry-tree." Whitman, *Leaves of Grass 1856*, ll. 24–25.

125. Clifton, "mulberry fields," ll. 1–3.

126. Clifton, "mulberry fields," ll. 6–7.

127. Clifton, "mulberry fields," l. 8.

128. Clifton, "mulberry fields," ll. 15–17.

129. Lucille Clifton, "won't you celebrate with me," in *The Collected Poems of Lucille Clifton*, 427.

130. Whitman, *Leaves of Grass 1856*, ll. 1–2.

131. Clifton, "won't you celebrate with me," l. 5.

132. Clifton, "won't you celebrate with me," ll. 6–7.

133. Clifton, "won't you celebrate with me," ll. 12–14.

134. Clifton, "won't you celebrate with me," ll. 10–12.

135. Clifton, "what has been made," in *The Collected Poems of Lucille Clifton*, 632, ll. 1–2.

136. Jane Hirshfield, "Optimism," in *The Ecopoetry Anthology*, ed. Ann Fisher-Worth and Laura-Gray Street (San Antonio, TX: Trinity University Press, 2013), 329.

137. Clifton, "what has been made," l. 9.

138. Clifton, "what has been made," ll. 10–11.

139. Whitman, *Leaves of Grass 1855*, l. 121.

140. Haraway, *Staying with the Trouble*, 143.

141. Haraway, *Staying with the Trouble*, 150.

142. Whitman, *Leaves of Grass 1855*, ll. 1331–33.

143. Langston Hughes, *The Collected Poems of Langston Hughes*, ed. Arnold Rampersad and David Rossel (New York: Vintage, 1995), 46, 547–48.

144. George B. Hutchinson, "The Whitman Legacy and the Harlem Renaissance," in *Walt Whitman: The Centennial Essays*, ed. Ed Folsom (Iowa City: University of Iowa Press, 1994), 212–13.

2. JOYFUL FRUGALITY: THOREAU, DICKINSON, AND THE PLEASURES OF NOT CONSUMING

1. Nathaniel Hawthorne, "Earth's Holocaust," *Graham's Lady's and Gentleman's Magazine (1843–1844)* 25, no. 5 (May 1844): 193.

2. Hawthorne, "Earth's Holocaust," 195, 195, 193, 195.

3. Hawthorne, "Earth's Holocaust," 200.

4. Frederic Jameson, "Future City," *New Left Review* 21 (May–June 2003): 76, attributes this remark to an unnamed "somebody."

5. Karl Marx, *Capital*, vol. 1. [1867], trans. Ben Fowkes (New York: Penguin, 1992), 742.

6. Alexis Shotwell's commitment to "thinking about complicity and compromise as a starting point for action" is particularly relevant here, as is Donna Haraway's career-long, "no-nonsense commitment to faithful accounts of a 'real' world," or what Haraway has more recently characterized as "staying with the trouble." Alexis Shotwell, *Against Purity: Living Ethically in Compromised Times* (Minneapolis: University of Minnesota Press, 2016), 5; Donna Haraway, *Simians, Cyborgs, and Women: The Re-Invention of Nature* (New York: Routledge, 1991), 187; Donna Haraway, *Staying with the Trouble: Making Kin in the Chthulucene* (Durham, NC: Duke University Press, 2016), 1. Susan Wendell's critique of self-sufficiency as an ableist fantasy in *The Rejected Body: Feminist Philosophical Reflections on Disability* (New York: Routledge, 1996) is also helpful here. While antebellum frugality was bound up with a valorization of self-sufficiency, I am arguing in this chapter for a "joyful frugality" that disentangles happiness from consumerism and is an ethical paradigm precisely because it recognizes entanglement and interdependence.

7. Joyce Appleby, "Moderation in the First Era of Popular Consumption," in *Thrift and Thriving in America: Capitalism and the Moral Order from the Puritans to the Present*, ed. Joshua J. Yates and James Davidson Hunter (New York: Oxford University Press, 2011), 139–59.

8. "As late as 1800, 85 percent of America's manufactured goods were produced in the household, and the bulk of these goods was consumed either by the family that made them or by a neighboring household in the same community. But by the 1830s, this figure had been reduced dramatically. For many people, within a single generation, the household had ceased to be the basic unit of production." Stephen Nissenbaum, *Sex, Diet, and Debility in Jacksonian America: Sylvester Graham and Health Reform* (Westport, CT: Greenwood, 1980), 4.

9. R. Douglas Hurt, *American Agriculture: A Brief History*, rev. ed. (West Lafayette, IN: Purdue University Press, 2002), 72.

10. Jürgen Habermas, *The Structural Transformation of the Public Sphere: An Inquiry into a Category of Bourgeois Society*, 1st MIT Press paperback ed. (Cambridge, MA: MIT Press, 1991), 3.

11. Hurt, *American Agriculture*, 73, 117.

12. Hurt, *American Agriculture*, 73.

13. Jefferson, quoted in Hurt, *American Agriculture*, 50.

14. Hurt, *American Agriculture*, 48–54.

15. As Habermas, Michael McKeon, and others have shown, a sense of privacy and market detachment came to characterize the *intimsphäre* of the conjugal family home during the eighteenth century. Habermas, *The Structural Transformation of the Public Sphere*, 28–29; Michael McKeon, *The Secret History of Domesticity: Public, Private, and the Division of Knowledge* (Baltimore, MD: Johns Hopkins University Press, 2005), part 1.

16. See Linda Kerber, "The Republican Mother: Women and the Enlightenment—An American Perspective," *American Quarterly* 28, no. 2 (Summer 1976): 187–205.

17. Lydia Maria Child, *The American Frugal Housewife: Dedicated to Those Who Are Not Ashamed of Economy*, 12th ed. (Boston: Carter, Hendee & Co., 1833), 89, 4–5, 108.

18. According to Jeanne Boydston, through the middle of the nineteenth century, working-class wages typically remained low, and it was only the wife's unpaid household labor that elevated them above subsistence level. Similarly, Boydston argues that middle-class salaried incomes needed the supplement of unpaid household labor in the form of a competent housewife in order to provide the surplus that translated into financial security from the vicissitudes of capitalism. Jeanne Boydston, *Home and Work: Housework, Wages, and the Ideology of Labor in the Early*

Republic (New York: Oxford University Press, 1990), 130–37. In other words, "continued engagement by the middle-class urban housewife in many of the activities of her farm mistress forbears was what made possible her family's acquisition of the closest approximation to traditional nonmarket rural independence that a market-dominated urban world offered." Keith Stavley and Kathleen Fitzgerald, *America's Founding Food: The Story of New England Cooking* (Chapel Hill: University of North Carolina Press, 2004), 132.

19. Child, *The American Frugal Housewife*, 7.
20. Child, *The American Frugal Housewife*, 109.
21. Child, *The American Frugal Housewife*, 96, 110.
22. For more on the etymological development of "economy," see Habermas, *The Structural Transformation of the Public Sphere*, 20.
23. Child, *The American Frugal Housewife*, 99.
24. Child, *The American Frugal Housewife*, 103.
25. Child, *The American Frugal Housewife*, 111.
26. Kenneth Allen Robinson, *Thoreau and the Wild Appetite* (New York: AMS, 1985), 12.
27. For more on Graham's life, see Karen Iacobbo and Michael Iacobbo, "Sylvester Graham, Grahamism, and Grahamites," in *Vegetarian America: A History* (Westport, CT: Praeger, 2004), 15–70; or Nissenbaum, *Sex, Diet, and Debility in Jacksonian America*, 13–14. For an analysis of the troubling gender and imperialist potential of Graham's program, see Kyla Tompkins, "Sylvester Graham's Imperial Dietetics," *Gastronomica* 9, no. 1 (Winter 2009): 50–60. By contrast, Nissenbaum and Sokolow offer more favorable evaluations of the Grahamite movement's effects on women. Jayme Sokolow, *Eros and Modernization: Sylvester Graham, Health Reform, and the Origins of Victorian Sexuality in America* (Rutherford, NJ: Fairleigh Dickinson University Press, 1983), 165.
28. Because Sylvester Graham was the first public person to advocate stridently for its consumption, "Graham flour" was the name antebellum Americans attached to unrefined, whole-grain flour. Such flour had not needed a special nomenclature in earlier periods because it was only in the antebellum period that superfine "white" flour was invented.
29. Iacobbo and Iacobbo, *Vegetarian America*, 49.
30. Sylvester Graham, *Lectures on the Science of Human Life* (New York: Fowler & Wells, 1839), 516.
31. Graham, *Lectures on the Science of Human Life*, 299.
32. Graham, *Lectures on the Science of Human Life*, 576.
33. Graham, *Lectures on the Science of Human Life*, 479, 558.
34. Graham, *Lectures on the Science of Human Life*, 42.

35. Graham, *Lectures on the Science of Human Life*, 253.

36. Michel Foucault, *The History of Sexuality*, vol. 2: *The Use of Pleasure*, trans. Robert Hurley (New York: Vintage, 1990), 30–31.

37. Eileen Joy, "Improbable Manners of Being," *GLQ: A Journal of Lesbian and Gay Studies* 21, nos. 2–3 (June 2015): 222.

38. Graham, *Lectures on the Science of Human Life*, 493.

39. Michael Warner, *Publics and Counterpublics* (New York: Zone, 2005), 273.

40. See Michelle C. Neely, "Embodied Politics: Antebellum Vegetarianism and the Dietary Economy of *Walden*," *American Literature* 85, no. 1 (2013): 38–39.

41. Graham, *Lectures on the Science of Human Life*, 256.

42. Graham, *Lectures on the Science of Human Life*, 256, 257.

43. Graham, *Lectures on the Science of Human Life*, 261.

44. Lynn Avery Hunt, *Inventing Human Rights: A History* (New York: Norton, 2007), 26–34.

45. Elizabeth B. Clark, "'The Sacred Rights of the Weak': Pain, Sympathy, and the Culture of Individual Rights in Antebellum America," *Journal of American History* 82, no. 2 (September 1995): 463–93. See also Britt Rusert, *Fugitive Science: Empiricism and Freedom in Early African American Culture* (New York: New York University Press, 2017), 65–112; and Cristin Ellis, *Antebellum Posthuman: Race and Materiality in the Mid–Nineteenth Century* (New York: Fordham University Press, 2018), 23–35.

46. For Garrison's interest in Graham, see the *Liberator* (Boston) of March 11, 1837; November 21, 1845; and December 20, 1839. Nissenbaum, *Sex, Diet, and Debility*, 143, also points out that Garrison elected to stay in New York City's "Graham Boardinghouse" when he had occasion to travel to the city.

47. Henry David Thoreau, *Walden*, ed. James Lyndon (Princeton, NJ: Princeton University Press, 1971), 45. The epigraph for this section appears on 64–65.

48. See, for instance, Robert A. Gross, "The Great Bean Field Hoax: Thoreau and the Agricultural Reformers," in *Critical Essays on Henry David Thoreau's Walden*, ed. Joel Myerson (Boston: G. K. Hall, 1988), 193–202.

49. Brian Walker, "Thoreau on Democratic Cultivation," *Political Theory* 29, no. 2 (April 2001): 155, discusses Thoreau's agricultural "cultivation as a mode of democratic practice" and "advice giving" more generally as "a mode of literature friendly to the expansion of the democratic imagination," while Ruth Lane, "Standing 'Aloof' from the State: Thoreau on Self-Government," *Review of Politics* 67, no. 2 (Spring 2005): 283, reads *Walden* as a presentation of a "specific model of self-government, *individual* self-government, that

occurs under the frequently irrelevant roof provided by liberal democratic state institutions."

50. Sacvan Bercovitch, _The American Jeremiad_ (Madison: University of Wisconsin Press, 1978); Michael T. Gilmore, _American Romanticism and the Marketplace_ (Chicago: University of Chicago Press, 1985).

51. Gilmore, _American Romanticism and the Marketplace_, 42.

52. Gilmore, _American Romanticism and the Marketplace_, 36.

53. Appleby, "Moderation in the First Era of Popular Consumption," 139–59.

54. Joanna Cohen, _Luxurious Citizens: The Politics of Consumption in Nineteenth-Century America_ (Philadelphia: University of Pennsylvania Press, 2017), 4–5.

55. Kathryn Schulz, "Pond Scum: Henry David Thoreau's Moral Myopia," _New Yorker_, October 19, 2015.

56. Schulz, "Pond Scum."

57. For an even-handed direct rebuttal, see Donovan Hahn, "Everybody Hates Henry," _New Republic_, October 21, 2015. For an in-depth exploration of the contemporary tendency to misread or misrepresent Thoreau's political commitments specifically, see James Finley, "#ReclaimHDT," Thoreau Society, https://www.thoreausociety.org/news-article/reclaimhdt -james-finley.

58. In a typical instance, Richard J. Schneider, "Walden," in _The Cambridge Companion to Henry David Thoreau_, ed. Joel Myerson (New York: Cambridge University Press, 1995), 100, writes, "most readers find 'Higher Laws,' the most obviously Transcendentalist chapter in [_Walden_], to be exasperating in its puritanic insistence on the virtues of a vegetarian diet."

59. The best discussion of Thoreau's diet comes in Robinson, _Thoreau and the Wild Appetite_, 12–14. Nissenbaum, _Sex, Diet, and Debility_, xi, notes in passing that Thoreau was essentially following the Grahamite diet at Walden Pond, and David Reynolds's recent history of Jacksonian America, _Waking the Giant: America in the Age of Jackson_, 1st ed. (New York: Harper, 2008), 259, connects Graham to Thoreau's diet, although only to suggest (erroneously) that Thoreau "went beyond" Graham. Stephen Adams and Barbara Adams, "Thoreau's Diet at Walden," in _Studies in the American Renaissance_, ed. Joel Myerson (Charlottesville: University Press of Virginia, 1990), 243–60, also briefly discuss Alcott and Graham but focus solely on whether Thoreau's diet at Walden Pond was nutritionally adequate. Laura Dassow Walls, "As You Are Brothers of Mine: Thoreau and the Irish," _New England Quarterly_ 88, no. 1 (March 2015): 5–36, touches on Thoreau's interest in consumerism in the context of his writing about the Irish.

60. William Gleason highlights this generic interplay in "Re-Creating Walden: Thoreau's Economy of Work and Play," *American Literature* 65, no. 4 (1993): 673–701.

61. Thoreau, *Walden*, 8.

62. Thoreau, *Walden*, 9, 13, 14, 35.

63. Thoreau, *Walden*, 14–15.

64. Lance Newman, "Thoreau's Materialism and Environmental Justice," in *Thoreau at Two Hundred: Essays and Reassessments*, ed. Kristen Case and K. P. Van Englen (Cambridge: Cambridge University Press, 2016), 21.

65. Thoreau, *Walden*, 5.

66. Thoreau, *Walden*, 196.

67. Thoreau, *Walden*, 66.

68. Thoreau, *Walden*, 65–66.

69. Thoreau, *Walden*, 31.

70. For much more on this, see Neely, "Embodied Politics," 41–44.

71. Thoreau, *Walden*, 13.

72. Thoreau, *Walden*, 92.

73. Thoreau, *Walden*, 31.

74. Thoreau, *Walden*, 61.

75. Thoreau, *Walden*, 9.

76. Is it sheer coincidence that the name of this chapter, "Baker Farm," connects Thoreau's cautionary tale of thrift and home economy to the great enemy of those virtues, by Sylvester Graham's account, the public baker? Or that the family Thoreau encounters, the Fields, are nominally connected to the source of independence so essential to the *oikodespotes* and (in a slightly different sense) the vegetarian citizen?

77. Michael West, "Scatology and Eschatology: The Heroic Dimensions of Thoreau's Wordplay," *PMLA* 89, no. 5 (October 1974): 1049.

78. Thoreau, *Walden*, 205.

79. Thoreau, like Whitman in *Leaves of Grass*, goes out of his way to point out that he is a "loafer," but in Thoreau's case, the epithet has the advantage of being a Grahamite pun.

80. Thoreau, *Walden*, 205.

81. Thoreau, *Walden*, 223.

82. Thoreau, *Walden*, 69.

83. Marx, *Capital*, 1:719.

84. Lance Newman, *Our Common Dwelling: Henry Thoreau, Transcendentalism, and the Class Politics of Nature* (New York: Palgrave Macmillan, 2005), 136; Laura Dassow Walls, *Henry David Thoreau: A Life* (Chicago: University of Chicago Press, 2017), 161–62.

85. Thoreau, *Walden*, 8.

86. Three popular examples of this trend are Dave Bruno's "100 Thing Challenge," TEDxClaremontColleges, 2012; Courtney Carver's "Project 333," Be More with Less (blog), October 1, 2010; and Sheena Matheiken's "Uniform Project," http://www.theuniformproject.com/.

87. Bruce Stadfeld argues that consumption produces spaces "both public and private" that in turn yield "new relations within society and between society and nature." Quoted in Matthew W. Klingle, "Spaces of Consumption in Environmental History," *History and Theory* 42, no. 4 (December 2003): 99.

88. In *Your Money or Your Life*, Robin and Dominguez's central insight is that "cost" is the amount of "life energy" it takes to earn, own, and maintain an item—a version of Thoreau's argument about cost and wage labor in *Walden*. Like Thoreau, their solution is to advocate a shift in consciousness about capitalism and consumerism that leads to a frugal lifestyle that, they promise, can ultimately free any individual from needing to work (again, a version of Thoreau's *Walden* experiment). While Thoreau is never cited as a primary source of inspiration, even the phrase "your money or your life" is lifted from a passage of "Resistance to Civil Government." Vicki Robin and Joe Dominguez, *Your Money or Your Life: Nine Steps to Transforming Your Relationship to Money and Achieving Financial Independence* (1992; New York: Penguin, 2008).

89. Eighteenth-century physicians such as George Cheyne theorized the human body as a machine and made novel dietary recommendations based on the philosophy of the mechanical body, so Thoreau may also be playing with and against this earlier physiological theory. Trudy Eden, *The Early American Table: Food and Society in the New World* (DeKalb: Northern Illinois University Press, 2008), 85–98.

90. Thoreau, *Walden*, 90.

91. Shannon L. Mariotti, *Thoreau's Democratic Withdrawal: Alienation, Participation, and Modernity* (Madison: University of Wisconsin Press, 2010), 23.

92. Thoreau, *Walden*, 74.

93. Thoreau, *Walden*, 7.

94. Henry David Thoreau, "Resistance to Civil Government," in *Reform Papers*, ed. Wendell Glick (Princeton, NJ: Princeton University Press, 1973), 69.

95. Thoreau, "Resistance to Civil Government," 87.

96. Walter Benn Michaels, "*Walden*'s False Bottoms," in *Critical Essays on Henry David Thoreau's* Walden, ed. Joel Myerson (Boston: G. K. Hall, 1988), 137.

97. Michaels, "*Walden's* False Bottoms," 139.

98. Thoreau, "Resistance to Civil Government," 74.

99. Henry David Thoreau, "Slavery in Massachusetts," in *Reform Papers*, ed. Wendell Glick (Princeton, NJ: Princeton University Press, 1973), 103.

100. Thoreau, "Resistance to Civil Government," 66, 80.

101. Klingle, "Spaces of Consumption in Environmental History," 109.

102. Jane Bennett, *Thoreau's Nature: Ethics, Politics, and the Wild* (1994; New York: Rowman and Littlefield, 2002), 42.

103. Thoreau, *Walden*, 10.

104. Thoreau, *Walden*, 323.

105. Emily Dickinson, *The Poems of Emily Dickinson*, ed. R.W. Franklin (Cambridge, MA: Belknap, 1999), F1447, l. 1. All subsequent Dickinson poems in this chapter are excerpted from this edition.

106. Emily Dickinson, *Letters of Emily Dickinson*, ed. Thomas H. Johnson (Cambridge, MA: Harvard University Press, 1997), 474.

107. Higginson calls Dickinson's life "abnormal" in reflection on his acquaintance with the poet. Thomas Wentworth Higginson, "Emily Dickinson's Letters," *Atlantic Monthly* 68 (October 1891): 453. No scholar has done more to disrupt this version of Dickinson than Martha Nell Smith, whose *Open Me Carefully: Emily Dickinson's Intimate Letters to Susan Huntington Dickinson* (Paris: Paris Press, 1998) and other works have mounted the most compelling challenge to the widespread conception of Emily Dickinson as loveless, lonely, and producing her poetry in isolation. Magdalena Zapedowska, "Dickinson's Delight," *Emily Dickinson Journal* 21, no. 1 (2012): 1–24, is another recent exception to the critical tendency to read misery into Dickinson's life and work. Zapedowska highlights the almost total critical blindness to Dickinson's engagement with happiness and then compellingly argues for a Dickinsonian "poetic subjectivity that originates in delight" (20).

108. Dickinson, F1447, ll. 1–2.

109. Dickinson, *Letters*, 137.

110. Nancy Harris Brose et al., *Emily Dickinson: A Profile of the Poet as Cook, with Selected Recipes* (Amherst, MA: Hamilton Newall, 1976), 1.

111. See Heather Kirk Thomas, "Emily Dickinson's 'Renunciation' and Anorexia Nervosa," *American Literature* 60, no. 2 (May 1988): 205–25; or Vivian K. Pollak, "Thirst and Starvation in Emily Dickinson's Poetry," *American Literature* 51, no. 1 (March 1979): 33–49. Barbara Antonina Clarke Mossberg has also written about Dickinson's "aesthetics of anorexia" in *Emily Dickinson: When a Writer Is a Daughter* (Bloomington: Indiana University Press, 1982), 135–46.

112. Elizabeth Andrews, "'This Foreshadowed Food': Representations of Food and Hunger in Emily Dickinson's American Gothic," in *Culinary*

Aesthetics and Practices in Nineteenth-Century American Culture, ed. Marie Drews and Monika Elbert (New York: Palgrave Macmillan, 2009), 212.

113. Erica Fretwell, "Emily Dickinson in Domingo," *J19: The Journal of Nineteenth-Century Americanists* 1, no. 1 (Spring 2013): 71–96, is a recent example of what might be yielded from a more balanced account of Dickinson and food. Fretwell argues that "to address how Dickinson incorporated gustatory taste into her work is to dispel the myth of the ascetic Emily Dickinson" and replace it with "an *aesthetic* Emily Dickinson" (73). While I admire Fretwell's project, in this chapter I am not seeking to "dispel" "the ascetic Emily Dickinson" so much as to explore that asceticism in its rich nineteenth-century context. Joan Burbick, "Emily Dickinson and the Economics of Desire," *American Literature* 58, no. 3 (October 1986): 362, offers yet another context in her analysis of Dickinson's representations of desire: "sexual frugality."

114. David S. Reynolds, "Black Cats and Delirium Tremens: Temperance and the American Renaissance," in *Serpent in the Cup: Temperance in American Literature*, ed. David S. Reynolds and Debra J. Rosenthal (Amherst: University of Massachusetts Press, 1997), 54.

115. Dickinson, *Letters*, 3.

116. Dickinson, *Letters*, 240, 715, 717. In one of her earliest letters, Dickinson describes learning how to make bread, "the staff of life" (a phrase Graham also often used). *Letters*, 20.

117. "We are just thro' dinner, Austin, I want to write so much that I omit digestion, and a *dyspepsia* will probably be the result." Dickinson, *Letters*, 137.

118. Edward Hitchcock, *Dyspepsy Forestalled and Resisted, or, Lectures on Diet, Regimen, and Employment: Delivered to the Students of Amherst College, Spring Term, 1830* (Amherst, MA: J. S. & C. Adams, 1831), 27.

119. Hitchcock, *Dyspepsy Forestalled and Resisted*, 28.

120. Elizabeth Hewett, "Economics," in *Emily Dickinson in Context*, ed. Eliza Richards (Cambridge: Cambridge University Press, 2013), 188–97; Betsy Erkkila, "Emily Dickinson and Class," *American Literary History* 4, no. 1 (Spring 1992): 1–27; Peter Stoneley, "'I—Pay—in Satin Cash—': Commerce, Gender, and Display in Dickinson's Poetry," *American Literature* 72, no. 3 (2000): 575–94. These critics are part of a larger sea change in Dickinson criticism, as more and more scholars see Dickinson's poetry as engaging public as well as private concerns. Mastroianni, Marrs, Richardson, and others have compellingly established Dickinson as a Civil War poet, for instance.

121. Hewett, "Economics," 190.

122. Dickinson, F748, ll. 1–4.

123. Dickinson, F748, ll. 5–12.

124. Dickinson, F748, ll. 13–16.

125. Dickinson, F806, ll. 1–4.

126. See, for example, Dickinson, F207, "I taste a liquor never brewed—"; or F1351, "A Bee his Burnished Carriage."

127. Dickinson, F626, ll. 1–9.

128. Dickinson, F870, ll. 3–6.

129. For more examples of Dickinson's tendency to celebrate desire over possession, see Burbick, "Emily Dickinson and the Economics of Desire," 367–69. Burbick's argument differs fundamentally from mine in that she argues that "the speaker is finally left without the ability to have; only a fantasy about the ideal is possible. . . . Temporary deferment, leading to a more valued or idealized gratification, becomes instead a permanent impoverishment, if not a psychic or physical wounding" (369).

130. Dickinson, F1447, ll. 1–4.

131. Dickinson's idea of delighting in desire is the exact opposite of the way desire is ordinarily conceived. For instance, John Locke in *An Essay Concerning Human Understanding* (New York: Penguin, 2004), 235–36, claims that desire "spoil[s] the relish, even of those good things which we have." For background on Dickinson's conception of desire and its relation to her "lyric self," see Roland Hagenbüchle, "'Sumptuous—Despair': The Function of Desire in Emily Dickinson's Poetry," *Emily Dickinson Journal* 5, no. 2 (Fall 1996): 1–9.

132. Dickinson, F1447, ll. 5–8.

133. Elizabeth Petrino, "Allusion, Echo, and Literary Influence in Emily Dickinson," *Emily Dickinson Journal* 19, no. 1 (2010): 85, outlines Dickinson's knowledge of "Ode on a Grecian Urn."

134. Qtd. in Sara Ahmed, *The Promise of Happiness* (Durham, NC: Duke University Press, 2010), 30.

135. Ahmed, *The Promise of Happiness*, 13.

136. Ahmed, *The Promise of Happiness*, 59.

137. Ahmed, *The Promise of Happiness*, 164.

138. Dickinson, F1267, ll. 1–4.

139. Dickinson, F851, ll. 1–2.

140. Dickinson, F851, ll. 6, 4.

141. Dickinson, F1311, ll. 1–2.

142. Dickinson, F1311, l. 6.

143. Dickinson, F1311, ll. 7, 8.

144. Daniel Miller, *Consumption and Its Consequences* (London: Polity, 2012), 72.

145. Dickinson, F645, ll. 1–12.

146. Sylvia Plath, "A Birthday Present," in *Ariel* (New York: Harper and Row, 1965), 42–44, ll. 1–10.

3. THE PROBLEM WITH PRESERVATION: AESTHETICS AND SANCTUARY
IN CATLIN, PARKMAN, ERDRICH, MELVILLE, AND BYATT

1. Roderick Nash, *Wilderness and the American Mind*, 4th ed. (New Haven, CT: Yale University Press, 2001), 96–121.

2. "Howling wilderness" is Michael Wigglesworth's phrase, quoted in Hans Huth, *Nature and the American: Three Centuries of Changing Attitudes*, 2nd ed. (Lincoln: University of Nebraska Press, 1990), 6. For the full scope of Huth's argument, see 54–164, 210–12.

3. Ken Burns, *The National Parks: America's Best Idea* (Arlington: PBS, 1998).

4. William Cronon, "The Trouble with Wilderness," in *Uncommon Ground: Rethinking the Human Place in Nature*, ed. William Cronon (New York: Norton, 1995), 69–90; Mark David Spence, *Dispossessing the Wilderness: Indian Removal and the Making of the National Parks* (Oxford: Oxford University Press, 1999).

5. See Stefan Bechtel, *Mr. Hornaday's War* (Boston: Beacon, 2012), 150–67; Rachel Adams, *Sideshow U.S.A: Freaks and the American Cultural Imagination* (Chicago: University of Chicago Press, 2001), 31–44.

6. Rose Hanna Shell, "Introduction: Finding the Soul in the Skin," in *The Extermination of the American Bison* (Washington, DC: Smithsonian Institution Press, 1889).

7. Andrew C. Isenberg, *The Destruction of the Bison: An Environmental History, 1750–1920* (Cambridge: Cambridge University Press, 2000).

8. David D. Smits, "The Frontier Army and the Destruction of the Buffalo, 1865–1883," *Western Historical Quarterly* 25, no. 3 (Autumn 1994): 328.

9. Bechtel, *Mr. Hornaday's War*, 36.

10. Later in his career, Hornaday would spearhead live bison preservation in zoos and elsewhere.

11. James John Audubon, "The Pinnated Grouse," in *The Audubon Reader*, ed. Richard Rhodes (New York: Everyman's Library, 2006), 42.

12. Audubon, "The Pinnated Grouse," 40–53.

13. Audubon, "The Pinnated Grouse," 46, 42, 45, 53.

14. James John Audubon, "Account of the Method of Drawing Birds Employed by J. J. Audubon, Esq. F.R.S.E. in a Letter to a Friend," in *John James Audubon: Writings and Drawings*, ed. Christoph Irmscher (New York: Library of America, 1999), 754.

15. Audubon, "Account of the Method of Drawing Birds," 758.

16. George Catlin, *Letters and Notes on the Manners, Customs, and Conditions of North American Indians*, 2 vols. (New York: Dover, 1973), 1:2–3.

17. Catlin, *Letters and Notes*, 1:260.

18. Catlin, *Letters and Notes*, 1:2.
19. Catlin, *Letters and Notes*, 1:2.
20. Catlin, *Letters and Notes*, 1:2.
21. Catlin, *Letters and Notes*, 1:4.
22. Catlin, *Letters and Notes*, 1:6.
23. Catlin, *Letters and Notes*, 1:10.
24. Catlin, *Letters and Notes*, 1:260.
25. Catlin, *Letters and Notes*, 1:261.

26. Rochelle Johnson, *Passions for Nature: Nineteenth-Century America's Aesthetics of Alienation* (Athens: University of Georgia Press, 2009), 2–10, 186–87. Johnson reads Thomas Cole, Andrew Jackson Downing, and Ralph Waldo Emerson as emblematic expressions of this popular aesthetic and identifies "a counteraesthetics" that values nature for its "physicality" in the work of Susan Fenimore Cooper and Henry David Thoreau (3).

27. Huth, in *Nature and the American*, describes Catlin's proposal as "prophetic" and "progressive" (134), and even Spence, in *Dispossessing the Wilderness*, takes an extremely rosy view of Catlin's park proposal. Perhaps because Spence's interest is in creating a contrast between the antebellum writers and artists such as Thomas Cole, John James Audubon, and George Catlin, who viewed Indians as a "natural" part of the wilderness, and those parks advocates who supported and eventually enforced Indian removal from "park land," Spence represents Catlin's park plan as a remarkably culturally sensitive "hop[e] that some effort might be expended to protect the cultural autonomy of more distant tribes." "Ultimately," Spence continues, "Catlin's proposal represented a significant departure from the ambivalent hope and resignation that characterized antebellum society, and his concern for the lands and peoples he encountered in the West would soon find echoes in the experiences of others who followed in his footsteps" (16). Although I recognize Catlin's frequent openness to the Native cultures he encounters, I do not find his proposal to be the "significant departure from the ambivalent hope and resignation that characterized antebellum society" that Spence represents it to be.

28. Note Catlin's typical characterization of Native American lands as "idle." Despite the many forms of land use Catlin records throughout his book, including agriculture, the lack of property antebellum Americans would recognize as "private" and large-scale farming nevertheless renders the plains "idle."

29. Catlin, *Letters and Notes*, 1:261–62.

30. At least according to Catlin.

31. Catlin, *Letters and Notes*, 1:263. For more on white faith in and the fetishization of the so-called disappearing Indian, see Brian W. Dippie, *The*

Vanishing American: White Attitudes and U.S. Indian Policy (Lawrence: University Press of Kansas, 1982).

32. Catlin, *Letters and Notes*, 1:263.

33. Catlin, *Letters and Notes*, 1:262.

34. Catlin, *Letters and Notes*, 1:261–62.

35. Catlin, *Letters and Notes*, 1:262.

36. Catlin, *Letters and Notes*, 1:16.

37. Susan Sontag, *On Photography* (New York: Picador, 1973), 12.

38. Catlin, *Letters and Notes*, 1:26–27.

39. Catlin, *Letters and Notes*, 1:247.

40. Catlin, *Letters and Notes*, 1:237.

41. Mark Twain, *Roughing It*, ed. Richard Bucci, Victor Fisher, Michael B. Frank, and Kenneth M. Sanderson (Berkeley: University of California Press, 1993), 127.

42. Twain, *Roughing It*, 128–29.

43. Francis Parkman Jr., *The Oregon Trail* (Oxford: Oxford University Press, 1996), 108.

44. Parkman Jr., *The Oregon Trail*, 171.

45. Parkman Jr., *The Oregon Trail*, 86–87.

46. Parkman Jr., *The Oregon Trail*, 32.

47. Philip Fisher, *Hard Facts: Setting and Form in the American Novel* (Oxford: Oxford University Press, 1987), 24.

48. Fisher, *Hard Facts*, 131–32.

49. Richard Slotkin, *Regeneration through Violence: The Mythology of the American Frontier, 1600–1860* (Norman: University of Oklahoma Press, 1973), 418.

50. Parkman Jr., *The Oregon Trail*, 151.

51. Philip G. Terrie, "The Other Within: Indianization on the Oregon Trail," *New England Quarterly* 64, no. 3 (September 1991): 376–92.

52. Slotkin, *Regeneration through Violence*, 156, has observed that "on an extended hunt for a single beast, the hunter is forced to follow in the animal's footsteps, to eat when he eats, sleep when he sleeps, and move when he moves," a phenomenon that "contributes to that mysterious sense of identification between hunter and hunted that so many writers have remarked."

53. Parkman Jr., *The Oregon Trail*, 300.

54. Parkman Jr., *The Oregon Trail*, 317.

55. Terrie, "The Other Within," 377–78.

56. Parkman Jr., *The Oregon Trail*, 237.

57. Louise Erdrich, *Shadow Tag* (New York: Harper Perennial, 2010), 21.

58. Erdrich, *Shadow Tag*, 11.

59. Erdrich, *Shadow Tag*, 31.

60. Erdrich, *Shadow Tag*, 44–45.

61. Erdrich, *Shadow Tag*, 46.

62. Erdrich, *Shadow Tag*, 37–38.

63. Erdrich, *Shadow Tag*, 37.

64. Erdrich, *Shadow Tag*, 60.

65. Erdrich, *Shadow Tag*, 170.

66. Erdrich, *Shadow Tag*, 171.

67. Erdrich, *Shadow Tag*, 135.

68. Erdrich, *Shadow Tag*, 141.

69. James Audubon, "The Passenger Pigeon," in *The Audubon Reader*, 70.

70. Herman Melville, *Moby-Dick*, Longman critical ed., ed. John Bryant and Haskell Springer (New York: Pearson, 2009), 499.

71. For instance, John Levi Barnard, "The Cod and the Whale: Melville in the Time of Extinction," *American Literature* 89, no. 4 (December 2017): 851–79, reads *Moby-Dick* as a parable of the commodification of sea life that has led to our current crisis of marine overfishing and endangerment.

72. Melville, *Moby-Dick*, 405.

73. Melville, *Moby-Dick*, 405.

74. Daniel Cressey, "World's Whaling Slaughter Tallied at 3 Million," *Scientific American*, March 15, 2015.

75. Charles Darwin, *On the Origin of the Species by Means of Natural Selection* (London: John Murray, 1860), 110. For a more thorough contextualization of Melville's view of extinction in its own time, see Timothy Sweet, "'Will He Perish?' *Moby-Dick* and Nineteenth-Century Extinction Discourse," in *Above the American Renaissance: David S. Reynolds and the Spiritual Imagination in American Literary Studies*, ed. Harold K. Bush and Brian Yothers (Amherst: University of Massachusetts Press, 2018), 87–93.

76. Melville, *Moby-Dick*, 74, 311.

77. Melville, *Moby-Dick*, 184.

78. Melville, *Moby-Dick*, 269.

79. Melville, *Moby-Dick*, 404.

80. Thomas L. Altherr, "Drunk with the Chase: Francis Parkman and *Moby-Dick*," *Melville Society Extracts* 58 (1984): 8–9.

81. Melville, *Moby-Dick*, 404.

82. Melville, *Moby-Dick*, 405.

83. Melville, *Moby-Dick*, 403, 405.

84. Barnard, "The Cod and the Whale," 864; Melville, *Moby-Dick*, 402.

85. Melville, *Moby-Dick*, 404.

86. Melville, *Moby-Dick*, 405.

87. Melville, *Moby-Dick*, 405.

88. "Scientists Shocked by Arctic Permafrost Thawing 70 Years Sooner Than Predicted," *Guardian*, June 18, 2019.

89. World Wildlife Fund, "Living Planet Report 2018: Aiming Higher" (2018), 7.

90. Elizabeth Kolbert, *The Sixth Extinction: An Unnatural History* (New York: Henry Holt, 2014), 17.

91. See Elizabeth Schultz, "Melville's Environmental Vision in Moby-Dick," *ISLE: Interdisciplinary Studies in Literature and the Environment* 7, no. 1 (2000): 97–113; Philip Armstrong, "*Moby-Dick* and Compassion," *Society and Animals* 12, no. 1: 19–37; Philip Armstrong, *What Animals Mean in the Fiction of Modernity* (New York: Routledge, 2008).

92. Melville, *Moby-Dick*, 270.

93. Melville, *Moby-Dick*, 270–71.

94. Melville, *Moby-Dick*, 269, 271.

95. I generally agree with Schultz's claim in "Melville's Environmental Vision in Moby-Dick" that Melville's "environmental vision" is "one based on an understanding of a unity between humanity and nature, a unity derived from an emotional and social kinship," but I disagree with her conclusion that "he indicates an intrinsic and irresistible interdependency among diverse species of life" insofar as Melville dismisses the possibility of whale endangerment and extinction by taking refuge in a fantasy of species-level preservation (100). My reading is closer to Armstrong's in *What Animals Mean in the Fiction of Modernity*, and I agree with Armstrong that Schultz and others "overestimate [*Moby-Dick*'s] anxiety about species extinction" (104).

96. David Quammen, *The Song of the Dodo: Island Biogeography in an Age of Extinction* (New York: Scribner, 1997).

97. Melville, *Moby-Dick*, 248. Sweet in "'Will He Perish?'" argues, compellingly, that Ishmael argues against whale extinction by positing human extinction as the more likely event (a supposition partially borne out by the fate of the *Pequod*). Sweet's reading raises the question of whether the effects of a kind of suicidal misanthropy are not worse for the nonhuman world rather than better. While it might seem as if a deep-ecology decentering of the human could be useful to combat anthropocentric violence, Sweet's account of *Moby-Dick* suggestively implies that, having given up on humanity, it becomes difficult to act or care for the nonhuman world in any meaningful way.

98. A. S. Byatt, "Sea Story," *Guardian*, March 15, 2013.

99. Byatt, "Sea Story."

100. Byatt, "Sea Story."

101. Byatt, "Sea Story."

102. Byatt, "Sea Story."

103. Melville, *Moby-Dick*, 248.

104. Timothy Morton, *Hyperobjects: Philosophy and Ecology after the End of the World* (Minneapolis: University of Minnesota Press, 2013).

105. Byatt, "Sea Story."

106. Melville, *Moby-Dick*, 499.

107. Melville, *Moby-Dick*, 248.

108. In the final chapter of *Moby-Dick*, Starbuck tells Ahab, "Moby Dick seeks thee not. It is thou, thou, that madly seekest him!" Melville, *Moby-Dick*, 496.

109. Byatt, "Sea Story."

110. Byatt, "Sea Story."

111. Byatt, "Sea Story."

112. "And of all these things the Albino whale was the symbol. Wonder ye then at the fiery hunt?" Melville, *Moby-Dick*, 185.

113. Byatt, "Sea Story."

114. Michael Ziser and Julie Sze, "Climate Change, Environmental Aesthetics, and Global Environmental Justice Cultural Studies," *Discourse* 29, no. 2/3 (2007): 407.

115. Ziser and Sze, "Climate Change, Environmental Aesthetics, and Global Environmental Justice Cultural Studies," 407.

116. Stacy Alaimo, "Oceanic Origins, Plastic Activism, and New Materialism at Sea," in *Material Ecocriticism*, ed. Serenella Iovino and Serpil Oppermann (Bloomington: Indiana University Press, 2014), 187. See also Stacy Alaimo, *Exposed: Environmental Politics and Pleasures in Posthuman Times* (Minneapolis: University of Minnesota Press, 2016), esp. its conclusion.

117. Alaimo, "Oceanic Origins, Plastic Activism, and New Materialism at Sea," 187.

118. Alaimo, "Oceanic Origins, Plastic Activism, and New Materialism at Sea," 193.

119. Bechtel, *Mr. Hornaday's War*, 161.

120. John Berger, "Why Look at Animals?" in *About Looking* (New York: Vintage, 1980), 23.

121. Henry David Thoreau, *Journal*, vol. 1, *1837–1844*, ed. John C Broderick et al. (Princeton, NJ: Princeton University Press, 1981), 472.

122. Henry David Thoreau, *The Maine Woods*, ed. Joseph J. Moldenhauer (Princeton, NJ: Princeton University Press, 1972), 71.

123. Cronon, "The Trouble with Wilderness," 88–90.

124. John G. Neihardt, *Black Elk Speaks: Being the Life Story of a Holy Man of the Oglala Sioux*, premier ed. (Albany: State University of New York Press, 2008), 9.

4. RADICAL PET KEEPING: CRAFTS, WILSON, AND LIVING WITH OTHERS IN THE ANTHROPOCENE

1. See Jason Moore, "Name the System! Anthropocenes and the Capitalocene Alternative," Jasonwmoore.wordpress.com, October 9, 2016.

2. Donna Haraway, "Anthropocene, Capitalocene, Plantationocene, Chthulucene," *Environmental Humanities* 6 (2015): 159–65.

3. Jamie Lorimer, *Wildlife in the Anthropocene: Conservation after Nature* (Minneapolis: University of Minnesota Press, 2015), critiques and modifies the Anthropocene without rejecting it entirely. Nicholas C. Kawa, "Amazonia in the Anthropocene." https://nicholaskawa.files.wordpress.com/2017/02 /amazonia-and-the-anthropocene-uc-taft-talk.pdf, draws upon his field work in the Amazonia to critique the Anthropocene through a contrast with "rural Amazonians [who] typically acknowledge the agency of a wide number of non-human others that challenge human intentions and desires" (5).

4. Peter Karieva et al., "Domesticated Nature: Shaping Landscapes and Ecosystems for Human Welfare," *Science* 316, no. 5833 (2007): 1866, 1869.

5. John Asafu-Adjaye et al., "An Ecomodernist Manifesto," Ecomodern-ism.org, April 2015, 6.

6. In that optimistic best-case scenario, people like Martin Rees, an astronomer and former president of the Royal Society, have argued, "The dawn of the Anthropocene epoch would then mark a one-off transformation from a natural world to one where humans jumpstart the transition to electronic (and potentially immortal) entities, that transcend our limitations and eventually spread their influence far beyond the Earth." While this technologically driven vision of human mastery may bring comfort to some, it's unappealing and unrealistic to many others. Damian Carrington, "The Anthropocene Epoch: Scientists Declare Human-Influenced Age," *Guardian*, August 29, 2016.

7. Val Plumwood, *Feminism and the Mastery of Nature* (New York: Routledge, 1994), 104–19.

8. Kawa, "Amazonia in the Anthropocene," 24.

9. Cited in Cynthia Willett, *Interspecies Ethics* (New York: Columbia University Press, 2014), 5.

10. Ursula Heise, *Imagining Extinction: The Cultural Meanings of Endangered Species* (Chicago: University of Chicago Press, 2016), 18.

11. John Berger, "Why Look at Animals?" in *About Looking* (New York: Vintage, 1980), 14.

12. Lydia Maria Child, "A Letter from Mrs. Child to 'Our Jessie.'" *Liberator* 41 (October 11, 1861).

13. Frederick Douglass, *Narrative of the Life of Frederick Douglass, an American Slave* (New York: Penguin, 2014), is an emblematic instance. See, e.g., 39, 84, 90, 105–6, 144.

14. Prominent abolitionists also engaged in animal-welfare activism, so such rejections of kinship did not necessarily entail rejecting sympathy for nonhuman animals. Diane L. Beers, *For the Prevention of Cruelty: The History and Legacy of Animal Rights Activism in the United States* (Athens: Swallow Press/Ohio University Press, 2006), 45–58.

15. Augusta Rohrbach, "'A Silent Unobtrusive Way': Hannah Crafts and the Literary Marketplace," in *In Search of Hannah Crafts: Critical Essays on* The Bondwoman's Narrative, ed. Henry Louis Gates Jr. and Hollis Robbins (New York: BasicCivitas Books, 2004), 13.

16. Mart A. Stewart, "Slavery and the Origins of African American Environmentalism," in *"To Love the Wind and the Rain": African Americans and Environmental History*, ed. Dianne D. Glave and Mark Stoll (Pittsburgh, PA: University of Pittsburgh Press, 2006), 9–20; Kimberly K. Smith, *African American Environmental Thought* (Lawrence: University Press of Kansas, 2007); and Scott Giltner, "Slave Hunting and Fishing in the Antebellum South," in *"To Love the Wind and the Rain,"* 21–36.

17. Dylan C. Penningroth, *The Claims of Kinfolk: African American Property and Community in the Nineteenth-Century South* (Chapel Hill: University of North Carolina Press, 2003), 46.

18. Michael Lundblad, "From Animal to Animality Studies," *PMLA* 124, no. 2 (2009): 497.

19. Jennifer Mason, *Civilized Creatures: Urban Animals, Sentimental Culture, and American Literature, 1850–1900* (Baltimore, MD: Johns Hopkins University Press, 2005); Annie Dwyer, "Animal Autobiography and the Domestication of Human Freedom," *Arizona Quarterly* 71, no. 2 (Summer 2015): 1–30; Elizabeth Barnes, "Drowning (in) Kittens: The Reproduction of Girlhood in Victorian America," *American Literature* 86, no. 2 (2014): 305–31; and Brigitte Nicole Fielder, "Animal Humanism: Race, Species, and Affective Kinship in Nineteenth-Century Abolitionism," *American Quarterly* 65, no. 3 (2013): 487–514.

20. Susan J. Pearson, *The Rights of the Defenseless: Protecting Animals and Children in Gilded Age America* (Chicago: University of Chicago Press, 2011), 1–10; Beers, *For the Prevention of Cruelty,* 23–90.

21. Dana D. Nelson, *The Word in Black and White: Reading "Race" in American Literature, 1638–1867* (Oxford: Oxford University Press, 1992), 7.

22. Ezra Tawil, *The Making of Racial Sentiment* (Cambridge: Cambridge University Press, 2006), 49. See also George M. Frederickson, *The Black Image in the White Mind: The Debate on Afro-American Character and Destiny, 1817–1914* (New York: Harper & Row, 1971), 74.

23. Frederickson, *The Black Image in the White Mind,* 107.

24. Josiah Clark Nott, *Types of Mankind: Or Ethnological Researches, Based upon the Ancient Monuments, Paintings, Sculptures, and Crania of Races* (Philadelphia: Lippincott, Grambo & Co., 1854), 457.

25. Nott, *Types of Mankind*, 458–59.

26. David Walker, *Appeal to the Coloured Citizens of the World*, ed. Peter P. Hinks (University Park: Pennsylvania State University Press, 2000), 12, xxvii.

27. Walker, *Appeal to the Coloured Citizens of the World*, 12.

28. Walker, *Appeal to the Coloured Citizens of the World*, 9.

29. Walker, *Appeal to the Coloured Citizens of the World*, 64.

30. Walker, *Appeal to the Coloured Citizens of the World*, 78.

31. Colin Dayan, *The Law Is a White Dog: How Legal Rituals Make and Unmake Persons* (Princeton, NJ: Princeton University Press, 2011), 113–27, offers a more full account of this dynamic. David Brion Davis, *The Problem of Slavery in the Age of Emancipation* (New York: Vintage, 2014), 3–44, offers an historical overview of the role of animalization in Western European conceptions of slavery. Dwyer discusses the post-Reconstruction use of animalization in the United States to criminalize Blackness.

32. David Armitage, "John Locke, Carolina, and the 'Two Treatises of Government,'" *Political Theory* 32, no. 5 (2004): 607.

33. Davis, *The Problem of Slavery in the Age of Emancipation*, 33.

34. Wayne Glausser, "Three Approaches to Locke and the Slave Trade," *Journal of the History of Ideas* 51, no. 2 (1990): 200–4.

35. James Farr, "'So Vile and Miserable an Estate': The Problem of Slavery in Locke's Political Thought," *Political Theory* 14, no. 2 (1986): 277–80.

36. John Locke, *Second Treatise*, in *Two Treatises of Government*, ed. Peter Laslett (Cambridge: Cambridge University Press, 1960), 271.

37. Locke, *Second Treatise*, 382–83.

38. Locke, *Second Treatise*, 377.

39. Locke, *Second Treatise*, 284.

40. Orlando Patterson, *Slavery and Social Death: A Comparative Study* (Cambridge, MA: Harvard University Press, 1982), 5.

41. Patterson, *Slavery and Social Death*, 5.

42. Frederickson, *The Black Image in the White Mind*, 58.

43. Mason, *Civilized Creatures*, 1–12; Katherine C. Grier, *Pets in America: A History* (New York: Harcourt, 2006), 74–112.

44. Elizabeth Barnes, *States of Sympathy: Seduction and Democracy in the American Novel* (New York: Columbia University Press, 1997), xi.

45. See Dana Nelson, *National Manhood: Capitalist Citizenship and the Imagined Fraternity of White Men* (Durham, NC: Duke University Press, 1998); and Frederickson, *The Black Image in the White Mind*.

46. Robyn Wiegman, *American Anatomies: Theorizing Race and Gender* (Durham, NC: Duke University Press, 1995), 62–69. Michael Warner, "The Mass Public and the Mass Subject," in *Habermas and the Public Sphere*, ed. Craig Calhoun (Cambridge, MA: MIT Press, 1992), 377–401.

47. The exploitation of the labor of enslaved people has directed critical attention to comparisons between slaves and specifically laboring creatures such as horses and cattle. Yet many antebellum pets also had household labor functions, although sentimental attachment was the primary justification for keeping animals in the family, in the nineteenth century as today. Grier, *Pets in America*, 12, 26–27. Applying the trope of the pet to enslaved or indentured Black Americans tended to mystify their labor-based exploitation, but the "child" metaphor operated similarly.

48. For more on this see Lesley Ginsberg, "Slavery and the Gothic Horror of Poe's 'The Black Cat,'" in *American Gothic: New Interventions in a National Narrative*, ed. Robert K. Martin and Erick Savoy (Ames: University of Iowa Press, 1998), 99–128, who offers a complementary discussion of pet keeping and slavery.

49. See, for example, the newspaper account of a man who tells a friend, when contemplating the purchase of an enslaved child, "I mean to bring her up *well*. She'll be a pet for the children." "Democratic Slave Markets," *Liberator* 31 (August 1, 1856): 1.

50. Herman Melville, "Benito Cereno," in *Benito Cereno, Billy Budd, Sailor and Other Stories* (New York: Bantam, 1981), 136.

51. "Breakfast to Mr. Frederick Douglass," *Liberator* 9 (February 27, 1846): 1.

52. James Caitlin publishes a jeremiad against "the pet institution of our government" in *Frederick Douglass' Paper* in 1852. A *Liberator* review of *Aunt Phillis' Cabin* from the same year calls slavery "the pet system of this republic" ("Random Thrusts," *Liberator* 36 [September 3, 1852]: 1), and an 1854 *Liberator* report by Susan B. Anthony "from the land of slavery" again uses the phrase "pet institution" ("Slavery and Reform," *Liberator* 15 [April 14, 1854]: 1). There are many more examples throughout the 1850s and into the 1860s.

53. "I Also Am a Man," *London Patriot*, July 26, 1860; repr. *Liberator* 33 (August 17, 1860): 1.

54. "Colorphobia," *The Liberator* 25 (June 22, 1849): 1.

55. "The Cat and the Kitten," *Liberator* 47 (November 23, 1833): 1.

56. Robert S. Levine, "Trappe(d): Race and Genealogical Haunting in *The Bondwoman's Narrative*," in *In Search of Hannah Crafts: Critical Essays on* The Bondwoman's Narrative, ed. Henry Louis Gates Jr. and Hollis Robbins (New York: BasicCivitas Books, 2004), 278.

57. Hannah Crafts, *The Bondwoman's Narrative*, ed. Henry Louis Gates Jr. (New York: Warner Books, 2002), 10, 11–12, 108–9, 161–62.

58. While Rose is not explicitly labeled a "pet" in this scene, later in the novel another enslaved woman, Lizzy, is described as having been "the pet of a rich family," a description that could just as easily be applied to Rose before this incident. Crafts, *The Bondwoman's Narrative*, 34.

59. Crafts, *The Bondwoman's Narrative*, 21.

60. The dog's "whiteness" is a suggestive bit of evidence that Sir Clifford (or some other white man) may be the father of Rose's child, since the dog is Rose's daughter's "memorial" and synechdotal stand-in. But it's also a reminder of the hollowness of white claims of paternalistic "kinship" with the persons they enslave. Rose is a kind of suffering mammy figure in this scene, and her love for her "white child" (Sir Clifford's son, whom she nursed) and even the white child's love for her (Sir Clifford's son begs his father to spare Rose) has no effect on Rose's fate.

61. Crafts, *The Bondwoman's Narrative*, 21–22.

62. Crafts, *The Bondwoman's Narrative*, 22.

63. Crafts, *The Bondwoman's Narrative*, 23–24.

64. The scene acts as a "primal scene" of slavery in Hartman's sense: a "terrible spectacle [that] dramatizes the origin of the subject and demonstrates that to be a slave is to be under the brutal power and authority of another." Saidiya Hartman, *Scenes of Subjection: Terror, Slavery, and Self-Making in Nineteenth-Century America* (Oxford: Oxford University Press, 1997), 3.

65. Yellin has noted the many plot similarities between Crafts's and Stowe's novels, but she does not discuss the pet-keeping murder in Crafts's novel as one of these similarities, despite Stowe's novel containing a scene in which George's enslaver orders George to drown his pet dog. Jean Fagen Yellin, "*The Bondwoman's Narrative* and *Uncle Tom's Cabin*," in *In Search of Hannah Crafts: Critical Essays on* The Bondwoman's Narrative, ed. Henry Louis Gates Jr. and Hollis Robbins (New York: BasicCivitas Books, 2004), 106–14. Yellin argues that although "Stowe's best-seller certainly helped shape it, *The Bondwoman's Narrative* makes a very different statement about slavery and racism in nineteenth-century America" (114), and Crafts's modifications to the scene of pet murder certainly support that difference.

66. Crafts, *The Bondwoman's Narrative*, 6.

67. Crafts, *The Bondwoman's Narrative*, 200.

68. Laura Brace, *The Politics of Property: Labour, Freedom, and Belonging* (New York: Palgrave Macmillan, 2004), 162.

69. Chancellor Harper, "Harper on Slavery," in *The Pro-Slavery Argument; as Maintained by the Most Distinguished Writers of the Southern States, Containing the Several Essays, on the Subject, of Chancellor Harper, Governor Hammond, Dr. Simms, and Professor Dew* (Charleston: Walker, Richards & Co., 1852), 56–57.

70. Josephine Donovan and Carol J. Adams, "Introduction," in *The Feminist Care Tradition in Animal Ethics*, ed. Josephine Donovan and Carol J. Adams (New York: Columbia University Press, 2007), 9.

71. Donovan and Adams, "Introduction," 2.

72. Susanne Kappeler, "Speciesism, Racism, Nationalism . . . or the Power of Scientific Subjectivity," in *Animals and Women: Feminist Theoretical Explorations*, ed. Carol J. Adams and Josephine Donovan (Durham, NC: Duke University Press, 1995), 330–31.

73. Kappeler, "Speciesism, Racism, Nationalism," 323.

74. Jacques Derrida, *The Animal That Therefore I Am*, ed. Marie-Louise Mallet, trans. David Wills (New York: Fordham University Press, 2008), 29.

75. Derrida, *The Animal That Therefore I Am*, 34.

76. Derrida, *The Animal That Therefore I Am*, 91.

77. Donna Haraway, *When Species Meet* (Minneapolis: University of Minnesota Press, 2007), 78.

78. Haraway, *When Species Meet*, 67.

79. Haraway, *When Species Meet*, 71.

80. Crafts, *The Bondwoman's Narrative*, 45.

81. Crafts, *The Bondwoman's Narrative*, 93.

82. Crafts, *The Bondwoman's Narrative*, 101.

83. Crafts, *The Bondwoman's Narrative*, 101–2.

84. Crafts, *The Bondwoman's Narrative*, 100, 101.

85. Crafts, *The Bondwoman's Narrative*, 118–23.

86. Crafts, *The Bondwoman's Narrative*, 116.

87. Crafts, *The Bondwoman's Narrative*, 206.

88. William Andrews, "Hannah Crafts's Sense of an Ending," in *In Search of Hannah Crafts: Critical Essays on* The Bondwoman's Narrative, ed. Henry Louis Gates Jr. and Hollis Robbins (New York: BasicCivitas Books, 2004), 35–36.

89. Crafts, *The Bondwoman's Narrative*, 17 (emphasis added).

90. Crafts, *The Bondwoman's Narrative*, 114–15.

91. Crafts, *The Bondwoman's Narrative*, 120.

92. Michele Navakas, "Antebellum Coral," *American Literature* 91, no. 2 (2019): 280, has recently argued that coral disrupts racial taxonomies and "the fixed fact" of racial difference in antebellum culture and *Uncle Tom's Cabin* specifically, a project that similarly suggests we have much to learn about ideas of race, humanity, and animacy in the nineteenth century.

93. Harriet E. Wilson, *Our Nig; or, Sketches from the Life of a Free Black* (New York: Vintage, 2002), 3, 30, 74–75.

94. Wilson, *Our Nig*, 139.

95. Wilson, *Our Nig*, 6.

96. Katherine Clay Bassard, "Harriet E. Wilson's *Our Nig* and the American Racial Dream-Text," in *Female Subjects in Black and White: Race, Psychoanalysis, Feminism*, ed. Elizabeth Abel, Barbara Christian, and Helene Moglen (Berkeley: University of California Press, 1997), 187–200.

97. Wilson, *Our Nig*, 28.

98. Wilson, *Our Nig*, 30.

99. Wilson, *Our Nig*, 37.

100. Wilson, *Our Nig*, 36.

101. Wilson, *Our Nig*, 71.

102. Wilson, *Our Nig*, 40.

103. Wilson, *Our Nig*, 41.

104. Wilson, *Our Nig*, 49–50.

105. Wilson, *Our Nig*, 74–75.

106. Wilson, *Our Nig*, 61.

107. Wilson, *Our Nig*, 74.

108. Wilson, *Our Nig*, 129.

109. Walter D. Mignolo, "Sylvia Wynter: What Does It Mean to Be Human?" in *Sylvia Wynter: On Being Human as Praxis*, ed. Katherine McKittrick (Durham, NC: Duke University Press, 2015), 106–22.

110. Édouard Glissant, "For Opacity," in *Poetics of Relation*, trans. Betsy Wing (Ann Arbor: University of Michigan Press, 1997), 190.

111. Audre Lorde, "The Master's Tools Will Never Dismantle the Master's House," in *This Bridge Called My Back: Writings by Radical Women of Color*, 4th ed., ed. Cherríe Moraga and Gloria Anzaldúa (Albany: SUNY Press, 2015), 95.

112. Combahee River Collective, "A Black Feminist Statement," in *This Bridge Called My Back: Writings by Radical Women of Color*, 4th ed., ed. Cherríe Moraga and Gloria Anzaldúa (Albany: SUNY Press, 2015), 215.

113. See Weheliye's vital analysis of Wynter and other Black feminists' critiques of "the human as coterminus with the white liberal subject." Alexander G. Weheliye, *Habeas Viscus: Racializing Assemblages, Biopolitics, and Black Feminist Theories of the Human* (Durham, NC: Duke University Press, 2014), 22.

114. Diana Leong, "The Mattering of Black Lives: Octavia Butler's Hyperempathy and the Promise of the New Materialisms," *Catalyst: Feminism, Theory, Technoscience* 2 (2016): 1–35.

115. J. Michael Scott et al., "Recovery of Imperiled Species under the Endangered Species Act: The Need for a New Approach," *Frontiers in Ecology and the Environment* 3, no. 7 (September 2005): 383–89.

116. Holly Doremus, "Restoring Endangered Species: The Importance of Being Wild," *Harvard Environmental Literature Review* 23 (1999): 1.

117. J. Michael Scott et al., "Conservation-Reliant Species and the Future of Conservation," *Conservation Letters* 3 (2010): 94.

118. Jon Mooallem, *Wild Ones: A Sometimes Dismaying, Weirdly Reassuring Story about Looking at People Looking at Animals in America* (New York: Penguin, 2013), 97.

119. Mooallem, *Wild Ones*, 201–7.

120. Mooallem, *Wild Ones*, 115.

121. Lorimer, *Wildlife in the Anthropocene*, 3.

122. Lauret Edith Savoy, *Trace: Memory, History, Race, and the American Landscape* (Berkeley: Counterpoint, 2015), 39–47.

123. Julietta Singh, *Unthinking Mastery: Dehumanism and Decolonial Entanglements* (Durham, NC: Duke University Press, 2018), 1.

124. Singh, *Unthinking Mastery*, 3.

125. Weheliye, *Habeas Viscus*, 8.

CODA. EMBRACING GREEN TEMPORALITIES: INDIGENOUS SUSTAINABILITIES, ANGLO-AMERICAN UTOPIAS

1. Eric Lombardi, "One Man's 20-Year Pursuit of Zero Waste in America," Waste360.com, September 3, 2015.

2. T. Curran and I. D. Williams, "A Zero-Waste Vision for Industrial Networks in Europe," *Journal of Hazardous Materials* 207–208 (2012): 3.

3. Sunpreet Singh, Seeram Ramakrishna, and Munish Kumar Gupta, "Towards Zero-Waste Manufacturing: A Multidisciplinary Review," *Journal of Cleaner Production* 168, no. 1 (December 2017): 1230.

4. T. Curran and I. D. Williams, "A Zero-Waste Vision for Industrial Networks in Europe," 3.

5. Upton Sinclair, *The Jungle* (New York: Penguin, 2006), 108, 109.

6. Sinclair, *The Jungle*, 109.

7. Sinclair, *The Jungle*, 111, see also 135.

8. Naomi Klein, *This Changes Everything: Capitalism vs. the Climate* (New York: Simon & Schuster, 2015), 169.

9. Paul Wapner, "Climate of the Poor: Suffering and the Moral Imperative to Reimagine Resilience," in *Reimagining Climate Change*, ed. Paul Wapner and Hilal Elver (New York: Routledge, 2016), 138.

10. Wapner, "Climate of the Poor," 138.

11. Klein, *This Changes Everything*, 164.

12. Robin Wall Kimmerer, *Braiding Sweetgrass: Indigenous Wisdom, Scientific Knowledge, and the Teachings of Plants* (Minneapolis, MN: Milkweed, 2013), 173–201. Kyle Whyte, "What Do Indigenous Knowledges Do for Indigenous Peoples?" in *Traditional Ecological Knowledge: Learning from Indigenous Practices for Environmental Sustainability*, ed. Melissa K. Nelson

and Dan Shilling (Cambridge: Cambridge University Press, 2018), 57–61; Melissa K. Nelson, "Introduction: Lighting the Sun of Our Future—How These Teachings Can Provide Illumination," in *Original Instructions: Indigenous Teachings for a Sustainable Future* (Rochester, VT: Bear & Company, 2008), 1–19.

13. Kimmerer, *Braiding Sweetgrass*, 183.

14. Kimmerer, *Braiding Sweetgrass*, 183–84, 185.

15. Kimmerer, *Braiding Sweetgrass*, 183.

16. See Nelson, *Original Instructions*, for some of the possible areas of learning and exchange.

17. Aldo Leopold, *A Sand County Almanac and Sketches Here and There* (Oxford: Oxford University Press, 1949), 204.

18. Leopold, *A Sand County Almanac*, 201.

19. Lauret Edith Savoy, *Trace: Memory, History, Race, and the American Landscape* (Berkeley, CA: Counterpoint, 2015), 33.

20. Savoy, *Trace*, 33–34.

21. Qtd. in Savoy, *Trace*, 44.

22. Savoy, *Trace*, 44.

23. Dan Shilling, "Introduction: The Soul of Sustainability," in *Traditional Ecological Knowledge: Learning from Indigenous Practices for Environmental Sustainability*, ed. Melissa K. Nelson and Dan Shilling (Cambridge: Cambridge University Press, 2018), 11.

24. Whyte, "What Do Indigenous Knowledges Do for Indigenous Peoples?," 62, 66.

25. Kyle Whyte, Chris Caldwell, and Marie Schaefer, "Indigenous Lessons about Sustainability Are Not Just for 'All Humanity,'" in *Sustainability: Approaches to Environmental Justice and Social Power*, ed. Julie Sze (New York: New York University Press, 2018), 149–79.

26. Whyte, Caldwell, and Schaefer, "Indigenous Lessons about Sustainability," 75–77.

27. Kyle Whyte, "Our Ancestors' Dystopia Now: Indigenous Conservation and the Anthropocene," in *The Routledge Companion to the Environmental Humanities*, ed. Ursula K. Heise, John Christensen, and Michelle Niemann (New York: Routledge, 2017), 207.

28. Langston Hughes, *The Collected Poems of Langston Hughes*, ed. Arnold Rampersad and David Rossel (New York: Vintage, 1995), 189.

29. Hughes, *The Collected Poems of Langston Hughes*, 191.

30. Sierra Club online store, https://store.sierraclub.org/make-america -green-again-bumper-sticker-p344.aspx.

31. Hughes, *The Collected Poems of Langston Hughes*, 191.

32. José Esteban Muñoz, *Cruising Utopia: The Then and There of Queer Futurity* (New York: New York University Press, 2009), 56.

33. Ernst Bloch and Theodor Adorno, "Something's Missing," in *The Utopian Function of Art and Literature*, trans. Jack Zipes and Frank Mecklenburg (Cambridge, MA: MIT Press, 1988), 12.

34. Bloch and Adorno, "Something's Missing," 12.

35. Ruth Levitas, *The Concept of Utopia* (Syracuse, NY: Syracuse University Press, 1990), 4.

36. Levitas, *The Concept of Utopia*, 5.

37. Levitas, *The Concept of Utopia*, 6; see Ernst Bloch, *The Principle of Hope*, vols. 1 and 2, trans. Neville Plaice, Stephen Plaice, and Paul Knight (Cambridge, MA: MIT Press, 1995); and Ernst Bloch, *The Spirit of Utopia*, trans. Anthony A. Nassar (Palo Alto, CA: Stanford University Press, 2000); Bloch and Adorno, "Something's Missing"; Lucy Sargisson, *Contemporary Feminist Utopianism* (New York: Routledge, 1996); Margaret Whitford, *Luce Irigaray: Philosophy in the Feminine* (New York: Routledge, 1991).

38. Levitas, *The Concept of Utopia*, 6.

39. Levitas, *The Concept of Utopia*, 8.

40. Sargisson, *Contemporary Feminist Utopianism*, 52.

41. Rebecca Solnit, Hope in the Dark: Untold Histories, Wild Possibilities (Chicago: Haymarket, 2016), 79

42. Qtd. in Solnit, *Hope in the Dark*, 79.

43. Lydia Millet, *Magnificence: A Novel* (New York: Norton, 2013), 255.

Adams, Rachel. *Sideshow U.S.A: Freaks and the American Cultural Imagination.* Chicago: University of Chicago Press, 2001.

Adams, Stephen, and Barbara Adams. "Thoreau's Diet at Walden." In *Studies in the American Renaissance*, ed. Joel Myerson, 243–60. Charlottesville: University of Virginia Press, 1990.

Adamson, Joni. "We Have Never Been *Anthropos*." In *Environmental Humanities: Voices from the Anthropocene*, ed. Serpil Opperman and Serenella Iovino. New York: Rowman and Littlefield, 2017.

Ahmed, Sara. *The Promise of Happiness.* Durham, NC: Duke University Press, 2010.

Alaimo, Stacy. *Exposed: Environmental Politics and Pleasures in Posthuman Times.* Minneapolis: University of Minnesota Press, 2016.

———. "Oceanic Origins, Plastic Activism, and New Materialism at Sea." In *Material Ecocriticism*, ed. Serenella Iovino and Serpil Oppermann, 186–203. Bloomington: Indiana University Press, 2014.

———. "Sustainable This, Sustainable That: New Materialisms, Posthumanism, and Unknown Futures." *PMLA* 127, no. 3 (2012): 558–64.

Altherr, Thomas L. "Drunk with the Chase: Francis Parkman and *Moby-Dick*." *Melville Society Extracts* 58 (1984).

Andrews, Elizabeth. "'This Foreshadowed Food': Representations of Food and Hunger in Emily Dickinson's American Gothic." In *Culinary Aesthetics and Practices in Nineteenth-Century American Culture*, ed. Marie Drews and Monika Elbert. New York: Palgrave Macmillan, 2009.

Andrews, William. "Hannah Crafts's Sense of an Ending." In *In Search of Hannah Crafts: Critical Essays on* The Bondwoman's Narrative, ed. Henry Louis Gates Jr. and Hollis Robbins, 30–42. New York: BasicCivitas Books, 2004.

Anthony, Susan B. "Slavery and Reform." *Liberator* 15 (April 14, 1854): 1.

Appleby, Joyce. "Moderation in the First Era of Popular Consumption." In *Thrift and Thriving in America: Capitalism and the Moral Order from the Puritans to the Present*, ed. Joshua J. Yates and James Davidson Hunter, 139–59. New York: Oxford University Press, 2011.

Armitage, David. "John Locke, Carolina, and the 'Two Treatises of Government.'" *Political Theory* 32, no. 5 (2004): 602–27.

Armstrong, Philip. "*Moby-Dick* and Compassion." *Society and Animals* 12, no. 1: 19–37.

———. *What Animals Mean in the Fiction of Modernity*. New York: Routledge, 2008.

Asafu-Adjaye, John, et al. "An Ecomodernist Manifesto." Ecomodernism .org, April 2015.

Aspiz, Harold. *Walt Whitman and the Body Beautiful*. Urbana: University of Illinois Press, 1980.

"At the Exhibition at Topsfield, Mass." *National Advocate*, November 10, 1824, 1.

Audubon, James John. "Account of the Method of Drawing Birds Employed by J. J. Audubon, Esq. F.R.S.E. in a Letter to a Friend." In *John James Audubon: Writings and Drawings*, ed. Christoph Irmscher, 753–64. New York: Library of America, 1999.

———. "The Passenger Pigeon." In *The Audubon Reader*, ed. Richard Rhodes, 64–72. New York: Everyman's Library, 2006.

———. "The Pinnated Grouse." In *The Audubon Reader*, ed. Richard Rhodes, 40–53. New York: Everyman's Library, 2006.

Barnard, John Levi. "The Cod and the Whale: Melville in the Time of Extinction." *American Literature* 89, no. 4 (December 2017): 851–79.

Barnes, Elizabeth. "Drowning (in) Kittens: The Reproduction of Girlhood in Victorian America." *American Literature* 86, no. 2 (2014): 305–31.

———. *States of Sympathy: Seduction and Democracy in the American Novel*. New York: Columbia University Press, 1997.

Bassard, Katherine Clay. "Harriet E. Wilson's *Our Nig* and the American Racial Dream-Text." In *Female Subjects in Black and White: Race, Psychoanalysis, Feminism*, ed. Elizabeth Abel, Barbara Christian, and Helene Moglen, 187–200. Berkeley: University of California Press, 1997.

Bearak, Max, and David Lynch. "African Nations Are Fed Up with the West's Hand-Me-Downs. But It's Tough to Keep Them Out." *Washington Post*, May 29, 2018.

Bechtel, Stefan. *Mr. Hornaday's War*. Boston: Beacon, 2012.

Beers, Diane L. *For the Prevention of Cruelty: The History and Legacy of Animal Rights Activism in the United States*. Athens: Swallow Press/Ohio University Press, 2006.

Benjamin, Walter. *Illuminations: Essays and Reflections*. Ed. Hannah Arendt. Trans. Harry Zohn. New York: Schocken, 1968.

Bennett, Jane. *Thoreau's Nature: Ethics, Politics, and the Wild*. 1994; repr. New York: Rowman and Littlefield, 2002.

———. "Whitman's Sympathies." *Political Research Quarterly* 69, no. 3 (September 2016): 607–20.

Bercovitch, Sacvan. *The American Jeremiad*. Madison: University of Wisconsin Press, 1978.

Berger, John. "Why Look at Animals?" In *About Looking*, 3–28. New York: Vintage, 1980.

Bittman, Mark. *A Bone to Pick: The Good and Bad News about Food, with Wisdom and Advice on Diets, Food Safety, GMOs, Farming, and More*. New York: Clarkson Potter, 2015.

Bloch, Ernst. *The Principle of Hope*, vols. 1 and 2. Trans. Neville Plaice, Stephen Plaice, and Paul Knight. Cambridge, MA: MIT Press, 1995.

———. *The Spirit of Utopia*. Trans. Anthony A. Nassar. Palo Alto, CA: Stanford University Press, 2000.

Bloch, Ernst, and Adorno, Theodor. "Something's Missing." In *The Utopian Function of Art and Literature*, trans. Jack Zipes and Frank Mecklenburg. Cambridge, MA: MIT Press, 1988.

"Books." *Brooklyn Daily Eagle*, June 28, 1847.

Boydston, Jeanne. *Home and Work: Housework, Wages, and the Ideology of Labor in the Early Republic*. New York: Oxford University Press, 1990.

Brace, Laura. *The Politics of Property: Labour, Freedom, and Belonging*. New York: Palgrave Macmillan, 2004.

"Breakfast to Mr. Frederick Douglass." *Liberator* 9 (February 27, 1846): 1.

Brose, Nancy Harris, et al. *Emily Dickinson: A Profile of the Poet as Cook, with Selected Recipes*. Amherst, MA: Hamilton Newall, 1976.

Bruno, Dave. "The 100 Things Challenge." TEDxClaremontColleges, 2012.

Buell, Laurence. *The Environmental Imagination: Thoreau, Nature Writing, and the Formation of American Culture*. Cambridge, MA: Belknap, 1996.

———. *Writing for an Endangered World: Literature, Culture, and Environment in the U.S.* Cambridge, MA: Harvard University Press, 2001.

Burbick, Joan. "Emily Dickinson and the Economics of Desire." *American Literature* 58, no. 3 (October 1986): 361–78.

Burns, Ken. *The National Parks: America's Best Idea*. Arlington, VA: PBS, 1998.

Byatt, A. S. "Sea Story." *Guardian*, March 15, 2013.

Cancian, Dan. "Malaysia Has Started Returning Tons of Trash to the West: We Will Not Be the Dumping Ground of the World." *Newsweek*, May 28, 2019.

Carrington, Damian. "The Anthropocene Epoch: Scientists Declare Human-Influenced Age." *Guardian*, August 29, 2016.

Carver, Courtney. "Project 333." Be More with Less (blog). October 1, 2010.

"The Cat and the Kitten." *Liberator* 47 (November 23, 1833): 1.

Catlin, George. *Letters and Notes on the Manners, Customs, and Conditions of North American Indians.* 2 vols. New York: Dover, 1973.

Catlin, James. *Frederick Douglass' Paper.* Issue 45 (October 29, 1852): 1.

Child, Lydia Maria. *The American Frugal Housewife: Dedicated to Those Who Are Not Ashamed of Economy.* 12th ed. Boston: Carter, Hendee & Co., 1833.

———. "A Letter from Mrs. Child to 'Our Jessie.'" *Liberator* 41 (October 11, 1861).

Clark, Elizabeth B. "'The Sacred Rights of the Weak': Pain, Sympathy, and the Culture of Individual Rights in Antebellum America." *Journal of American History* 82, no. 2 (September 1995): 463–93.

Clark, Timothy. *Ecocriticism on the Edge: The Anthropocene as a Threshold Concept.* London: Bloomsbury, 2015.

Clifton, Lucille. *The Collected Poems of Lucille Clifton, 1965–2010.* Ed. Kevin Young and Michael S. Glaser. Rochester, NY: BOA Editions, 2012.

Cock, Jacklyn. "'Green Capitalism' or Environmental Justice? A Critique of the Sustainability Discourse." *Focus* 63 (November 2011): 45–51.

Cohen, Jeffrey Jerome, and Lowell Duckert. *Veer Ecology: A Companion for Environmental Thinking.* Minneapolis: University of Minnesota Press, 2017.

Cohen, Joanna. *Luxurious Citizens: The Politics of Consumption in Nineteenth-Century America.* Philadelphia: University of Pennsylvania Press, 2017.

"Colorphobia." *Liberator* 25 (June, 22 1849): 1.

Combahee River Collective. "A Black Feminist Statement." In *This Bridge Called My Back: Writings by Radical Women of Color,* 4th ed., ed. Cherríe Moraga and Gloria Anzaldúa, 201–18. Albany: SUNY Press, 2015.

"Cows." *Connecticut Mirror,* July 12, 1824, 2.

Crafts, Hannah. *The Bondwoman's Narrative.* Ed. Henry Louis Gates Jr. New York: Warner Books, 2002.

Cressey, Daniel. "World's Whaling Slaughter Tallied at 3 Million." *Scientific American,* March 15, 2015.

Cronon, William. "The Trouble with Wilderness." In *Uncommon Ground: Rethinking the Human Place in Nature,* ed. William Cronon, 69–90. New York: Norton, 1995.

Curran, T., and I. D. Williams, "A Zero-Waste Vision for Industrial Networks in Europe." *Journal of Hazardous Materials* 207–208 (2012): 3–7.

Davis, David Brion. *The Problem of Slavery in the Age of Emancipation.* New York: Vintage, 2014.

Davis, Zoe, and Heather Todd. "On the Importance of a Date, or Decolonizing the Anthropocene." *ACME: An International Journal for Critical Geographies* 16, no. 4 (2017): 761–80.

Dawson, Ashley. "Biocapitalism and Deextinction." In *After Extinction,* ed. Richard Grusin, 173–200. Minneapolis: University of Minnesota Press, 2018.

Darwin, Charles. *On the Origin of the Species by Means of Natural Selection.* London: John Murray, 1860.

Dayan, Colin. *The Law Is a White Dog: How Legal Rituals Make and Unmake Persons.* Princeton, NJ: Princeton University Press, 2011.

"Democratic Slave Markets." *Liberator* 31 (August 1, 1856): 1.

Derrida, Jacques. *The Animal That Therefore I Am.* Ed. Marie-Louise Mallet. Trans. David Wills. New York: Fordham University Press, 2008.

———. "'Eating Well,' or the Calculation of the Subject." In *Points . . . Interviews, 1974–1994,* ed. Elisabeth Weber, trans. Peggy Kamuf et al., 255–87. Stanford, CA: Stanford University Press, 1995.

Dickinson, Emily. *Letters of Emily Dickinson.* Ed. Thomas H. Johnson. Cambridge, MA: Harvard University Press, 1997.

———. *The Poems of Emily Dickinson.* Ed. R.W. Franklin. Cambridge, MA: Belknap, 1999.

Dimock, Wai Chee. "Historicism, Presentism, Futurism." *PMLA* 133, no. 2 (2018): 257–63.

Dippie, Brian W. *The Vanishing American: White Attitudes and U.S. Indian Policy.* Lawrence: University Press of Kansas, 1982.

Donovan, Josephine, and Carol J. Adams. "Introduction." In *The Feminist Care Tradition in Animal Ethics,* ed. Josephine Donovan and Carol J. Adams, 1–20. New York: Columbia University Press, 2007.

Dooren, Thom van. *Flight Ways: Life and Loss at the Edge of Extinction.* New York: Columbia University Press, 2014.

Doremus, Holly. "Restoring Endangered Species: The Importance of Being Wild." *Harvard Environmental Literature Review* 23 (1999).

Douglass, Frederick. *Narrative of the Life of Frederick Douglass, an American Slave.* New York: Penguin, 2014.

Dowie, Mark. *Conservation Refugees: The Hundred-Year Conflict between Global Conservation and Native Peoples.* Cambridge, MA: MIT Press, 2009.

Dwyer, Annie. "Animal Autobiography and the Domestication of Human Freedom." *Arizona Quarterly* 71, no. 2 (Summer 2015): 1–30.

Eden, Trudy. *The Early American Table: Food and Society in the New World.* DeKalb: Northern Illinois University Press, 2008.

Ellis, Cristin. *Antebellum Posthuman: Race and Materiality in the Mid–Nineteenth Century.* New York: Fordham University Press, 2018.

Erdrich, Louise. *Shadow Tag.* New York: Harper Perennial, 2010.

Erkkila, Betsy. "Emily Dickinson and Class." *American Literary History* 4, no. 1 (Spring 1992): 1–27.

———. *Whitman the Political Poet.* Oxford: Oxford University Press, 1989.

Farr, James. "'So Vile and Miserable an Estate': The Problem of Slavery in Locke's Political Thought." *Political Theory* 14, no. 2 (1986): 263–89.

Fielder, Brigitte Nicole. "Animal Humanism: Race, Species, and Affective Kinship in Nineteenth-Century Abolitionism." *American Quarterly* 65, no. 3 (2013): 487–514.

Finley, James. "#ReclaimHDT." https://www.thoreausociety.org/news -article/reclaimhdt-james-finley.

Fisher, Philip. *Hard Facts: Setting and Form in the American Novel.* Oxford: Oxford University Press, 1987.

Fletcher, Angus. *A New Theory for American Poetry: Democracy, the Environment, and the Future of the Imagination.* Cambridge, MA: Harvard University Press, 2004.

Foer, Jonathan Safran. *Eating Animals.* New York: Little, Brown, 2009.

Foucault, Michel. *The History of Sexuality.* Vol. 2: *The Use of Pleasure.* Trans. Robert Hurley. New York: Vintage, 1990.

Frederickson, George M. *The Black Image in the White Mind: The Debate on Afro-American Character and Destiny, 1817–1914.* New York: Harper & Row, 1971.

Fretwell, Erica. "Emily Dickinson in Domingo." *J19: The Journal of Nineteenth-Century Americanists* 1, no. 1 (Spring 2013): 71–96.

Friedmann, Karen J. "Victualling Colonial Boston." *Agricultural History* 47, no. 3 (July 1973): 189–205.

Gadgil, Madhav, and Ramachandra Guha. *Ecology and Equity: The Use and Abuse of Nature in Contemporary India.* New York: Routledge, 1995.

Garrard, Greg. *Ecocriticism.* New York: Routledge, 2012.

Gerhardt, Christine. *A Place for Humility: Whitman, Dickinson, and the Natural World.* Iowa City: University of Iowa Press, 2014.

Gilmore, Michael T. *American Romanticism and the Marketplace.* Chicago: University of Chicago Press, 1985.

Giltner, Scott. "Slave Hunting and Fishing in the Antebellum South." In *"To Love the Wind and the Rain": African Americans and Environmental History*, ed. Dianne D. Glave and Mark Stoll, 21–36. Pittsburgh, PA: University of Pittsburgh Press, 2006.

Ginsberg, Lesley. "Slavery and the Gothic Horror of Poe's 'The Black Cat.'" In *American Gothic: New Interventions in a National Narrative*, ed. Robert K. Martin and Erick Savoy, 99–128. Iowa City: University of Iowa Press, 1998.

Glausser, Wayne. "Three Approaches to Locke and the Slave Trade." *Journal of the History of Ideas* 51, no. 2 (1990): 199–216.

Gleason, William. "Re-Creating Walden: Thoreau's Economy of Work and Play." *American Literature* 65, no. 4 (1993): 673–701.

Glissant, Édouard. "For Opacity." In *Poetics of Relation*, trans. Betsy Wing, 189–94. Ann Arbor: University of Michigan Press, 1997.

Glotfelty, Cheryll. "Foreword." In *Veer Ecology: A Companion for Environmental Thinking*. Minneapolis: University of Minnesota Press, 2017.

Graham, Sylvester. *Lectures on the Science of Human Life*. New York: Fowler & Wells, 1839.

———. *Letter to the Hon. Daniel Webster, on the Compromises of the Constitution*. Northampton, MA: Hopkins, Bridgeman & Co., 1850.

Grier, Katherine C. *Pets in America: A History*. New York: Harcourt, 2006.

Gross, Robert A. "The Great Bean Field Hoax: Thoreau and the Agricultural Reformers." In *Critical Essays on Henry David Thoreau's Walden*, ed. Joel Myerson, 193–202. Boston: G. K. Hall, 1988.

Gruesz, Kirsten Silva. *Ambassadors of Culture: The Transamerican Origins of Latino Writing*. Princeton, NJ: Princeton University Press, 2002.

Guha, Ramachandra. "Radical Environmentalism and Wilderness Preservation: A Third World Critique" (1997). In *The Futures of Nature*, ed. Libby Robin, Sverker Sörlin, and Paul Warde, 409–31. New Haven, CT: Yale University Press, 2013.

Habeggar, Alfred. *My Wars Are Laid Away in Books: The Life of Emily Dickinson*. New York: Modern Library, 2002.

Habermas, Jürgen. *The Structural Transformation of the Public Sphere: An Inquiry into a Category of Bourgeois Society*. 1st MIT Press paperback ed. Cambridge, MA: MIT Press, 1991.

Hagenbüchle, Roland. "'Sumptuous—Despair': The Function of Desire in Emily Dickinson's Poetry." *Emily Dickinson Journal* 5, no. 2 (Fall 1996): 1–9.

Hahn, Donovan. "Everybody Hates Henry." *New Republic*, October 21, 2015.

Haraway, Donna. "Anthropocene, Capitalocene, Plantationocene, Chthulucene." *Environmental Humanities* 6 (2015): 159–65.

———. *Simians, Cyborgs, and Women: The Re-Invention of Nature*. New York: Routledge, 1991.

———. *Staying with the Trouble: Making Kin in the Chthulucene*. Durham, NC: Duke University Press, 2016.

———. *When Species Meet*. Minneapolis: University of Minnesota Press, 2007.

Harper, Chancellor. "Harper on Slavery." In *The Pro-Slavery Argument; as Maintained by the Most Distinguished Writers of the Southern States, Containing the Several Essays, on the Subject, of Chancellor Harper, Governor Hammond, Dr. Simms, and Professor Dew*. Charleston, SC: Walker, Richards & Co., 1852.

Hartman, Saidiya. *Scenes of Subjection: Terror, Slavery, and Self-Making in Nineteenth-Century America*. Oxford: Oxford University Press, 1997.

Hawthorne, Nathaniel. "Earth's Holocaust." *Graham's Lady's and Gentleman's Magazine (1843–1844)* 25, no. 5 (May 1844): 193–200.

Heise, Ursula. *Imagining Extinction: The Cultural Meanings of Endangered Species*. Chicago: University of Chicago Press, 2016.

Hewett, Elizabeth. "Economics." In *Emily Dickinson in Context*, ed. Eliza Richards, 188–97. Cambridge: Cambridge University Press, 2013.

Higginson, Thomas Wentworth. "Emily Dickinson's Letters." *Atlantic Monthly* 68 (October 1891): 444–56.

Hinks, Peter P. "Introduction." In *Appeal to the Coloured Citizens of the World*, by David Walker, ed. Peter P. Hinks, xi–xliv. State College: Pennsylvania State University Press, 2000.

Hirshfield, Jane. "Optimism." In *The Ecopoetry Anthology*, ed. Ann Fisher-Worth and Laura-Gray Street, 329. San Antonio, TX: Trinity University Press, 2013.

Hitchcock, Edward. *Dyspepsy Forestalled and Resisted, or, Lectures on Diet, Regimen, and Employment: Delivered to the Students of Amherst College, Spring Term, 1830*. Amherst, MA: J. S. & C. Adams, 1831.

"Hog Slaughter in Cincinnati." *Pensacola Gazette*, February 23, 1839, 1.

Hohn, Donovan. "Everybody Hates Henry." *New Republic*, October 21, 2015.

Hughes, Langston. *The Collected Poems of Langston Hughes*. Ed. Arnold Rampersad and David Rossel. New York: Vintage, 1995.

Hunt, Lynn Avery. *Inventing Human Rights: A History*. New York: Norton, 2007.

Hurt, R. Douglas. *American Agriculture: A Brief History*. Rev. ed. West Lafayette, IN: Purdue University Press, 2002.

Hutchinson, George B. "The Whitman Legacy and the Harlem Renaissance." In *Walt Whitman: The Centennial Essays*, ed. Ed Folsom, 201–16. Iowa City: University of Iowa Press, 1994.

Huth, Hans. *Nature and the American: Three Centuries of Changing Attitudes*. 2nd ed. Lincoln: University of Nebraska Press, 1990.

"I Also Am a Man." *London Patriot*, July 26, 1860; repr. *Liberator* 33 (August 17, 1860): 1.

Iacobbo, Karen, and Michael Iacobbo. "Sylvester Graham, Grahamism, and Grahamites." In *Vegetarian America: A History*, 15–70. Westport, CT: Praeger, 2004.

Isenberg, Andrew C. *The Destruction of the Bison: An Environmental History, 1750–1920*. Cambridge: Cambridge University Press, 2000.

Jacoby, Karl. "Slaves by Nature? Domestic Animals and Human Slaves." *Slavery and Abolition* 15 (1994): 89–97.

James, Jennifer C. "Ecomelancholia: Slavery, War, and Black Ecological Imaginings." In *Environmental Criticism for the Twenty-First Century*, ed. Stephanie LeMenager, Teresa Shewry, and Ken Hiltner, 163–78. New York: Routledge, 2011.

Jameson, Frederic. "Future City." *New Left Review* 21 (May/June 2003): 65–79.

Johnson, Rochelle. *Passions for Nature: Nineteenth-Century America's Aesthetics of Alienation*. Athens: University of Georgia Press, 2009.

Joy, Eileen. "Improbable Manners of Being." *GLQ: A Journal of Lesbian and Gay Studies* 21, nos. 2–3 (June 2015): 221–24.

Kappeler, Susanne. "Speciesism, Racism, Nationalism . . . or the Power of Scientific Subjectivity." In *Animals and Women: Feminist Theoretical Explorations*, ed. Carol J. Adams and Josephine Donovan. Durham, NC: Duke University Press, 1995.

Karieva, Peter, Sean Watts, Robert McDonald, and Tim Boucher. "Domesticated Nature: Shaping Landscapes and Ecosystems for Human Welfare." *Science* 316, no. 5833 (2007): 1866–69.

Kawa, Nicholas C. "Amazonia in the Anthropocene." https://nicholaskawa .files.wordpress.com/2017/02/amazonia-and-the-anthropocene-uc-taft -talk.pdf.

Kenner, Robert, Elise Pearlstein, and Kim Roberts. *Food, Inc.* Dir. Robert Kenner. New York: Magnolia Pictures, 2008.

Kerber, Linda. "The Republican Mother: Women and the Enlightenment— An American Perspective." *American Quarterly* 28, no. 2 (Summer 1976): 187–205.

Killingsworth, M. Jimmie. *Walt Whitman and the Earth: A Study in Ecopoetics*. Iowa City: University of Iowa Press, 2004.

———. *Whitman's Poetry of the Body: Sexuality, Politics, and the Text*. Chapel Hill: University of North Carolina Press, 1989.

Kimmerer, Robin Wall. *Braiding Sweetgrass: Indigenous Wisdom, Scientific Knowledge, and the Teachings of Plants*. Minneapolis, MN: Milkweed Editions, 2013.

Klammer, Martin. *Whitman, Slavery, and the Emergence of Leaves of Grass*. University Park: Pennsylvania State University Press, 1995.

Klein, Naomi. *This Changes Everything: Capitalism vs. the Climate*. New York: Simon & Schuster, 2015.

Klingle, Matthew W. "Spaces of Consumption in Environmental History." *History and Theory* 42, no. 4 (December 2003): 94–110.

Kolbert, Elizabeth. *The Sixth Extinction: An Unnatural History*. New York: Henry Holt, 2014.

Kornbluh, Anna, and Benjamin Morgan. "Introduction: Presentism, Form, and the Future of History." *BO2: An Online Journal*, October 4, 2016.

Lane, Ruth. "Standing 'Aloof' from the State: Thoreau on Self-Government." *Review of Politics* 67, no. 2 (Spring 2005): 283–310.

Larkin, Phillip. "The Trees." In *Collected Poems*, ed. Anthony Thwaite, 124. New York: Noonday, 1993.

Lawrence, D. H. *Studies in Classic American Literature*. New York: Thomas Selzter, 1923.

LeMenager, Stephanie. *Living Oil: Petroleum Culture in the American Century*. Oxford: Oxford University Press, 2014.

Leong, Diana. "The Mattering of Black Lives: Octavia Butler's Hyperempathy and the Promise of the New Materialisms." *Catalyst: Feminism, Theory, Technoscience* 2 (2016): 1–35.

Leopold, Aldo. *A Sand County Almanac and Sketches Here and There*. Oxford: Oxford University Press, 1949.

Levine, Robert S. "Trappe(d): Race and Genealogical Haunting in *The Bondwoman's Narrative*." In *In Search of Hannah Crafts: Critical Essays on The Bondwoman's Narrative*, ed. Henry Louis Gates Jr. and Hollis Robbins, 276–94. New York: BasicCivitas Books, 2004.

Levitas, Ruth. *The Concept of Utopia*. Syracuse, NY: Syracuse University Press, 1990.

Locke, John. *An Essay Concerning Human Understanding*. New York: Penguin, 2004.

———. *Two Treatises of Government*, ed. Peter Laslett. Cambridge: Cambridge University Press, 1960.

Lombardi, Eric. "One Man's Pursuit of Zero Waste in America." Waste360.com, September 3, 2015.

Lorde, Audre. "The Master's Tools Will Never Dismantle the Master's House." In *This Bridge Called My Back: Writings by Radical Women of Color*, 4th ed., ed. Cherríe Moraga and Gloria Anzaldúa, 94–97. Albany: SUNY Press, 2015.

Lordi, Emily J. "'[B]lack and Going on Women': Lucille Clifton, Elizabeth Alexander, and the Poetry of Grief." *Palimpsest: A Journal on Women, Gender, and the Black International* 6, no. 1 (2017): 44–68.

Lorimer, Jamie. *Wildlife in the Anthropocene: Conservation after Nature*. Minneapolis: University of Minnesota Press, 2015.

Luciano, Dana. "The Inhuman Anthropocene." *Avidly: A Channel of the Los Angeles Review of Books*, March 22, 2015.

Lundblad, Michael. "From Animal to Animality Studies." *PMLA* 124, no. 2 (2009): 496–502.

"A Machine for Milking Cows!" Globe, August 5, 1833, 2.

Malm, Andreas. *The Progress of This Storm: Nature and Society in a Warming World*. London: Verso, 2018.

Mariotti, Shannon L. *Thoreau's Democratic Withdrawal: Alienation, Participation, and Modernity*. Madison: University of Wisconsin Press, 2010.

Marrs, Cody. *Nineteenth-Century American Literature and the Long Civil War*. Cambridge: Cambridge University Press, 2015.

Marx, Karl. *Capital*. Vol. 1. Trans. Ben Fowkes. New York: Penguin, 1992.

Marx, Leo. *The Machine in the Garden: Technology and the Pastoral Ideal in America*. Oxford: Oxford University Press, 1964, 2000.

Maslan, Mark. *Whitman Possessed: Poetry, Sexuality, and Popular Authority*. Baltimore, MD: Johns Hopkins University Press, 2001.

Mason, Jennifer. *Civilized Creatures: Urban Animals, Sentimental Culture, and American Literature, 1850–1900*. Baltimore, MD: Johns Hopkins University Press, 2005.

Mastroianni, Dominic. *Politics and Skepticism in Antebellum American Literature*. Cambridge: Cambridge University Press, 2014.

Matheiken, Sheena. "The Uniform Project." TheUniformProject.com, 2018.

McFarland, Maria. "Decomposing City: Walt Whitman's New York and the Science of Life and Death." *ELH* 74, no. 4 (Winter 2007): 799–827.

McKeon, Michael. *The Secret History of Domesticity: Public, Private, and the Division of Knowledge*. Baltimore, MD: Johns Hopkins University Press, 2005.

McKibben, Bill. *Eaarth: Making Life on a Tough New Planet*. New York: St. Martin's Griffin, 2010.

McWilliams, James E. *A Revolution in Eating: How the Quest for Food Shaped America*. New York: Columbia University Press, 2005.

Meeham, Sean Ross. ""Nature's Stomach": Emerson, Whitman, and the Poetics of Digestion." *Walt Whitman Quarterly Review* 28, no. 3 (2011): 97–121.

Melville, Herman. *Benito Cereno, Billy Budd, Sailor and Other Stories*. New York: Bantam, 1981.

———. *Moby-Dick*. Longman Critical ed. Ed. John Bryant and Haskell Springer. New York: Pearson, 2009.

———. "The Paradise of Bachelors and the Tartarus of Maids." In *Tales, Poems, and Other Writings*, ed. John Bryant, 147–67. New York: Modern Library, 2002.

Mentz, Steve. "After Sustainability." *PMLA* 127, no. 3 (May 2012): 586–92.

Michaels, Walter Benn. "*Walden's* False Bottoms." In *Critical Essays on Henry David Thoreau's Walden*, ed. Joel Myerson, 131–47. Boston: G. K. Hall, 1988.

Mignolo, Walter D. "Sylvia Wynter: What Does It Mean to Be Human?" In *Sylvia Wynter: On Being Human as Praxis*, ed. Katherine McKittrick, 106–23. Durham, NC: Duke University Press, 2015.

"Milking Cows." *Daily Scioto Gazette* 242 (September 13, 1850): 1.

Miller, Daniel. *Consumption and Its Consequences*. London: Polity, 2012.

Millet, Lydia. *Magnificence: A Novel*. New York: Norton, 2013.

Milman, Oliver. "Since China's Ban, Recycling in the U.S. Has Gone Up in Flames." *Wired.com*, February 27, 2019.

Mooallem, Jon. *Wild Ones: A Sometimes Dismaying, Weirdly Reassuring Story about Looking at People Looking at Animals in America.* New York: Penguin, 2013.

Moore, Jason, ed. *Anthropocene or Capitalocene: Nature, History, and the Crisis of Capitalism.* Oakland: PM, 2016.

———. "Name the System! Anthropocenes and the Capitalocene Alternative." Jasonwmoore.wordpress.com, October 9, 2016.

Morton, Timothy. *Humankind: Solidarity with Nonhuman People.* London: Verso, 2017.

———. *Hyperobjects: Philosophy and Ecology after the End of the World.* Minneapolis: University of Minnesota Press, 2013.

Mossberg, Barbara Antonina Clarke. *Emily Dickinson: When a Writer Is a Daughter.* Bloomington: Indiana University Press, 1982.

Mouffe, Chantal. *Agonistics: Thinking the World Politically.* London: Verso, 2013.

"Mr. Graham." *Liberator* 7, no. 11 (March 11, 1837): 43.

Munasinghe, Mohan. "Exploring the Linkages between Climate Change and Sustainable Development: A Challenge for Transdisciplinary Research." *Conservation Ecology* 5, no. 1: 14.

Muñoz, José Esteban. *Cruising Utopia: The Then and There of Queer Futurity.* New York: New York University Press, 2009.

Nash, Roderick. *Wilderness and the American Mind.* 4th ed. New Haven, CT: Yale University Press, 2001.

Navakas, Michele. "Antebellum Coral." *American Literature* 91, no. 2 (2019): 263–93.

Neely, Michelle C. "Embodied Politics: Antebellum Vegetarianism and the Dietary Economy of *Walden*." *American Literature* 85, no. 1 (2013): 33–60.

Neihardt, John G. *Black Elk Speaks: Being the Life Story of a Holy Man of the Oglala Sioux.* Premier ed. Albany: SUNY Press, 2008.

Nelson, Dana D. *National Manhood: Capitalist Citizenship and the Imagined Fraternity of White Men.* Durham, NC: Duke University Press, 1998.

———. *The Word in Black and White: Reading "Race" in American Literature, 1638–1867.* Oxford: Oxford University Press, 1992.

Nelson, Melissa K., ed. *Original Instructions: Indigenous Teachings for a Sustainable Future.* Rochester, VT: Bear & Company, 2008.

Newbury, Michael. "Fast Zombie/Slow Zombie: Food Writing, Horror Movies, and Agribusiness Apocalypse." *American Literary History* 24, no. 1 (Spring 2012): 87–114.

Newman, Lance. *Our Common Dwelling: Henry Thoreau, Transcendentalism, and the Class Politics of Nature.* New York: Palgrave Macmillan, 2005.

———. "Thoreau's Materialism and Environmental Justice." In *Thoreau at Two Hundred: Essays and Reassessments*, ed. Kristen Case and K. P. Van Englen. Cambridge: Cambridge University Press, 2016.

Nissenbaum, Stephen. *Sex, Diet, and Debility in Jacksonian America: Sylvester Graham and Health Reform*. Westport, CT: Greenwood, 1980.

Noble, Mark. "Whitman's Atom and the Crisis of Materiality in the Early *Leaves of Grass*." *American Literature* 81, no. 2 (June 2009): 253–79.

Nott, Josiah Clark. *Types of Mankind, or, Ethnological Researches, Based upon the Ancient Monuments, Paintings, Sculptures, and Crania of Races*. Philadelphia: Lippincott, Grambo & Co., 1854.

Oppermann, Serpil. "Compost." In *Veer Ecology: A Companion for Environmental Thinking*, ed. Jeffrey Jerome Cohen and Lowell Duckert, 136–150. Minneapolis: University of Minnesota Press, 2017.

Outka, Paul. "(De)composing Whitman." *Interdisciplinary Studies in Literature and Environment* 12, no. 1 (Winter 2005): 41–60.

———. "Whitman and Race ('He's Unclear, He's Queer, Get Used to It')." *Journal of American Studies* 36, no. 2 (August 2002): 293–318.

Parkman, Francis Jr. *The Oregon Trail*. Oxford: Oxford University Press, 1996.

Patterson, Orlando. *Slavery and Social Death: A Comparative Study*. Cambridge, MA: Harvard University Press, 1982.

Pearson, Susan J. *The Rights of the Defenseless: Protecting Animals and Children in Gilded Age America*. Chicago: University of Chicago Press, 2011.

Penningroth, Dylan C. *The Claims of Kinfolk: African American Property and Community in the Nineteenth-Century South*. Chapel Hill: University of North Carolina Press, 2003.

Petrino, Elizabeth. "Allusion, Echo, and Literary Influence in Emily Dickinson." *Emily Dickinson Journal* 19, no. 1 (2010): 80–102.

Philippon, Daniel J. "'I Only Seek to Put You in Rapport': Message and Method in Walt Whitman's *Specimen Days*." In *Reading the Earth: New Directions in the Study of Literature and the Environment*, ed. Michael P. Branch et al., 179–93. Moscow: University of Idaho Press, 1998.

Phillips, Dana. "Nineteenth-Century Racial Thought and Whitman's 'Democratic Ethnology of the Future.'" *Nineteenth-Century Literature* 49, no. 3 (December 1994): 289–320.

Phillis, Yannis A., and Luc A. Andriantiatsaholiniaina. "Sustainability: An Ill-Defined Concept and Its Assessment Using Fuzzy Logic." *Ecological Economics* 37 (2001): 435–56.

Pinkus, Karen. "Thinking Diverse Futures from a Carbon Present." *symploke* 21, nos. 1–2 (2013): 195–206.

Plath, Sylvia. "A Birthday Present." In *Ariel*, 42–44. New York: Harper and Row, 1965.

Plumwood, Val. *Feminism and the Mastery of Nature*. New York: Routledge, 1994.

Pollak, Vivian K. "Thirst and Starvation in Emily Dickinson's Poetry." *American Literature* 51, no. 1 (March 1979): 33–49.

Pollan, Michael. *The Omnivore's Dilemma: A Natural History of Four Meals*. New York: Penguin, 2011.

Powell, Daniel. "Finding Solutions to China's E-waste Problem." *Our World*, April 8, 2013.

Pratt, Lloyd. *The Strangers Book: The Human of African American Literature*. Philadelphia: University of Pennsylvania Press, 2016.

Price, Kenneth, ed. *Walt Whitman: The Contemporary Reviews*. Cambridge: Cambridge University Press, 1996.

Puig de la Bellacasa, Maria. *Matters of Care: Speculative Ethics in More Than Human Worlds*. Minneapolis: University of Minnesota Press, 2017.

Quammen, David. *The Song of the Dodo: Island Biogeography in an Age of Extinction*. New York: Scribner, 1997.

"Random Thrusts." *Liberator* 36 (September 3, 1852): 1.

Rasula, Jed. *This Compost: Ecological Imperatives in American Poetry*. Athens: University of Georgia Press, 2002.

Reynolds, David. "Black Cats and Delirium Tremens: Temperance and the American Renaissance." In *Serpent in the Cup: Temperance in American Literature*, ed. David S. Reynolds and Debra J. Rosenthal, 22–57. Amherst: University of Massachusetts Press, 1997.

———. *Waking the Giant: America in the Age of Jackson*. 1st ed. New York: Harper, 2008.

———. *Walt Whitman's America: A Cultural Biography*. New York: Knopf, 1995.

Richards, Eliza. "Correspondent Lines: Poetry, Journalism, and the Civil War." *ESQ: A Journal of the American Renaissance* 54, no. 1–4 (2008): 145–70.

Ritvo, Harriet. "At the Edge of the Garden: Nature and Domestication in Eighteenth- and Nineteenth-Century Britain." *Huntington Library Quarterly* 55, no. 3 (Summer 1992): 363–78.

Robin, Vicki, and Joe Dominguez. *Your Money or Your Life: Nine Steps to Transforming Your Relationship to Money and Achieving Financial Independence*. 1992; repr., New York: Penguin, 2008.

Robinson, Kenneth Allen. *Thoreau and the Wild Appetite*. New York: AMS, 1985.

Rohrbach, Augusta. "'A Silent Unobtrusive Way': Hannah Crafts and the Literary Marketplace." In *In Search of Hannah Crafts: Critical Essays on The Bondwoman's Narrative*, ed. Henry Louis Gates Jr. and Hollis Robbins, 3–15. New York: BasicCivitas Books, 2004.

Rosenthal, Elisabeth. "Lead from Old U.S. Batteries Sent to Mexico Raises Risks." *New York Times*, December 8, 2011.

Rossiter, Margaret W. *The Emergence of Agricultural Science: Justus Liebig and the Americans, 1840–1880.* New Haven, CT: Yale University Press, 1975.

Rusert, Britt. *Fugitive Science: Empiricism and Freedom in Early African American Culture.* New York: New York University Press, 2017.

Sachs, Aaron. *Arcadian America: The Death and Life of an Environmental Tradition.* New Haven, CT: Yale University Press, 2013.

Sánchez-Eppler, Karen. "'To Stand Between': A Political Perspective on Whitman's Poetics of Merger and Embodiment." *ELH* 56, no. 4 (Winter 1989): 923–49.

———. *Touching Liberty: Abolition, Feminism, and the Politics of the Body.* Berkeley: University of California Press, 1993.

Sargisson, Lucy. *Contemporary Feminist Utopianism.* New York: Routledge, 1996.

Savoy, Lauret Edith. *Trace: Memory, History, Race, and the American Landscape.* Berkeley, CA: Counterpoint, 2015.

Schlosser, Eric. *Fast Food Nation: The Dark Side of the All-American Meal.* Rev. ed. New York: Mariner Books, 2012.

Schneider, Richard J. "Walden." In *The Cambridge Companion to Henry David Thoreau,* ed. Joel Myerson, 92–106. New York: Cambridge University Press, 1995.

Schultz, Elizabeth. "Melville's Environmental Vision in Moby-Dick." *ISLE: Interdisciplinary Studies in Literature and the Environment* 7, no. 1 (2000): 97–113.

Schulz, Kathryn. "Pond Scum: Henry David Thoreau's Moral Myopia." *New Yorker,* October 19, 2015.

"Scientists Shocked by Arctic Permafrost Thawing 70 Years Sooner Than Predicted." *Guardian,* June 18, 2019.

Scott, J. Michael, Dale D. Goble, Aaron M. Haines, John A. Wiens, and Maile C. Neel. "Conservation-Reliant Species and the Future of Conservation." *Conservation Letters* 3 (2010): 91–97.

Scott, J. Michael, Dale D. Goble, John A. Wiens, David S. Wilcove, Michael Bean, and Timothy Male. "Recovery of Imperiled Species under the Endangered Species Act: The Need for a New Approach." *Frontiers in Ecology and the Environment* 3, no. 7 (September 2005): 383–89.

Sears, Clara Endicott. *Bronson Alcott's Fruitlands.* Bedford, MA: Applewood, 2004.

Seymore, Nicole. *Bad Environmentalism: Irony and Irreverence in the Ecological Age.* Minneapolis: University of Minnesota Press, 2018.

Shell, Rose Hanna. "Introduction: Finding the Soul in the Skin." In *The Extermination of the American Bison.* Washington, DC: Smithsonian Institution Press, 1889.

Shilling, Dan. "Introduction: The Soul of Sustainability." In *Traditional Ecological Knowledge: Learning from Indigenous Practices for Environmental Sustainability*, ed. Melissa K. Nelson and Dan Shilling, 3–14. Cambridge: Cambridge University Press, 2018.

Shoot, Brittany. "China's Ban on Imported Recyclables Is Drowning U.S. Cities in Trash." *Fortune.com*, March 20, 2019.

Shotwell, Alexis. *Against Purity: Living Ethically in Compromised Times*. Minneapolis: University of Minnesota Press, 2016.

Sinclair, Upton. *The Jungle*. New York: Penguin, 2006.

Singh, Julietta. *Unthinking Mastery: Dehumanism and Decolonial Entanglements*. Durham, NC: Duke University Press, 2018.

Singh, Sunpreet, Seeram Ramakrishna, and Munish Kumar Gupta. "Towards Zero-Waste Manufacturing: A Multidisciplinary Review." *Journal of Cleaner Production* 168, no. 1 (December 2017): 1230–43.

Slotkin, Richard. *Regeneration through Violence: The Mythology of the American Frontier, 1600–1860*. Norman: University of Oklahoma Press, 1973.

Smith, Kimberly K. *African American Environmental Thought*. Lawrence: University Press of Kansas, 2007.

Smith, Martha Nell. *Open Me Carefully: Emily Dickinson's Intimate Letters to Susan Huntington Dickinson*. Paris: Paris Press, 1998.

Smits, David D. "The Frontier Army and the Destruction of the Buffalo, 1865–1883." *Western Historical Quarterly* 25, no. 3 (Autumn 1994): 312–38.

Sokolow, Jayme. *Eros and Modernization: Sylvester Graham, Health Reform, and the Origins of Victorian Sexuality in America*. Rutherford, NJ: Fairleigh Dickinson University Press, 1983.

Solnit, Rebecca. *Hope in the Dark: Untold Histories, Wild Possibilities*. Chicago: Haymarket, 2016.

Sontag, Susan. *On Photography*. New York: Picador, 1973.

Spence, Mark David. *Dispossessing the Wilderness: Indian Removal and the Making of the National Parks*. Oxford: Oxford University Press, 1999.

Stavley, Keith, and Kathleen Fitzgerald. *America's Founding Food: The Story of New England Cooking*. Chapel Hill: University of North Carolina Press, 2004.

Stewart, Mart A. "Slavery and the Origins of African American Environmentalism." In *"To Love the Wind and the Rain": African Americans and Environmental History*, ed. Dianne D. Glave and Mark Stoll, 9–20. Pittsburgh, PA: University of Pittsburgh Press, 2006.

Stoneley, Peter. "'I—Pay—in Satin Cash—': Commerce, Gender, and Display in Dickinson's Poetry." *American Literature* 72, no. 3 (2000): 575–94.

Strasser, Susan. *Waste and Want: A Social History of Trash*. New York: Henry Holt, 2000.

Sweet, Timothy. "'Will He Perish?' *Moby-Dick* and Nineteenth-Century Extinction Discourse." In *Above the American Renaissance: David S. Reynolds and the Spiritual Imagination in American Literary Studies*, ed. Harold K. Bush and Brian Yothers, 87–93. Amherst: University of Massachusetts Press, 2018.

TallBear, Kim. "An Indigenous Reflection on Working beyond the Human/ Not Human." *GLQ: A Journal of Lesbian and Gay Studies* 21, nos. 2–3 (June 2015): 230–35.

Tawil, Ezra. *The Making of Racial Sentiment*. Cambridge: Cambridge University Press, 2006.

Taylor, Jesse Oak. *The Sky of Our Manufacture: The London Fog in British Fiction from Dickens to Woolf.* Charlottesville: University of Virginia Press, 2016.

Terrie, Philip G. "The Other Within: Indianization on the Oregon Trail." *New England Quarterly* 64, no. 3 (September 1991): 376–92.

Thomas, Heather Kirk. "Emily Dickinson's 'Renunciation' and Anorexia Nervosa." *American Literature* 60, no. 2 (May 1988): 205–25.

Thomas, Keith. *Man and the Natural World: Changing Attitudes in England, 1500–1800*. London: Penguin, 1984.

Thomas, M. Wynn. "Weathering the Storm: Whitman and the Civil War." *Walt Whitman Quarterly Review* 15, no. 2 (Fall 1997): 87–109.

Thoreau, Henry David. *Journal*. Vol. 1: *1837–1844*. Ed. John C Broderick et al. Princeton, NJ: Princeton University Press, 1981.

———. *The Maine Woods*. Ed. Joseph J. Moldenhauer. Princeton, NJ: Princeton University Press, 1972.

———. *Reform Papers*. Ed. Wendell Glick. Princeton, NJ: Princeton University Press, 1973.

———. *Walden*. Ed. James Lyndon. Princeton, NJ: Princeton University Press, 1971.

Todd, Zoe. "Commentary: The Environmental Anthropology of Settler Colonialism, Part I." *Environment and Anthropology Society Engagement Blog*, April 11, 2017, https://aesengagement.wordpress.com/2017/04/11 /commentary-the-environmental-anthropology-of-settler-colonialism-part-i/.

Tompkins, Kyla. "Sylvester Graham's Imperial Dietetics." *Gastronomica* 9, no. 1 (Winter 2009): 50–60.

Trexler, Adam. *Anthropocene Fictions: The Novel in a Time of Climate Change*. Charlottesville: University of Virginia Press, 2015.

"Trump Quiet as the UN Warns of Climate Change Catastrophe." *Guardian*, October 9, 2018.

Tsing, Anna Lowenhaupt. *The Mushroom at the End of the World: On the Possibility of Life in Capitalist Ruins*. Princeton, NJ: Princeton University Press, 2015.

Tsing, Anna Lowenhaupt, Heather Swanson, Elaine Gan, and Nils Bubandt. *Arts of Living on a Damaged Planet: Monsters of the Anthropocene*. Minneapolis: University of Minnesota Press, 2017.

Turner, James. *Reckoning with the Beast: Animals, Pain, and Humanity in the Victorian Mind*. Baltimore, MD: Johns Hopkins University Press, 1980.

Turpin, Zachary. "Introduction to Walt Whitman's 'Manly Health and Training.'" *Walt Whitman Quarterly Review* 33, no. 3 (Spring 2016): 147–83.

Twain, Mark. *Roughing It*. Ed. Richard Bucci, Victor Fisher, Michael B. Frank, and Kenneth M. Sanderson. Berkeley: University of California Press, 1993.

United Nations World Commission on Environment and Development. *Our Common Future*. Oxford: Oxford University Press, 1987.

Unti, Bernarde Oreste. "The Quality of Mercy: Organized Animal Protection in the United States, 1866–1930." PhD diss., American University, 2002.

Walker, Brian. "Thoreau on Democratic Cultivation." *Political Theory* 29, no. 2 (April 2001): 155–89.

Walker, David. *Appeal to the Coloured Citizens of the World*. Ed. Peter P. Hinks. University Park: Pennsylvania State University Press, 2000.

Wallace, Molly. *Risk Criticism: Precautionary Reading in an Age of Environmental Uncertainty*. Ann Arbor: University of Michigan Press, 2016.

Walls, Laura Dassow. "As You Are Brothers of Mine: Thoreau and the Irish." *New England Quarterly* 88, no. 1 (March 2015): 5–36.

———. *Henry David Thoreau: A Life*. Chicago: University of Chicago Press, 2017.

Wapner, Paul. "Climate of the Poor: Suffering and the Moral Imperative to Reimagine Resilience." In *Reimagining Climate Change*, ed. Paul Wapner and Hilal Elver, 131–49. New York: Routledge, 2016.

Warner, Michael. "The Mass Public and the Mass Subject." In *Habermas and the Public Sphere*, ed. Craig Calhoun, 377–401. Cambridge, MA: MIT Press, 1992.

———. *Publics and Counterpublics*. New York: Zone, 2005.

Watson, Ivan. "China: The Electronic Wastebasket of the World." CNN, May 30, 2013.

Weheliye, Alexander G. *Habeas Viscus: Racializing Assemblages, Biopolitics, and Black Feminist Theories of the Human*. Durham, NC: Duke University Press, 2014.

Wendell, Susan. *The Rejected Body: Feminist Philosophical Reflections on Disability*. New York: Routledge, 1996.

West, Michael. "Scatology and Eschatology: The Heroic Dimensions of Thoreau's Wordplay." *PMLA* 89, no. 5 (October 1974): 1043–64.

Whitford, Margaret. *Luce Irigaray: Philosophy in the Feminine*. New York: Routledge, 1991.

Whitley, Edward. "'A Long Missing Part of Itself': Bringing Lucille Clifton's *Generations* into American Literature." *MELUS* 26, no. 2 (Summer 2001): 47–64.

Whitman, Walt. "The Eighteenth Presidency!" In *Walt Whitman: Complete Poetry and Collected Prose*, ed. Justin Kaplan, 1307–25. New York: Library of America, 1982.

———. *Leaves of Grass: A Textual Variorum of the Printed Poems*. Vol. 1: *Poems, 1855–1856*. Ed. Sculley Bradley, Harold W. Blodgett, Arthur Golden, and William White. New York: New York University Press, 1980.

———. *Leaves of Grass: The First (1855) Edition*. New York: Penguin, 2005.

———. *Leaves of Grass and Other Writings*. Ed. Michael Moon. New York: Norton, 2002.

———. [Mose Velsor, pseud.]. "Manly Health and Training, with Off-Hand Hints Toward Their Conditions." Ed. Zachary Turpin. *Walt Whitman Quarterly Review* 33, no. 3 (2016): 184–310.

Whyte, Kyle. "Our Ancestors' Dystopia Now: Indigenous Conservation and the Anthropocene." In *The Routledge Companion to the Environmental Humanities*, ed. Ursula K. Heise, John Christensen, and Michelle Niemann, 206–15. New York: Routledge, 2017.

———. "What Do Indigenous Knowledges Do for Indigenous Peoples?" In *Traditional Ecological Knowledge: Learning from Indigenous Practices for Environmental Sustainability*, ed. Melissa K. Nelson and Dan Shilling, 57–81. Cambridge: Cambridge University Press, 2018.

Whyte, Kyle, Chris Caldwell, and Marie Schaefer. "Indigenous Lessons about Sustainability Are Not Just for 'All Humanity.'" In *Sustainability: Approaches to Environmental Justice and Social Power*, ed. Julie Sze, 149–79. New York: New York University Press, 2018.

Wiegman, Robyn. *American Anatomies: Theorizing Race and Gender*. Durham, NC: Duke University Press, 1995.

Willett, Cynthia. *Interspecies Ethics*. New York: Columbia University Press, 2014.

Williams, Raymond. *The Country and the City*. Oxford: Oxford University Press, 1973.

Williams, William Carlos. "The Bare Tree" in *Selected Poems*, ed. Charles Tomlinson, 157. New York: New Directions, 1985.

Wilson, Harriet E. *Our Nig; or, Sketches from the Life of a Free Black*. New York: Vintage, 2002.

Wilson, Ivy G. "Organic Compacts, Form, and the Cultural Logic of Cohesion; or, Whitman Re-Bound." *ESQ* 54 (2008): 199–215.

World Wildlife Fund. "Living Planet Report 2018: Aiming Higher." 2018.

Yellin, Jean Fagen. *"The Bondwoman's Narrative* and *Uncle Tom's Cabin."* In *In Search of Hannah Crafts: Critical Essays on* The Bondwoman's Narrative, ed. Henry Louis Gates Jr. and Hollis Robbins. New York: BasicCivitas Books, 2004.

Zapedowska, Magdalena. "Dickinson's Delight." *Emily Dickinson Journal* 21, no. 1 (2012): 1–24.

Ziser, Michael, and Julie Sze. "Climate Change, Environmental Aesthetics, and Global Environmental Justice Cultural Studies." *Discourse* 29, no. 2/3 (2007): 384–410.

MICHELLE C. NEELY is Assistant Professor of English and Affiliate Faculty in Environmental Studies and American Studies at Connecticut College.

CPSIA information can be obtained
at www.ICGtesting.com
Printed in the USA
JSHW041350080621
15688JS00001B/90